## Advance Praise for *Manhood Manifesto*

"In our nearly four decades of friendship, I've found Mike to be candid, funny, and insightful. The wisdom he brings to every subject and every experience may appear irreverent at first. Eventually, it will settle into your soul in a way that informs the way you live your life. Mike Shereck makes a difference."
—Rory J. Clark, Founder and CEO of FOCUS SELLING®

"Mike brings gut-punching, brutally honest perspective to the world in a time when it is needed most. I have had the pleasure of working with him for two years and the journey has been transformative. His take on the gynocentric paradigm and the call to men to 'man up' will leave you with a new way of looking at the world. Don't miss the opportunity to read this book!"
—Rocco Cozza, Founder, the Cozza Law Group, PLLC and Author, *The A.L.P.H.A. Way*

"Challenge your conventional thinking and dive deeply into this book. Mike delivers a bold, creative, disruptive, controversial, and edgy opinion that will cause you not only to think, but act."
—Ted Kulawiak, Author, *21 Lessons Learned in Sales Management*

"This book is a must read for any leader who is committed to showing up more authentically and powerfully while standing in the fire of our modern world's

cancel culture. Only read this if you're ready to be fully expressed while risking getting arrows in your back."
—Peter Scott, Bestselling Author,
*The Fearless Mindset*

"Mike reinforces ideas that I don't have to be afraid of speaking my mind. This is important because in running for public office, things can get nasty. I don't allow that nastiness. I will always be able to answer, challenge, and come back. I insist stuff gets done in my community. This book speaks of the power of clarity and standing for one's own beliefs."
—Richard Leja, Berwyn City Council

"Mike just gets down to looking at values, principles, what we are in service of, and the integrity of what we're doing. He bases his coaching on these principles and I enjoy that we're not using all these crazy tools. Tools are great, but his book is about really simple coaching in the best way."
—Andrew Leonard, Father,
Husband, and Entrepreneur

"Being a twenty-one-year-old Black man from Chicago and being so different from Mike, his ability to connect with me and understand where I come from is exceptional. He seamlessly transitioned and made positive and powerful connections with us. Mike's book is the textbook for how he operates."
—Derrick Green, President, Phi Kappa
Sigma Fraternity, Beta Lambda Chapter

# MANHOOD MANIFESTO

## How Men Must Lead
## At Home, At Work,
## and in the Public Sphere

# MIKE SHERECK

BOMBARDIER

A BOMBARDIER BOOKS BOOK
An Imprint of Post Hill Press
ISBN: 978-1-64293-867-8
ISBN (eBook): 978-1-64293-868-5

Manhood Manifesto:
How Men Must Lead at Home, at Work, and in the Public Sphere
© 2021 by Mike Shereck
All Rights Reserved

Cover Design by Tiffani Shea

Post Hill Press
New York • Nashville
posthillpress.com

Published in the United States of America
1 2 3 4 5 6 7 8 9 10

# CONTENTS

**Part III**
**Doing the Work**

## Epilogue

## Appendix

# PREFACE

## by Jason D. Hill

Like all authentic ethical alpha males who also happen to be leaders, Mike Shereck is profoundly in love with this earth and with humanity at large. This love stems from the pivotal three foundations of masculinity Mike defines in his book, and which suffuse his moral character: the capacity to provide, the need to protect others, and the aspirational desire to leave a legacy.

It is these three foundations that have been the collective bedrock out of which our Western civilization has been forged; a civilization largely built by men. Our civilization has also been built from the best within men, from their noblest and most inspirational drives.

Today, those impulses are under attack. Masculinity and even manliness are under assault. We are witnessing, as Mike points out so eloquently in the ensuing pages of this inspiring book, the criminalization of growth, vitality, and development in young boys and men by a phalanx of radical feminists and *woke* progressives whose sole goal is to feminize men and neuter them for the sake of advancing their own goals and of achieving not equality and parity with men but, rather, raw, naked brute power. By advancing a gynocentric paradigm that has the effect of neutering men and making them apologists for their masculinity, these individuals are the original misanthropes and destroyers of our civilization. Mike exposes them. Mike develops a method in the style of Sun Tzu for how to undercut the strategy of these radical antimasculinists along with their coteries of male feminists who, like obsequious little Babbitts, prostrate themselves before the image of the castrated and useless male prototype championed as the antihero men should aspire to emulate in today's culture.

But this is not just a fighting book or one that will equip men to inoculate themselves against charges that they exhibit traits of "toxic masculinity." Mike's book has a calming spirit of reverence to it as well. It is a call for men to make a sacred covenant among themselves. A covenant to be the best version of themselves, to cultivate the virtues he clearly outlines that are unique to masculinity and, equally important, indispensable to the maintenance of our exceptional republic—the United States of America, and Western civilization itself. Where men have seen weakness in showing the feelings of vulnerability and pain behind rage and anger, Mike has shorn up the false beliefs behind such fears, and he has created a formula for transmuting such perceived weaknesses into a man's greatest strength.

Mike loves women. They are not his enemy. This is a book about creating strong men who can partner with and listen to strong women. Real men do not seek to diminish women. But real men have a purpose in life. It's what defines them. They have strong wills, and they do not allow anyone to stifle their wills. Mike has no tolerance for weak-willed individuals—men or women. In this respect, this book is for those who are strong or whose aspirational identities are being forged in the crucibles of strength, vitality, growth, indefatigability, and indomitability.

This is a book that will anger you, make you laugh, make you think, and above all, reevaluate what it means to be man in our world today when so many forces seem bent on making

manhood an outcast—and almost an outlaw. Read it with pleasure and a sense of humor. It is filled with funny anecdotes. Read
it with gravitas. It is chock full of kernels of wisdom and many
truths. Above all, read Mike's book with respect and gratitude.
Be grateful that one as courageous as Mike has assumed the
responsibility of debunking so many of the shibboleths, myths,
and downright lies and acts of treason committed against men.
Read it and be proud of your manhood—you've earned it. And
to the women who dare to pick it up, I say: behold the masculine
male—Yours is the glory!

# HOW THIS CAME ABOUT

*"Be the change you want to see in the world."*
—*Mahatma Gandhi*

In so many ways, I wish this book did not need to be written, and in so many ways this is why I am here. This is a discussion that needs to be had, and I am somewhat reluctantly the vehicle for it.

About three years ago, I found myself in a hotel meeting room with a group of humans who I would find out later were nothing but ballers. This was a group of truly special and powerful people; people of vision, people committed to making the lives of other people better. These were people whose authentic expression can only be described as "leaders." What was even more interesting was they were mostly women. Throughout the next two days something began to unfold. That unfolding is continuing to this day, and I believe will continue throughout the rest of my days on earth.

About an hour after it started I was called to the stage and asked, "Why are you here?" I did not have an answer that was not some form of bullshit. The truth was Deb had said I should show up; I had no idea of why I was there, other than I trusted Deb completely. Deb was a friend of mine and was working with me to market my recently published book and help me further develop "my brand."

*"The unexamined life is not worth living."*
—*Socrates*

I was in a workshop to develop my speaking skills; I had no desire to speak publicly. Why was I there then? I didn't know until I began interacting with "Tricia." Tricia Brouk is a world-renowned speaker's coach and a curator of TEDx Lincoln Square in New York City. What I learned was that I had a message that had never been shared, at least not the way I was sharing it. A message from me about men and to men. The message was one of responsibility, one of ownership, one of respect and honor and, most of all, authenticity.

*"What they don't realize is the greatest conflict you
will ever face will be the conflict with yourself."*
—*Chadwick Boseman*

As I began speaking, I had the experience of being used by something. I know, it sounds weird and "woo woo," and it was unlike any experience I had ever had. I don't like standing in front of twenty people, let alone two hundred or three hundred. What I discovered was an idea in its rawest form. That idea has been being refined and synthesized for the better part of two and a half years now. By the time you read this book it will have approached the third anniversary of Tricia saying, "So what? You are the one to do it." She said that after I said, "I didn't want to be that guy."

The message is *"The world needs men,"* and, most of all, *"The world needs masculine leadership."* That leadership is not the "dominant, win-at-all-costs, fear-based" leadership. The type of leadership I am speaking of is a clear, determined, vital, and powerful sense of leadership that moves others and brings people together. It is the type of leadership that listens to others and has limitless tolerance for imperfection. It is a leadership sourced by compassion and love. It is a leadership that is willing to release its position to examine a perspective it does not share, knowing it can always return to the place it held before. It is a leadership that trusts because the leader trusts himself, his intention, and his commitment. It is a leadership of integrity and valor. It is authentic. Most of all, the leader owns his actions even in error. There will be errors, breakdowns, and failure. The real test is how to handle that. This version of leadership is that the men will take complete responsibility in cleaning it up and restoring whatever needs to be restored and getting back at it. No drama, no complaining, no "hey look at me." The leadership we are speaking of is sourced by commitment and fueled by passion. That is what the book is about. It really isn't even a book. Welcome to the *Manhood Manifesto.*

When creating an environment of limitless compassion, there must be edges. That edge is "zero tolerance for bullshit." That edge must be there, or it will just be a giant cluster. You can see how thin that line is. Limitless compassion for imperfection and zero tolerance for bullshit. That line requires focus, attention, vitality, presence, and most of all a willingness to admit and clean up when mistakes are made, because they will be made. This version of leadership is grounded in strength. The source of that strength is not ego. Quite the contrary, the source comes through profound understanding of oneself and an understanding that we are on a constant journey of learning, growing, and developing as humans. As Mike Jenson says, "There is no top to the mountain."

Let me share with you how the book was written so you can understand, or at least *try* to understand, my intention and process. The book has three parts. Think of it as a construction project.

The first part is "Documenting Existing Conditions." In any project you are building something that is not there now. By nature you are disrupting what currently exists. You had better have a good understanding of what you are disrupting so you can deal with it effectively and understand the challenges. In construction, this is the real work. You miss this and you are in need of a constant barrage of change orders. Customers hate change orders because they get expensive and impact trust. It is best to be really direct and matter of fact in this area. This book/manifesto is no different.

The second part is "Root Cause Analysis." You want to understand how things got the way they are. In many construction projects you are attempting to "un-fuck" something. To un-fuck something, it works best if you understand how it got fucked up in the first place. That is what this section is about.

Section Three is "Doing the Work." I get it: you are guys, and you want to jump to the money shot. Do so if you must, but I really invite you to read the first two sections. They create context and provide a deeper understanding of the challenges and resistance we as men face. Resistance is essential for development. Einstein said, "If I had an hour to solve a problem I'd spend fifty-five minutes thinking about the problem and five minutes thinking about solutions." If we have an hour, we will spend forty minutes thinking and twenty minutes solving.

This book is a culmination of three years of focused work and sixty-five years of living. This is not a "how to." This book will ask you to begin looking. Looking at yourself and the folks around you, have you asked, "Are we doing the best we can?" "Are we utilizing this time on the planet in a way that celebrates the amazing gift it is and leaves us fulfilled, satisfied, and fully self-expressed?" If you complete this book and you answer those two question in the affirmative, drop to your knees and thank God; then keep on doing what you are doing. If your answer is less than a "hell yeah," the good news is you are still on this side of the turf. Join me and the guys with me and begin this journey with us. I promise it will be a good time.

*"Life is precious and urgent."*
—*Christopher Dennis McAuliffe*

Thank you for picking up this book. When it is over there will be some contact opportunity. I invite you to answer the opportunity. Thank you again.

# BEFORE WE BEGIN

*"In our families, we are finding that abandoning that sense of masculine entitlement actually enables us to live happier lives."*
—*Michael S. Kimmel*

I'm just gonna jump in. Men are under attack. Just check out the quote. The essence of masculinity is under attack. The being of the alpha male is under attack and often despised. Our efforts to address this constant attack are not working. We, as men, are failing.

We have failed to engage with this attack. We have allowed it to go on for too long, and we have allowed the activities that have given rise to the attack to continue. Not all of this attack is uncalled for. Some is, but not all. I am unwilling to admit defeat or concede.

The impact of these ongoing and continuous attacks is devastating. We are in the midst of an ongoing cultural war. Black vs. white, women vs. men, gay vs. straight, left vs. right, good vs. evil, up vs. down, in vs. out. It seems as if everything is polarized. There is almost no position one can have without near violent and aggressive opposition to it. This is out of control. We are a culture in nearly constant chaos.

Make no mistake, this war being waged upon us is *not* a war of ideology—it is a war about *power*. The power to control, the power to influence, the power to eliminate opposition, and most of all the power to end the American ideal, the quest for freedom and to eliminate individual liberty.

I assert that the reason for this volatility, uncertainty, ambiguity, and chaos begins with one thing: the absence of trustworthy, responsible masculine leadership. That void of leadership creates an absence of masculine presence and energy. We men have abdicated our roles as leaders and our responsibility as men. We have chosen expedience over leadership. We have chosen appeasement over working through it, and we have chosen short-term easy results over doing the right thing. We have acted confused. We have chosen comfort and convenience over investing long term to create an inviting and sustainable future for our children and our children's children. In short, we have sold out.

One can argue my last statements were in error or exaggerated. One can argue I am overreacting. That is possible. To address an issue you must own the issue. I choose to own this one. Our arrogance, our comfort, our cocksureness impacted our unwillingness to see what was right in front of our eyes. Well, guess what, brother? We were wrong. We fucked up.

I am not asserting this was always done willfully. In many cases we did not even realize what we were doing. I believe the tack we have taken was to "keep the peace." I believe we were thinking, *How bad can it get?* What has happened is that we have given an inch and "they" have taken miles. We are in the midst of a shit show—100 percent feces hitting the fan. I am not blaming anyone; I am just staying chill time is over. It is time for us to "man up."

That's OK; it has all led up to this time. *Manhood Manifesto: How Men Must Lead at Home, at Work, and in the Public Sphere.* This is more than a book; it is a manifesto. For those of you think a manifesto is a crazy rant, please do not let Ted Kaczynski ruin it for everyone. The definition of manifesto is "a written statement declaring publicly the intentions, motives, or views of the issuer." The issuer is me; there is no more accurate description than that. When you finish reading this book, you will be 100 percent clear on my commitment to manhood and masculine expression. You will fully understand what it takes to lead and that leadership is far more than a position. It is a mindset and a way of being. You will also be given an opportunity to discover and choose for yourself. This work is not written to convince you; it is written to inspire.

How it works is we are going to go on a journey. We are going to look at what it means to be a man; for real, dig in and look. We are really going to look at what masculinity is and what it isn't, and we are going to thoroughly look at this thing called "toxic masculinity." All too often the solution for "toxic masculinity" has been the reduction of masculine expression. I say no way. It makes no sense to me if the *issue* is the absence of responsible masculine expression that the *solution* is less or a more feminized version of masculinity. That seems completely insane and unworkable.

We will see how we got here: the choices made, the mindset we use, and the context we operated from. We will look at the forces that some may think are attacking us. The primary force is radical feminism. There is an element inside feminism that is the biggest issue: progressive left gynocentrism. We will dive deep into it and the impact it has had on men.

I don't believe feminism is the enemy—absolutely not. I think we have some work to do to create healthy alignment, lots of work. It takes two to tango, and there is no value in assigning blame. We need to wear this.

We will begin with "how men must lead at home, at work, and in the public sphere." At the core of leading is responsibility. With responsibility comes freedom. Masculinity and responsible masculine expression are the ultimate display of freedom.

## Vision for Manhood Manifesto

The vision of this book is to create a beginning toward shifting masculine expression for all men! That expression is one of authenticity based in self-awareness. That expression is one of responsibility and of service. Ultimately it is one of leadership—first in our own lives, and then in our homes, work, and community. That leadership I speak of is one that provides, protects, and leaves a legacy for future generations. This is a process for us to express ourselves in the most authentic way. This is not a one-size-fits-all conversation. It is essential in this "movement" that we create partnership with our true partners, women. We do that not by being less of a man; we do that by establishing the most authentic expression of manhood possible. My belief is when men are more masculine, woman can embrace their true feminine expression and be more of themselves.

### *The Mission*

We are creating a movement. The movement is one of responsible expression of men and the expression of those men through our communities in the form of leadership no matter what position we hold. Ultimately this movement is in service of providing, protecting, and leaving a legacy.

## Our Values

Freedom: Freedom is the ultimate value; without freedom we do not have the ability to impact much. The most important part of freedom is to ensure our minds are free and open. Freedom is at the source of our God-given right of free will.

Trust: Trust is a gift, and it begins with us. If trust is missing, look in the mirror. It is ours to give and ours to create. Integrity is foundational to the trust we create.

Courage: Courage is not the absence of fear; courage is taking action in the face of fear. For most men, courage is the ultimate expression of vulnerability.

Integrity: Before we can honor anything we must honor ourselves. The ultimate demonstration of that is honoring our word. Honoring does not mean being perfect; it means *honoring*. If you fuck up, clean it up and move along.

Authenticity: This is whom the world interacts with. To achieve authenticity we must first know who we are and how goofy we can be; wear that and own it. Then we can be who we are truly called to be. When we err, clean it up and get back on it.

Responsibility: Own it. No excuses, you can only impact things you are engaged in. The greater responsibility we accept, the freer we are. The more freedom we experience, the more alive we are; the more alive we are, the more we are in touch with this amazing experience of being an American and being a man. The only way anything is going to change is if we "git some on us."

Belief in God (or at least something greater than yourself): I am a Christen, and I believe in Jesus as God. I am not here to sell you my beliefs. I am and will walk the talk and walk that line, and am OK with you holding me to account. (Though I will swear a fuck ton, I have gotten permission from above to do so.)

Finally, Fun: If this shit ain't fun, why in the hell are we doing it? Sometimes you have to walk through something really ugly to actually see how funny it is. The best joke I ever experienced had a three day setup, for a one-line punch line.

## Big-Ass Goals

1. Have men get how cool it is to be a man in America and then be responsible for keeping it cool.
2. Begin the process of cleaning up some of the stupid shit that guys have done in the past. (First goal: end physical, sexual, and emotional abuse in America.)
3. To begin the building of bridges across the divides that currently exist. (Special note: dudes are great at building stuff, so I think we got this one fully nutted.)
4. Have men get that the more they can fully be men, then the more women can fully be feminine and kids can fully be kids. I really look forward to what those results look like. Our owning who we are, and our masculinity, creates the opening for authenticity across the board.
5. To reduce the fear and eliminate all the taboo topics that have been created throughout our culture. (These are created because certain actions, thoughts, and words have generated fear. Out of fear has come prohibition or shame, which does no one any good and drives those actions more in the dark, thus creating more fear. See how this works?)
6. Create a community of men who keep this movement going long after I have ceased to exist on this planet.

7. Build real partnership with woman to build stronger families, stronger communities, stronger organizations, and, most of all, a stronger America.

*"The brick walls are there for a reason. The brick walls are not there to keep us out. The brick walls are there to give us a chance to show how badly we want something. Because the brick walls are there to stop the people who don't want it badly enough. They're there to stop the other people."*
—*Randy Pausch*

Thank you, Professor Pausch. I can only hope this book inspires a fraction of the people you have touched.

Mike Shereck
December 18, 2020
Naperville, IL

# PART I

## DOCUMENTATION OF EXISTING CONDITIONS

(Houston, We Got A Problem. We
are balls deep in the muck)
The Current View of Masculinity in America

"Transformation begins with a powerful relationship to what is so."

—Werner Erhard

## CHAPTER 1

# We're Not in Kansas Anymore

*"Angry white men are on the losing side of history,
which is poised to roll over them like a demo-
graphic steamroller. Theirs is a rearguard action,
the circling of wagons, Custer's last stand. In fact,
they've already lost."*
—*Michael S. Kimmel*

Welcome to the *Manhood Manifesto*. Manhood, men, and the
essence of masculinity are under attack. We are in the midst
of a political, cultural, and, in some ways, gender war. Some
will position this war as foundational between the political lib-
eral/progressive against the traditional and conservative agenda.
That explanation is too simple. The battle, the conflict, the war
that we are engaged in is one that man has been engaged in
since Adam took a bite of the apple. The battle is simply one of
freedom vs. one of desire, comfort, fulfillment of our ego, and
putting our wants before all other things. With freedom comes
responsibility. As humans we often conflate responsibility with
obligation. The temptations of comforts and desires are great,
and this is the existential question I believe we are all here to
answer. What do we choose?

This country was founded on the principles of freedom, equality, and liberty. This idea was also divinely inspired. We can lose sight that this country was created through a connection with our creator. That is usually where this thing falls off the rails, when we begin to put our ego and identity ahead of our purpose. Real freedom is messy. Real freedom is sometimes a complete shit show. Real freedom is an act of continual growth, development, and change. Real freedom requires diversity of thought and inclusion. That mess, that pain, that apparent chaos is just the beginning stage of creation and innovation. Often times in the midst of that, it is very human to want to quell the noise, control the situation, and stop the pain. I can assure you that is not what will serve us best. With freedom comes responsibility, and with great freedom great responsibility is required. America is the freest country in the world. The gap in the level of responsibility at which we operate and the level of freedom we have been granted is the source of the challenges, upset, and problems we face.

From the beginning of time there has always been a pull to control mankind by some arbitrary means. This started, if you believe the story, in the Garden of Eden. Man and woman, Adam and Eve, were granted complete freedom. To enjoy that freedom there was one constraint: do not eat the fruit of the apple tree. The serpent had a better idea. He shared with them how delicious the apple would be and how, by denying them the tasty deliciousness of that most awesome apple, God was just using them, oppressing them, and enslaving them. The serpent promised if they ate the apple and followed him, life would be a rock 'n' roll show. That was the first act of deception in the history of man. Well, we all know how the story ends, and it has been *Groundhog Day* ever since. You do not have to believe in the story. I mean, a talking serpent is a big lift. But the meaning of the story is what is most important. For freedom to exist there must be some constraints; otherwise it is chaos. The biggest challenge to freedom comes in the deception of the alternative.

As humans, we are addicted to consumption; to the new shiny thing, to whatever is sexy, tasty, cool, and attractive. We want more, bigger, awesome. That is how we have defined success. That is what has driven the show. Without external challenges and constraints, our desire for *more* can have freedom morph into some outrageous orgy of consumption. Our desire for more, for cooler, sexier, fancier, more luxurious is also how we can become manipulated. Our desire for external comfort and safety is the very thing that has cost us our full self-expression, our happiness, and our souls. It has cost us our ability to lead, and in doing so it has cost us our ability to shift and adapt. This addiction to comfort and safety is now becoming a threat to the greatest gift we have, our freedom. You may not see that yet; you may disagree with me. That is OK; hang in there—this is what the *Manhood Manifesto* is about.

This quest for materialism and material and financial success has led many, mostly men, to make some bad choices that were not in the best interest of other people. John Kennedy once said, "To whom much is given much is required." This battle against freedom has been bolstered by cries for "social justice" as well as an attack on "the patriarchy," an attack on "the systemic racism," an attack on "the toxic masculinity," an attack on capitalism and, in many ways, an attack on the America idea, Constitution, and American way of life. Unfortunately, men, predominantly white men with power and influence, have taken actions that have supplied ample evidence to create traction and agreement for these attacks. Through the absence of real inquiry, responsibility, and the doubling down of further justification and tone-deaf response, these actions have led to a level of rage that is creating a divide we have not seen in this country in over fifty years.

The only way to solve a problem is for us to own the problem. It does not matter if it is true or not. But consider there must be some level of truth to support the evidence and outrage. We must own the issue to be able to solve it, or we continue in the constant give and take of "he said, she said, they said."

We are in a new time. Please look at the chart in the appendix labeled "Manhood Manifesto Graph." What this shows, in theory, is that we are in a new realm of the human experience. There is more data, more information, and more misinformation than ever before. The strategy of *knowing* is far less effective than before. The reliance on experts and expertise is then less effective than ever before. The strategy of using artificial intelligence (AI) to manage it seems like it could work, but AI cannot catch up and actually accelerates the issue to a greater degree. We cannot continue playing the game in this way. Einstein is credited with saying that the definition of insanity is doing the same thing over and over and expecting different results.

The first question we must ask is "What is the problem?" The problem this manifesto looks to address is the problem with men. Men are about 50 percent of the population of this planet. To have 50 percent of the people be the root of the problem is a *big* issue. First we need to ask, are men really the problem? I don't think so, but let's accept that it is true. Men are the issue. But the truth is, the problem is the *story* around men and the reason that story existed. The real problem is the fear of men and particularly the fear of white, older, powerful men. The solution to the problem as provided by those who have the fear of men is fewer men in leadership, reduced levels of masculine expression, and the creation of quotas to replace men, in particular, with other types of people. Michael Kimmel's quote to introduce the chapter suggests that. This mentality has led to a rise in identity politics. The change that identity politics creates is only a superficial one, not a sustainable change that improves the lives of all living creatures. The sustainable change is a noble endeavor.

I am not denying there has been, if I can use a technical phrase, some epically fucked-up shit that men have done. Men have limitless capacity for evil and destruction. You can collect all the evidence you desire from slavery to rape to the destruction of the environment to war and genocide; yes, men have done all those things. I have no defense for that. Men have also created the art, buildings, and technology that have advanced the experience of being alive for all people throughout the years.

What we must accept is that the level to which men can go dark is equal to the level to which they can create light. That is the experience of being human. That is the essence of the yin and the yang. I believe the greatest creation of mankind is the idea and the creation of the United States of America. It was divinely inspired and created by committed and flawed men. The documents of that creation, the Declaration of Independence and the Constitution of the United States, are the foundational structure of the idea and experiment of the United States.

The United States is a work in process; thus the phrase "in order to form a more perfect union." As long as Americans are here, we will never be done. There is no arrival point for the United States of America. As a country we are always moving, evolving, growing, developing, failing, and recovering. That is what freedom looks like. There is no place on earth like this. Others have attempted to copy what we have, yet we are the original and we are ever changing. Sometimes it is a shit show. It has to be. It has to be so that we have access to our greatness. Being with the shit show is tough. It requires courage. Most of all it requires leadership. Given the new realm of human experience we are now in, it will require a new kind of leadership.

That leadership begins with completely owning all of it. That type of leadership begins with understanding and inquiry to fully understand. To understand, we must come from a place of inquiry, of not knowing, of curiosity. To do that requires an element of vulnerability, of courage, and of understanding you may not know. That type of leadership requires compassion, not empathy. Empathy is tricky. Empathy requires us to feel what others feel, and in doing so we lose objectivity. In losing objectivity and attaching to the subjective reality of the victimized, we too align and become victims of the deeds done to others. From the condition of victimhood it becomes very difficult to advocate for victims because we get too "into the weeds," and we then begin to personalize everything. This position also becomes very susceptible to deception. In the quest to relieve pain, any option may occur as acceptable. This is at the source of most of the complaints we see in America today. I believe operating with compassion is far more powerful. With compassion we do not feel what the victims feel, but we trust what they feel, and experience is true. This book is written from the space of dispassionate compassion and loving kindness. From that mentality and perspective we now have the ability to call bullshit on the unworkable and discover the deception. That is a difficult task when operating from empathy.

We are in a strange time in history. A wedge has been driven into our culture, separating us like we have never seen before. I understand the divide. I just don't think it needs to be there.

I think it harms all of us, especially the people it is aimed to support. The result of this divide has made men, particularly older, able-bodied, employed, somewhat successful White men, the villain. I don't include Black men, only because I am not one. I don't want to speak for them, but I know many Black guys who share my perspective. I don't believe the solution is as Michael Kimmel suggests. When you create a villain, you must have a victim.

The victims are everyone who aligns with the gynocentric paradigm. Their tactics are safety (lockdowns, defunding police, prison reform), social justice, equality, and now equity. As constructed, the victims include not only those who have been victimized, it also includes anyone who identifies with them. This does two things: it greatly increases the victim class, and it then takes justice from an individual right to a call for a social or overreaching solution. That is why social justice has become a perverted version of justice.

I get it. The collective call to "do something" has generated a public response both at a grass roots level and through the media. Whenever we hear that call of "doing something," it is always a cry for someone other than those who are the oppressed or the oppressors to take action. Often, the call to "do something" is looking for the government to step in. We have hundreds of years of history to show us "government intervention" usually does not work out for the better. Up until now we have had the collective intelligence to heed the restraint. I don't see today any differently. Again, insert Einstein quote on insanity.

What is needed is for men to step up. Throughout this book we will be pointing out where it is needed and where we have abdicated. Abdicating, disappearing, focusing only on what makes us wealthier, more powerful, or more influential can no longer be the reason for action. Nor can our desire for lust, self-intoxication, and acting like fifteen-year-old numbskulls in quest of "good times." To create the shift, it must occur within us first. We must begin with understanding who we are and why we do what we are doing. Knowing and living our "why" is the way we must lead and the way this divide will be bridged. We can no longer be so caught up in the how that we lose sight of the why. Welcome to *The Manhood Manifesto: How Men Must Lead at Home, at Work, and in the Public Sphere.*

Thank you for the gift of your time and attention. My pledge to you is this is a worthy endeavor.

## CHAPTER 2

# Winning at All Costs

*"The truth is that our finest moments are most likely to occur when we are feeling deeply uncomfortable, unhappy, or unfulfilled. For it is only in such moments, propelled by our discomfort, that we are likely to step out of our ruts and start searching for different ways or truer answers."*
—*M. Scott Peck*

We love winning. To the victor go the spoils. Western civilization has been built upon the toils of men risking their time, wealth, and honor to create and build success, wealth, and monuments of accomplishment. It has often gone well, and those men who risked have been rewarded—sometimes very well. They have won. In sports we celebrate winning. We hold parades for the champions, and they are invited to the White House for public celebrations. Champions are remembered, memorialized, and celebrated. Just ask yourself who were the six teams Michael Jordan and the Bulls beat in their championship run. That's right; I don't know either, and I don't care. That is our relationship to winning. It is summed up well in the great David Mamet play *Glengarry Glen Ross* when the sales manager, Blake, announces a new sales incentive. "To the winner, a new Cadillac. Second place, a set of steak knives."

Is winning fair? Do we care about the effort? If we are honest, we don't care—we just want the result. If you want to know who talks about "fairness," it's the losers. Losers are always the ones who will raise the flag of things being unfair. The problem with losers is oftentimes they think it is *their* turn to win without understanding how winning is achieved. That is the perspective of many losers. To understand that, all you have to do is get inside the mind of a Chicago Cubs fan prior to the arrival of Theo Epstein. They made losing part of their identity. What happens when people do not understand what it takes to win? They become comfortable with losing. There becomes a nobility to it or a comfort with it. Who hated the Washington Generals? No one. They were harmless; they could cause no upset; they were benign. The challenge, though, was no one wanted to grow up to be a Washington General nor did the team have many fans. Being comfortable with losing is surrendering without a fight. It is choosing to be safely enslaved vs. standing for what you believe and desire. Choosing safety over freedom is the mark of a loser.

That is the challenge with winning. Few really understand what winning is. Few understand what is needed to win consistently. Winning is a funny thing; sometimes you can get lucky and win: think of lottery winners. A few have achieved great wealth. Others, like members of the lucky sperm club, are also winners who did nothing except to be born into great wealth and privilege. Sometimes the cards fall right, and you win. Hell, the New York Jets and the Chicago Bears have both won Super Bowls and look at them today. Winning is what we all say we want. Sometimes we want it so much we will do pretty crazy things to win.

When we look at men and masculinity, we look at winning. One of the common complaints from those influenced by the gynocentric paradigm (adherents of which are typically radical feminists, your Black Life Matters folks, those who have a challenge identifying what gender they are, marginalized professional victims, the great white woke folks, and of course our highly sensitive and feminized men, also known as allies) is that the hypercompetitiveness and the quest for victory may cause harm.

There are others who make up the gynocentric paradigm, but you get the point—the folks who are really invested in the position of victimization and accepting losing as their lot in life. The complaint about men is that men, particularly alpha men, are hypercompetitive. What does that mean? Simply, nothing means more than winning. Winning is more important than relationships, health, and well-being, long-term stability, the health of the planet, and on and on. That singularity of purpose scares those who are comfortable with losing.

As someone who has erred on the side of winning, I understand the complaint and the impact of that. That is where we as men have to be responsible. We have had a good run. The '80s, the '90s, and even the first decade of the 2000s were good to us. Contrary to the beliefs of Barack Hussein Obama, the run does not have to end, and, like all growth curves, the winning and results begin to flatten out.

When a growth curve flattens out, it comes to a state of bifurcation. That state of bifurcation is a critical point; it is a point of choice. It is critical because remaining the same is not an option. If you choose sameness, the result is eventual extinction. We are at that state *now* and have been, I assert, since 2012. The lead-up was coming for quite some time, and the election of 2012 was the day when everything changed, and the war on men and masculinity was declared.

The problem is we did not see it until recently. Some did, but overall we have been complacent and comfortable, thinking, *And this too shall pass.* I know I was one of them. I asked the question, "How bad can it get?" Look around brothers. The answer is "pretty fucking bad." The time is now for us to step up, and it is no longer something we can ignore if we want to continue experiencing freedom for ourselves and more importantly for our kids and the generations to come. We have an opportunity to stand for freedom and the idea that is this great country. To do that there is some work to do. That is why I created this book, this manifesto.

First let's get clear on what a manifesto is. I know I spelled it out, and if you are a dude you did not read the introduction and went right to the chapters so you missed it. I can only imagine what you are like with foreplay. It is that eagerness to achieve, to "git 'er done," to "git some on ya" that makes you awesome and a dude. It is the single-mindedness, the rules don't apply, and the "I'm gonna do it my way." That is also the reason we are in a bit of a jam. Listen, I am one of you. I have yet to meet an instruction manual that needs to be read, and when I was in construction I only referred to the blueprints when we were really in a jam. I get it, I applaud it, and we need to wake up. We are on new terrain.

As stated earlier, here is the definition of manifesto: "a written statement declaring publicly the intentions, motives, or views of its issuer."

My declaration is that men shall reclaim and restore their manhood and leadership at home, at work, and in the public sphere. We step up and own it. No longer do we take a back seat, no longer are we cancelled, ignored, blamed, and attacked. No longer do we sit back passively, unwilling to step up and ignore the nonsense that is going on. We can't—the cost is too high.

In addition as we claim our leadership we do so by creating true partnership with the women who desire to partner with us. We are built and designed to partner with women—physically, emotionally, spiritually, and intellectually. That partnership must occur at home, and there is huge opportunity to partner with them at work and in the public sphere. I am speaking of *real* partnership not the politically correct claptrap that occurs throughout our current gynocentric culture.

I am unwilling to sit by and witness a bunch of incompetent buffoons beclown themselves and destroy all that we hold dear in this nation. What is missing is authentic responsible masculine leadership. What is missing is the return of manhood. That is what I am declaring. Today manhood is reinstated.

To do that we can sit here and whine and bitch about how it is not fair. No! That gets into the same argument of defending and justifying discussed earlier, and we do not grow and develop. Remember, we are in a state of bifurcation. That requires we adapt or die. We must adapt. The best way to adapt is to begin to understand not only who we are, but also the field of engagement. We will get into who we are and our own self-development throughout much of the book. Let's look at the field of play.

We have discussed the awesomeness of the '80s, '90s, and the first five to seven years of the new millennium. While we were kicking ass and taking names, things were changing behind us. They told us, and we did not listen. George H. W. Bush declared a new world order, and we thought, *That sounds nice.* It was the public declaration of a global, one-world government agenda, which is a direct attack on the US Constitution. Since then we have had Bush, Clinton, another Bush, and *almost* another Clinton, but instead we got Barack Hussein Obama and then almost another Clinton. Since 1992 we have had basically the same pro-globalist political system that has led to the decline of the middle class and freedom in this country. Thank God for Donald Trump and his interruption of that. We had no idea what a big deal it was for him to win. His mantra of "draining the swamp" sounded cool, but his pledge to do so was a real existential threat to those who are invested in the global agenda.

Why do you think the media went after him so hard because he made the comment of "grab them by the pussy?" That is what they say to grab headlines and create clicks on social media. It gives the suburban housewives in Naperville something to cackle about while they gather to consume their lattes and create excuses so they can go bang the twenty-four-year-old trainer from Lifetime Fitness at noon. Nobody cares what Trump did in 1999. He was out to turn the corrupt system on its ear. The challenge he represents is why he gets attacked. Those of us who are aligned with the ideas of freedom, independence, and sovereignty are why they attack us. Our independence and our willingness to go the extra mile to achieve are what scares the shit out of the opposition. That is why the gynocentric progressive left is filled with weak soy boys and feminized men.

The idea of strength, courage, responsibility, determination, and vitality is imposing. The progressive left gynocentric agenda is about power. Make no mistake: a desire for power is their objective. They know there is no way that in a direct confrontation or in a fair fight they would have a chance. They only way for them to win is to either cheat or create a false narrative. The false narrative they created was one of toxic masculinity and a corrupt patriarchal system. The results are the cries of toxic masculinity and systemic racism, systemic sexism, systemic misogyny, and of course the ultimate battle cry, the destruction of the planet.

The real crime is being too aggressive, too competitive, and too insensitive to the needs of others. Donald Trump is the poster child for the alpha male and the perfect target for their agenda and their attack. DJT is unapologetically aggressive, competitive, and committed to winning. He is also the master of the double down, which is both his biggest strength and biggest weakness. We will go into depth on the double down in a later chapter. As I noted, the preparation for the attack on freedom and men began as far back as 1992. The declaration was in November 2012. DJT staved them off a bit and showed the holes in their game. It is up to us to finish the job.

Saul Alinsky, an old radical communist from the 1960s, wrote the book *Rules for Radicals*. America, and the freedom it represents, has been under attack from its inception. Alexander Hamilton, one of the founding fathers, was a globalist. The nature of freedom is that we will always be under attack. It is a condition, and we must accept that. Again we had a good run, and, to paraphrase Dean Wormer, we got "fat, dumb, and lazy." Back to Saul Alinsky's *Rules for Radicals*, specifically rule #4: "Make the enemy live up to its own book of rules."

This is where we dropped the ball. This is where when we got fat, dumb, and lazy; we also got sloppy. When the going got tough we "shortcutted." One example is the concept of growth through actions that were not organic. Corporations began to see growth only through acquisition. The impact of that was always the loss of jobs—usually well-paying, highly skilled jobs. Often those jobs were moved overseas. The other impact was a reduction of customer service. Through the increase in the use of technology, we got a triple whammy: reduced customer service, fewer jobs, and a greater gap in human connection. The benefit was the bottom line, greater earnings, and, of course, better bonuses to the leaders of those organizations, as well as higher dividend and stock values for the shareholders. There was winning, but in its wake there was the beginning of destruction. Greed became the guiding influence. We lost sight of the things that made us successful: service and a sense of mission. But hey, we were getting paid—how bad can it be? That question again.

Wash, rinse, repeat that across the country; throw in NAFTA and the attacks on unions; and we begin to put pressure on the middle of the country in a way we had never seen before. The wins on Wall Street were not showing up on Main Street, but we did not talk about that because the media center of the world is about five miles north of Wall Street.

It wasn't just in the corporate sphere. We got into the habit of taking shortcuts everywhere, and Donald Trump was the guy who did that everywhere. From his bankruptcies to stiffing contractors to extramarital affairs to sexist comments and, of course, accusations of racism, he represented the narrative of toxic masculinity and a corrupt patriarch. He was not only the guy who was going to disrupt the swamp, he was also the guy who also represented everything wrong with the strong, independent, successful, vital, and determined man. The one criticism they nailed him on is that he left some messes in his wake. There have been times he was not responsible for his actions or his words. We can no longer operate in a "win at all cost" modality because the cost is far too high. This is an example of the cost of breaks in integrity.

For our declaration of "owning our manhood," we must be responsible. For us to be able to lead this nation, our families, and our organizations to the level of success and sustainability we so want and desire, we must own all of it. That does not mean we need to be perfect. There is no way we can be. We are dudes. Dudes are not perfect. Dudes are engaged, and when in engagement, they make errors. That is fine. When a mistake is made, a ball dropped, a mess created, there is just one thing to do: clean it up and keep on moving. To do that we must be aware.

The thing that separates winning from winning at all costs is the understanding of cost and the cleaning up of errors. That is it. To do that you must be present to the action you are taking. When you do that, every opportunity is a learning and growth opportunity. Isn't that what life is about? Thanks for being here, and thank you for joining in this movement. I am honored by you.

## CHAPTER 3

# Toxic Masculinity

*"When looking at the attributes associated with masculinity in the US, the same researchers identified the following: winning, emotional control, risk-taking, violence, dominance, playboy, self-reliance, primacy at work, power over women, disdain for homosexuality, and pursuit of status."*
—*Brené Brown*

I hate the phrase "toxic masculinity." The reason I hate it so much is that toxic has become a near predictive prefix to the word *masculinity*. I have so much respect for Brené Brown, and this quote has created an environment where calling masculinity *toxic* has become the norm.

As guys, we can get all pissed off or butt-hurt about it. What good will that do? We are in a new environment, an environment that is much more diverse, inclusive, and politically correct. We can bitch, but bitching makes no difference. We can carry on and ignore it, but in a way that will only support the ongoing narrative. If men want to make a difference, if we are committed to leading, if we want to fulfill on our commitment and make the contributions we are put here to make, we must listen to what is being said and take it on. I did not say agree. We need to listen so we can really understand the complaint. The reason we want to listen is because behind every complaint is a commitment, and inside that commitment is where the real alignment can take place—not in the bullshit ally stuff that is being force-fed to us.

The common label of "toxic masculinity" seems to re-place any expression of traditional masculinity. Those would include expressions of stoicism, strength, emotional control, self-sufficiency, absence of communication, or anything that can be describe as chauvinistic: which can include opening a door, referring to a gyno-American as a girl, or uttering any expression considered politically incorrect. We are not going to address this at this moment; we are going to begin by engaging in the heavy lifting first.

The real issues and the areas we must listen to are the sit-uations where our words or actions create fear or upset. Please know, we cannot be responsible for someone else's reaction, and as leaders it is incumbent upon us to be 100 percent responsible for the environment we create. There is an art to relinquishing the need to control someone else's reaction while owning 100 percent responsibility for the environment that response occurs within. This requires a powerful relationship with oneself along with the willingness and desire to be a full-grown adult.

In his book *Extreme Ownership,* former Navy SEAL Jocko Willink states there are no bad teams, only bad leaders. Leadership has two primary responsibilities. The first one is to set the mission, the vision, the purpose, and the reason that team exists. The team can be a work team, a social group, a family, or any group of people gathering together to create an experience. As men it is our job to be leaders no matter what our role is. We will never know when we will be called upon to be that leader who sets the agenda. It does not matter; we can demonstrate and live leadership in any role we have.

The second responsibility of leadership is to create and manage the environment. It can be at an office; it can be a field of play; it can be at a social gathering. Our responsibility as men is to create the environment where the mission, vision, purpose, or reason can be fulfilled and ensure that environment is maintained.

We are going to get into this in great detail throughout the book. The basic function of men is ultimately to provide, protect, and leave a legacy. You can see how creating the vision and mission, along with creating and managing the environment, is essential to those three core responsibilities. For now though, we are looking at "toxic masculinity."

The biggest complaints about traditional masculinity are as follows: aggression, sexual aggression or control, suppressed emotions, hypercompetitiveness, need to dominate, violence, isolation, low empathy, entitlement, and chauvinism and sexism. Or in other words, not being feminine.

These expressions of masculinity are believed to then be demonstrated in the following behaviors: bullying, expressions of anger, domestic violence, sexual assault, risky behavior, substance abuse, suicide, psychological trauma, and absence of real connection or relationships. These behaviors are all methods of control and maintaining some sense of order.

These complaints must be listened to. As I said earlier, we do not need to accept them as the truth, but we do need to listen and examine them. If we are going to make this world work toward meeting the commitment that this book encourages us to, we must do so in partnership with women. To create that partnership we must listen, and fully understand where they are coming from, what they *need* from us, and what they *desire* from us. We must withhold our judgements about them or the pain we have experienced in relationships with them. We must be responsible for any upset, unfulfilled expectations, thwarted intentions, or undelivered communications we have with them, or with other men.

What is also at the source of what is labeled "toxic masculinity" is our fear and desire to avoid shame. As men, shame is our kryptonite. Shame kills us. Shame has us experience ourselves as *less than* and question our value. Our antidote to shame is often arrogance, humor, dominance, or deflection. None of these responses is authentic or changes anything. That is the work we need to do. We must fully develop our self-awareness and understanding to begin this incredibly important job of establishing manhood and responsible masculine leadership in America.

The work is simply to begin the process of knowing ourselves. There is no top to this mountain. The process of self-discovery is an ongoing one, and the further we progress, the more we grow in relationship to our self. The real beauty is that the more we deepen our relationship with our self, the more capacity we have to deepen our relationships with others. The more capacity we have for intimacy, connection, and the ability to listen and really understand what is going on with others, the more those with whom we are in relationships will understand us. What I just described is the creation of empathy, which is one of the components identified as missing in "toxic masculinity."

Through the development of self-awareness, we become less afraid. We develop a much more powerful relationship not only to ourselves but also to the world around us. Werner Erhard has stated many times, "Transformation begins with a powerful relationship to what is so." That is such a simple and elegant phrase, and it is so powerful if you really listen to it. "A powerful relationship to what is so." That is simply *not* arguing with reality. Another way of saying it is being fully responsible for our triggers, our amygdala hijacks, and one of the most common male expressions (again identified as toxic), our anger. This is foundational to Daniel Goleman's book *Emotional Intelligence*. The emotionally intelligent person is one who both understands and is responsible for the impact of their words and actions. This is also expressed in Ekart Tolle's book *The Power of Now*.

When we become aware of the impact of our words and actions, we can shift the way that impact affects others. We can go from creating fear and upset to making the contribution we desire. When we can authentically communicate our position and do so in a way that is an expression of our vision and commitment, we have just entered into the arena of real leadership. Our communication goes from doing the right thing to being an authentic stand for what we are committed to. That is what is missing with men and our leadership today. That is what we will be addressing throughout the book and what our intention is to deliver to you and anyone who interacts with us.

In the meantime we need to address this issue with "toxic masculinity." As I said before, we have to accept it as is and deal with it from that standpoint. One of the issues is that the term "toxic masculinity" exists in a gynocentric paradigm. What do I mean when I say gynocentric? It is simple: gynocentrism is a dominant or exclusive focus on women in theory or practice; or to the advocacy of this focus. Anything can be considered gynocentric when it is concerned exclusively with a female (or feminist) point of view. Toxic masculinity is a total gynocentric point of view. Therefore toxic masculinity is a biased viewpoint. So what? That is the playing field we must operate on.

Let's begin with the big items on the list of issues with toxic masculinity: low empathy, chauvinism, and sexism. As we stated before, we will dig in deeper, when we develop a higher understanding of ourselves, and develop the self-awareness and relationship with ourselves, we will then have access to our own authentic expression. What that looks like is we will begin to speak and act more from our hearts. We will have the courage to say the things we know to say and take the actions we know to take that will be less imposing. We will begin to see things not as we think they "should be," but more as they truly are. When we do that we will recognize that people are people regardless of gender, sexual orientation, race, ethnicity, identified political affiliation, or whether they prefer dogs or cats, or the Stones or the Beatles. It won't matter. When we no longer get tripped up with that, the issues with empathy begin to evaporate.

Now is a good time to address sexual assault. This gets back to self-awareness. Until we get there, can we all just agree no means no? No matter what. I remember when I was a junior in high school, my hormones were raging and all I could think of was girls, and there was this one young lady whom I found alluring, to say the least. I had just gotten my driver's license and had borrowed my dad's car to take her on a date. We were going to the drive-in. In those days that was often considered a sign of consent.

The show began, and we began to make out. There is no doubt I was clumsy and awkward—I was a sixteen-year-old boy who went to Catholic school and was constantly told that sex was bad and to never get a girl knocked-up. Yep, I said it: "knocked-up" was a scientific term in the '70s. I was also hornier than a six-balled tomcat, and all I could think of was systematically circling the bases with this beautiful creature. Therein lies the first issue. This girl, who was my friend, someone I really cared for, became not so much a human—she became an object of my desire and my pleasure. I had no understanding of, and even less concern with, what her experience was. I did assume she was OK with it because she is the one who offered up the drive-in as an ideal place for our date. But all I could think of was "how was I going to score?" I did not even know what scoring really meant. Of course I didn't share my concerns or fear with her because that would make me look like I didn't know what I was doing, when in fact I had no clue.

While I was groping and clumsily trying to free her from the confines of her bra, as soon as I successful negotiated the two clasps of her upper-body underwear, she said, "No, don't." I stopped. I was in a state of immediate cognitive dissonance. I wanted to high-five and share with my buddies, my newfound skill of unclasping the most sacred of all treasure, and here I was with someone I truly cared for, respected, and admired, and she just expressed a personal boundary. I said OK. We spent the next ninety-plus minutes watching a movie neither of us cared for. I remember being numb, stunned, and confused. I did not know what to do, and in that moment of amygdala hijack, I did what I seldom do: I froze.

I took her home and kissed her good night. Two days later, on Monday morning, I went by her locker, as I did often before school. As on most mornings, she was holding court with all her sixteen-year-old-girlfriends, and they were chatting away. Except this day was different. When I got there, I realized they were talking about me, and when they realized I was there, they stopped. Why did they stop? They were laughing at me, saying I was scared, or something to that effect, and that I was afraid to "take her." What was left out was that she said, "No, don't," and I honored her statement. I was devastated. They were right—I was scared. I was also confused. Yes, I was clumsy, and I thought she and I were together in this. When she said no, I thought no meant no. I stopped, I did not know she wanted me to continue; I did not know what to think.

I share this story because part of the gynocentric paradigm we exist in is women have a complete say in their bodies and their experiences, which they should. However, it will not take long until women have a complete say in how men should be, and what is acceptable and not acceptable for men to do, think, and act. This is the source of the entire experience we call toxic masculinity. Remember the quotation, "Transformation begins with a powerful relationship to what is so." Please also remember we can only make changes within us; we cannot change another person. The last tenet to remember: there are no bad teams only bad leaders. These three tenets will be revisited over and over in this book.

How women think, how they communicate, and how they make choices are, in most cases, different than the way men act. We will not and cannot change how they operate, nor should we want to. It is my experience that women often speak in codes. Women have been known to say *yes* when they mean *no* and *no* when they mean *yes*. Are they lying? No. They are being women. Women are incredibly sensitive to their environments. The primary role of our amygdala is to keep us alive. The same holds true for women. When they sense fear, they will do, say, and act out in any way to ensure their survival.

Our job is to make sure they have the experience of being protected. We cannot be a threat to them—ever. We cannot be a threat to anyone ever unless it is warranted. One of the core responsibilities of masculinity is to protect. This is nonnegotiable. With that comes our agreement that we will never hit women or act out toward women or men in any expression of violence unless we are being attacked. We must never assault women sexually in any way. All sexual contact with women must be consensual. If they say no, it is no. No matter what. This does not mean we are to be wimps and worried; it just means we need to be present and respectful. What it mostly means is we are honoring ourselves and our word. I think that is the biggest issue with the gynocentric paradigm and the old school chivalry. We have throughout history put ourselves last, sacrificed ourselves, and not honored who we are.

In establishing manhood and responsible masculine leadership we need to put ourselves first. Not because we are better or because of our ego. For us to provide, protect, and leave a legacy, we must be in great condition. It is like putting the mask on first so we can assist others. Men have, in the past, not been responsible for their own well-being. Our well-being must be a priority for us. This is essential if we are to fulfill on our commitments to lead at home, at work, and in the public sphere.

In providing a protected and safe environment we are doing our job as men and leaders. What we are also doing is allowing the area to be a space that cultivates authentic expression. When we create a place that allows for authentic expression, what will show up is real connection, listening, and the possibility of intimacy. I am not just speaking of sexual interaction; I am speaking of two people connecting and experiencing each other, fully on the level of their soul. When that happens and someone is free to share their soul, we are in a new realm.

I want to address the issue of anger and the perception of anger by the gynocentric participant. Anger is an expression that is common in men. We use anger because if we actually expressed how we felt, especially at the time we are expressing anger, it would not be safe for us. What gynocentric people do not understand about anger is it masks our true emotions. It covers the pain and sorrow; it hides the heartbreak and disappointment, and it does not allow us to show the devastation we are experiencing at the break of trust. The gynocentric human especially does not understand anger when it is directed at them. I have asked them why it's so horrible for them because anger is only an emotion. In response to that question, what I get is some word salad about what is appropriate, mature, and so on.

Anger is a powerful expression. It is also used to mask what we truly feel. The mask is not only for the outside world; it masks the emotions for us. Throughout the years both men and women have not communicated directly about what we are experiencing and what we are committed to. I assert that this masking, this inauthenticity, is really the reason for the divide. We aren't owning who we are, and we really don't know who they are. Most of all we are not fully owning our experience of life. Any wonder we have issues?

This is why self-awareness is so important. When we become aware of and own who we are, it allows for authentic communication. We begin to reveal who we are and what we believe. It also allows us to reveal our commitments not only through words, but through our actions. It is the source of both courage and passion. It begins to create that protected space so others also can communicate from their heart. This is the practice we must take on. That practice begins with us connecting to and honoring who we are.

The last thing I want to address is in the area of competitiveness. In the gynocentric paradigm that our culture is currently constructed within, we have made competition and competing bad. We have already addressed the winning-at-all-costs mindset. Winning at all costs is not competition; it's tilting the playing field to reduce the competition. Competition builds character, provides resistance for growth, and allows us to learn about ourselves, our teammates, and those with whom we are competing. It also provides one of life's greatest lessons: the ability to manage defeat.

In the world of gynocentrism there is a weird relationship to competition, equality, fairness, and competing. The gynocentric expression says it is OK to compete, but the results must be "fair." "Fairness" means the outcome they want and not what is generated through the competition. At the core, the gynocentric structure wants the results—regardless of skill, practice, talent, or opportunity. To me this is nonsense, and you see it play out every day with quotas, affirmative action, and the ever important equality of outcomes. Today we have the popular expression of "systemic racism." This is just another outcry of the gynocentric paradigm that is impacting every aspect of our culture today.

The other unusual component I have seen around competition is the inability of the gynocentric population to be satisfied with anything that is not perfect. Perfectionism may be one of the most destructive human expressions we know. There is no winning. There is only judgment, assessment, and criticism. Perfectionism allows you to be right and have nothing at stake. Perfectionism is risk-free. It is also one of the saddest states anyone can live in. Perfectionism is unattainable and therefore impossible. It leaves the perfectionist in a state of constant frustration. It is a horrible way to live. It is a condition of safety because nothing is good enough, and so the perfectionist doesn't have to engage.

We cannot get triggered by these coded messages. What we must do is understand and address the commitment behind the complaints and judgments. We must continually practice listening. We must listen to what is behind the coded message, what is behind the complaint, what is the commitment they want us to understand. It will take work, and it is work that is required for us to be the leaders we are committed to being.

In summary of this chapter, it is simple: it is on us. First and foremost we need to develop our self-awareness and self-understanding. We cannot have a relationship with anyone if we aren't in good standing with our self. Next, under no circumstance do we initiate violence of any kind (unless there is an imminent threat). Next, no means no. If anyone says no to physical or emotional advances, stop. No, means no. I think a simple rule to end toxic masculinity, especially as we build our relationship with ourselves, is: "Don't be an asshole."

As we begin to own ourselves and our actions, we can begin to fully enjoy and utilize the freedoms bestowed upon us by God and begin to restore responsible leadership in this great country of ours.

CHAPTER 4

# American Exceptionalism

*"That America is an exceptional nation is unclear only to one who has not been taught its true history. It ceases to be exceptional only when its representative leaders cease to be exceptional. America, it has been said, is a nation of laws, not of men. The more it becomes a nation of men, the less it remains America."*

—*Ron Brackin*

About twenty years ago, September 12, 2001, America was a unified nation. We were unified by our sorrow of losing over three thousand of our brothers and sisters. We were united by the outrage of the blatant and unprovoked attack on our country and to the greatest city in the world, New York City. We were unified in our shock at the brazenness of the attack on the Pentagon, the center of political and military power in the world. We were unified in our love and commitment to this great country of ours. We were unified in our love, respect, and admiration for the brave men and woman of the NYPD and NYFD, and the other brave souls who rushed in as the first responders to the attack. We were unified in our commitment to not letting this gutless attack keep us from being who we truly are—Americans. We were unified in our love of our country, flaws and all. We loved the USA. We were also unified in our want and desire for retribution. Some could say vengeance; some could say we wanted blood.

We were pissed, and we were motivated. I remember seeing George W. Bush walking across the White House lawn on the evening of September 11 and thinking, *I'm glad he won, because he is a tough dude from Texas—better than wimpy ol' Al Gore.* Yep, I thought that. I also thought W was gonna kick some ass. At that time that was the myopic, shortsighted, win-at-all-costs mentality. Notice that I said, "Win at all costs." We just got our asses kicked, we were cheapshotted unexpectedly, and that is what we thought: we gotta win. What in God's name was there to win? That, my friends is the thinking of a reactive alpha male. One who is not quite fully mature. You hurt me, I will deliver a blow that you will not forget, I will kick your ass. This was not just W's mentality; this was the mentality of all of us.

Days after 9/11, the recruiting stations were blowing up. People from every walk of life—men and women—were signing up to defend the country. Pat Tillman and his twin brother signed up to become Rangers in the Army. Pat was a highly compensated defensive back with the Arizona Cardinals in the NFL. Pat was *that guy*, country over personal success. Pat was a hero; Pat lost his life in Afghanistan in what was later discovered to be the result of "friendly" fire. War is hell and unpredictable. It is not romantic—it is ugly. It is the ultimate breakdown in the human condition, and sometimes it happens.

Throughout the next few months there were other lesser attacks on our nation. There was the shoe bomber who attempted to light his shoe that was packed with explosives while traveling on an American Airlines airplane from Paris to Miami. There were anthrax attacks and attempted attacks on water and food supplies. American was under attack. The question becomes, why? The other question is, what do we do about it?

Why would people attack America? I want to invite you to look at America not as a land, but more as an idea. You can even look at it as an ideology. If you look there, you will find there have been few places on the planet and throughout history that are like America. American is a grand experiment. America is an experiment in freedom, in governing by the people and for the people. The idea of freedom is an elusive one, and an idea that make tyrants crazy. Self-governance, individual responsibility, personal sovereignty, and the consent of the governed are all unusual and uncommon ideas.

Throughout history, freedom has been difficult to maintain. It is and will always be susceptible to capture and destruction from larger, better-organized, and better-financed nations, countries, or ideologies. Most of the world, most of the time, has been ruled by tyrants, dictators, emperors, monarchs, or some version of totalitarianism. This structure, no matter what form, comes as a man or woman, a person or group of people, bestowing rights on you. The rights you have are not actually yours; they are granted to you by a leader, or a government, and you are allowed to live under their rule. This does not require oppression; people have consented to being ruled for centuries. Take most of Europe as an example. There is very little lifestyle difference between living in Europe and the States, other than in Europe you are required to "comply" to enjoy the freedoms afforded you by the government. Some could argue that those "freedoms," like five weeks of vacation and free health care, make compliance not a problem. More on that later in the chapter.

America is about freedom. Freedom to fully be yourself. Freedom to express yourself as authentically as one can. There is a bar in Scottsdale, Arizona, called the Rusty Spur Saloon. I think it is *the* most American place on the planet. It is run by this guy, who, I think the best way to describe him, is a "bit vulgar." I think that is how the world sees America—a bit vulgar. I think true human authenticity, human expression, can be a bit vulgar. I think vulgar is OK. I think at times it is needed, I think it both cleans things up and awakens us to the malaise and sameness that can occur.

Back to the Rusty Spur Saloon, what makes this place so American is not the great burgers or the horse that walks in the bar once in a while or the limitless supply of ice-cold long-neck beers. What make this place so unique and so American is the atmosphere. I have only been there during spring training. It is a place where Dodger and Giant fans can drink together, where White Sox and Cubs fans can share a table and talk shit to each other while laughing. Because in America it is OK to disagree and still respect one another and allow each other to ability to live and be free. What creates this atmosphere you ask? Strict adherence to three rules. They are (and they are not negotiable), per the owner:

> #1 Tip your bartenders and waitresses well, cuz I don't pay them shit.

> #2 If you cannot have fun here, it is your own damn fault.

> #3 Don't let your fun interfere with anyone else having fun.

Simple huh? Stupid too, until you look at what it really says.

Rule #1: "Tip your bartenders and waitresses well, cuz I don't pay them shit."

Let's not worry about his compensation structure. He is a small business owner, and he needs to attract talent because the talent interacts with the most important people to his business, his customers. So I am sure his comp program works for him because the place has been there for sixty years.

What is so American is the aspect of free enterprise. The waiters, waitresses, and barkeepers are all independent enterprises. They are free to interact with you in a way that is a complete expression of themselves and do so in a way that provides you maximum service. I've been in the place twenty-plus times, and I don't remember a specific service provider. What I do remember is each and every one was great, and I tipped them all a ton, like 50 percent of the bill, because it was worth it. Each time, the experience was great. That is free enterprise, my friends. People will pay for a great experience, a great product, and they will keep coming back. It is not about brand; it is not about any "relationship" that was created or any other marketing bullshit. It was about the *experience*. There is no greater experience anyone can have than being free and being able to freely be themselves. The Rusty Spur Saloon delivers on creating that environment for that to occur.

Rule #2: "If you cannot have fun, it is your own damn fault."

There is no complaint department. I think if there was, it would kindly tell you to fuck off. This place is politically incorrect; it is insensitive to the needs of many. It is loud, it is vulgar, it does not always smell that good, it is sexist, it is misogynistic (or can seem that way), and it is completely unconcerned with your opinion on how it looks. The Rusty Spur does not give a shit about diversity and inclusion, and it is as diverse and inclusive a place as you can find in Scottsdale. What really is noticeable, at least I noticed, is the relatively large number of mature adult women you will find in the crowd. This place is about freedom, choice, authenticity, fun, happiness, music, laughter, and beer. It is about humanity; it cannot be mandated, and you cannot be made to comply. There is an opportunity to have fun and enjoy yourself. It is up to you to accept that or not. They are perfectly fine with that. If you are not having fun, it is on you.

Rule #3: "Don't let your fun interfere with anyone else having fun."

This is my favorite rule. There are no rules really other than treat each other with respect. Manage your wake, have fun, and notice you are in a small bar with a lot of people. As I said, people from all over the country and all over the world come here to have fun and drink, often too much. Never have I seen even the hint of a fight or a brawl. Maybe because the patrons are mostly older humans, and with that much drinking, it is not always a constraint. Did I mention Arizona is an open-carry state? People get along because it is part of the social contract in being in the Rusty Spur. It is one of the three rules, and to enjoy yourself you must be responsible. What is easy to forget is with great freedom comes great responsibility. The Rusty Spur is complete freedom, and for it to last we, the patrons, must be responsible. Because God knows the owner is not. He is shit-faced and hitting on some twenty-five-year-old woman from Cincinnati.

Why do I bring up and spend that much time on the Rusty Spur Saloon? First it is not a sponsor, and it represents American exceptionalism. It represents freedom, and it represents American freedom. It is often said by many in the military that freedom is not free. Ronald Reagan, the greatest US president of my lifetime, once said, *"Freedom is never more than one generation away from extinction. We didn't pass it to our children in the bloodstream. It must be fought for, protected, and handed on for them to do the same, or one day we will spend our sunset years telling our children and our children's children what it was once like in the United States where men were free."*

Our freedom and American exceptionalism are not guaranteed. They must be worked for, and they are a constant work in process. There is not an arrival to freedom, no condition of "I got this handled." It is never handled. It is also never perfect. America and its exceptionalism are also highly flawed. When our nation was founded, we allowed slavery. There is no way in any argument that slavery is acceptable. Even the idea of slavery is anti-American. And yet, when America was founded, we had slavery and some of our founders had slaves.

America. The idea was a divine inspiration, developed and implemented by men—flawed human men. That does not reduce or limit the exceptional idea and the divine inspiration of its creation. It is from there that I completely reject the notion of the 1619 Project and the idea that America is inherently and structurally racist. There are and have always been racist men in the country and in government. Yes there have, but that does not mean the system is racist.

One of the great elements of freedom is for a country or system to be free, you must allow ideas that stand against freedom to exist. You must allow dissenting opinions to exist. That is the nature of freedom. It must be tested, it must be challenged, and it must be stressed for it to continue and for it to be as robust as it needs to be so people can be free and live the fullest lives possible. Through those tests, there will be failure—or else what good are tests? Failure, occasional systemic failure, is required for true freedom to live.

Today is no exception. We live in a time of great social divide. Some will say America is corrupt, it is time to change, it is time to shift the Constitution. There is a belief by some that President Trump was a despot, a tyrant, a man who wanted limitless authority. There are people who desire the decommissioning of police and the end of law and order as we know it. There are those who believe socialism, or some version of it, is what is needed for America to be truly free. There are those who believe everyone should be guaranteed a salary by the government and the borders should be open. These idea are all firmly against the idea of what America is. Yet these ideas must be shared, must be heard, and must be addressed. That is a testament to our freedom.

In what other country could this take place but here? In what other country could the mainstream press be in open opposition to the leader of the country? Could this happen in China? Of course not. In Russia and the Middle East, I am pretty sure opposition does not happen. South America, Africa, or how about New Zealand or Australia, anywhere in Europe? I don't believe so. That message would be censored. The expression of dissent and dislike for leadership is the key element in freedom, and we have structural components that not only allow for it but also call for it.

Now let's answer our second question about attacks on freedom: What do we do about it? The short answer is, we "be free." Live free, allow for freedom, and like most things make sure we have a strong foundation. How has the Rusty Spur stayed open for sixty years? It stays true to what they are. For us to remain free, we must stay true to who we are. That is what the rest of the book will deal with: how do we stay true to who we are, our ideals of freedom, when the world is changing by so much and so quickly. The answer is we adapt, we shift, and we stay true to who we are. We correct when we find ourselves not being that way. That brings us up to the first question: Why did they attack us?

The idea of America is and has been under constant attack since its inception. The idea of sovereignty is unique and scary. Joining up, especially with a larger more established entity, is a sound strategy for survival. It is not a great strategy if you are looking for more than survival. One of our founding fathers, Alexander Hamilton, was a proponent of aligning with Great Britain almost immediately after we won our freedom. His reason was economic stability. He was afraid the cost of the revolution and the resulting debt would make American un-sustainable. His solution, to provide safety and stability, was a sound idea except for the cost. The cost was our freedom, which we had just fought eight years for.

As long as we are free, there will be people who will be afraid of that. Freedom is scary. Real freedom is incorruptible and uncontrollable. That characteristic of freedom can also appear to be unpredictable. I assert it is not, but from the mindset of power and control I understand how it can seem that way. One of the challenges we will always face is the giving up of freedom for safety. We did it with smoking rules and with seat belt laws in our cars. I ride a Harley. Many states require riders to wear helmets. People who do not ride motorcycles cannot understand why someone would not wear a helmet. I would refer those people to rule #3 at the Rusty Spur.

After the 9/11 attack, with the best interest of the country in mind, President Bush, for all intents and purposes, suspended the Constitution and invoked new laws and policies that severely restricted our freedoms in some areas, especially travel. Transportation Safety Administration (TSA) is a direct result. The Department of Homeland Security, the single largest department in the federal government, was created as a result of 9/11. Think about it. Prior to 9/11 there was no such thing as Homeland Security, and after 9/11 it becomes the largest single government entity in an already swollen and bloated bureaucracy. Notice how fast things can change.

Fast-forward to March 2020 and the COVID-19 pandemic. We shut down the country, we destroyed the economy, we closed small business, and why? The pandemic. What was it, what is it? Do we really know? Notice the call for compliance, and listen to the rhetoric. Is this how an exceptional America responds or acts? I don't know. I have some opinions, and this is not about that. This chapter is to point to the thing that makes us great; what makes America exceptional is also highly fragile. What makes us fragile is our fear and our addiction to comfort and convenience.

We sacrificed our freedom for convenience. Through the use of Zoom, Amazon, and the various delivery operations like Door Dash, we have "adapted." Or have we? I assert we are at the precipice of losing this thing called freedom. We are at the edge of losing it—because men (you and me) have been OK with being comfortable. We have allowed the gynocentric concern for safety over freedom to run the show. We have allowed it to continue because we have disconnected. We have been more interested in the pursuit of our selfish and, at times, childish wants and desires, and abdicated our role as men and leaders.

We have failed. So what? That is the good news. For freedom to grow, we need to test the structure, and we need the test to be sufficient enough for it to fail. We have failed. That is the good news. Now is the time to restore responsible masculine leadership. Brothers, it is time to man up. This is the *Manhood Manifesto*; will you join me?

## CHAPTER 5

# Freedom without Responsibility (Boyz Gone Wild)

*"I love America more than any other country in the world and, exactly for this reason, I insist on the right to criticize her perpetually."*
—James Baldwin

Bill Clinton was the perfect president for America in the '90s. America had recovered from a horrible recession. Business was expanding due to the changes in technology and all that had provided, and the baby boomers were coming of age. Things seemed new and exciting, and it was time to shift from the more conservative and tried-and-tested ways. It was time to set ourselves free. Not only were we working, we were also driving business growth, innovation, and most of all consumption. The late '80s and all through the '90s we were the generation of "more." There was no such thing as too much of anything—especially a good time.

This "let the good times roll" mentality informed almost every decision. The idea of delayed gratification was so "old school." We were about progress, and we could not get there quickly enough. We were about getting what we wanted and scratching every itch. No one represented that better than our guy Bill. Slick Willie was the perfect captain for the pirate ship known as the USA. Though ideologically and politically Mr. Bill was a liberal, socially aware Democrat, the way he really rolled was a "laissez faire" capitalist. Like most things with Bill Clinton, what you saw was not necessarily what you got. It did not matter if it was environmental laws, corporate mergers and expansion, banking expansion, the removing of barriers for imports and the exporting of jobs, NAFTA, or even his famous "don't ask, don't tell." Bill was the guy to let things roll. He never met an opportunity he could not hold the door open to, and explain it in a way that had you think he had your best interests in mind. With Bill it was all about the paper—and paper was being made.

It wasn't about just money; it was about all things American. The constraints were lifted. The free love, free sex, drugs, and rock 'n' roll we so wanted in the late '60s and early '70s was now available. You want some blow? Done! A little X? Here you go! You name it, we got it—and not only did you get it from the street dealer, it was going Main Street. Big pharma became the biggest dealer of all time. What was great, you could now run it all through your insurance. Feeling a bit tired? Here you go! A bit anxious? We got something for you! And stressed? No problem! "Oh boy, is this great" was the battle cry. We were living in the time of greatness, where the hippie desires of sex, drugs, and rock 'n' roll, met the capitalist nirvana of never-ending consumption. Yep—we had arrived; we had achieved Utopia!

There was another phenomenon occurring at this time. Corporations were shifting their focus from being mission- or product-driven to being shareholder-driven. Share price was all that mattered. Simultaneously, companies were also switching from pensions to 401(k)s. We had a say in how we invested and what we invested in. Who gives a shit if we don't understand a damn thing about investing—it is just more for me! When the purpose at the time is "more," more is good.

Economic laws still played a role back then. With new interest in Wall Street and new investors with more money going into it, there is only one way for stocks to go, and that is up. Stocks going up meant you were making money, and before long we all thought we were rich. It did not matter what the company did. If they spun it right and it sounded cool, people bought the stocks. We made "more" paper, we were rich, or at least we thought we were, and, more importantly, we acted like it.

> *The Master said, "If your conduct is determined solely by considerations of profit you will arouse great resentment.*
>
> *—Confucius*

As we continued to grow wealthy, we continued to spend more. As we spent more we needed to make more money, so we got a new job. Sometimes that job required us to relocate, so we moved. Sometimes we went just a few miles and other times we moved across the country. We did this to "achieve our dream"; we did this for our career. We did it to chase the dragon of consumption. The idea of working for a company for your entire career and retiring with the gold watch, the pension, and the retirement luncheon was done. Show me the money! That is how we thought wealth was acquired.

This constant desire did not stop with jobs or cars or homes or drugs; it was personal, too. That cute blonde you worked with who was hot. What would it hurt if I banged her? She didn't care; she got to hang with a high-profile guy who treated her well. All the while, we were chasing, consuming, and gaining "more." It was not just men anymore with that behavior; women were in the work force, and some of them realized they possessed a secret weapon. That weapon was their sexuality. Some women became very successful and weaponized their sexuality for all kinds of reasons: monetary gain, career success, and access to power were all common reasons.

There were people in our lives who were not seeing it quite the way we were. This narrative of consumption seemed great and was fun, and it impacted our families. Divorce increased, homes broke up, and people were left in the wake. This happened everywhere. Work environments became mercenary encampments, no longer put together to serve a mission. They existed for one thing: personal reward and career development. All bets were off; everything was on the table. It was all about "me." I had to get mine!

This desire for personal success and personal achievement at just about any cost was typical. The work team you assembled, who moved across country to be led by you, fully understood that if you had a better opportunity you would be gone in a nanosecond. Or so we believed. The truth was, a ton of people were left in our wake. Friends, neighbors, wives, girlfriends, moms, dads, brothers, sisters, and, most of all, children who were impacted by the mercurial and impulsive unfulfillable desire for *more* that the achievement-oriented alpha male had. Bottom line, there was a body count. We justified it because we had 4,000-square-foot homes and BMWs. But what that cost was our relationships.

Relationships are what life is about, yet we tend to not realize it until they are damaged. It is what we do about it when we awaken. We can justify all we want if that makes us feel better. We can be pissed, but at whom? The most damaged relationships are with the kids. They witnessed all of it. You wonder why the millennials are the way they are? They witnessed the limitless bullshit we put them through, and they witnessed it through the eyes of an eight-year-old. Yes, we trained them, and they adapted. They adapted to survive the insanity that they witnessed. They are products of the lifestyles, beliefs, actions, and words they witnessed from us, that was all informed by our never-ending desire to consume more.

The core thing that was missing during this time for most men was responsibility. What I mean by that is understanding the relationship of responsibility to freedom. We had a very limited relationship to freedom. We thought freedom was status, money, power, influence, access, or more stuff. We became addicted to those things and realized that was not *freedom*; it was just another set of chains. Where we failed was not understanding the key to our freedom lies within us, not external to us. We just traded one set of chains for another. Those of us who live long enough are granted the opportunity to shift that. We are gifted the opportunity to correct the damage we did in our relationships. It begins with restoring our relationship to ourselves. When we do that we understand the gift that responsibility is and what it can provide.

This book is about restoring responsibility in masculine leadership. It is about establishing authentic manhood. It is not burdensome, nor is it shameful, though often that is the first place we go. Shame is really dangerous because it is the gateway to denial, which starts the cycle all over again. Through restoring the relationship in ourselves, and understanding all that we are and all that we are not, we are beginning that process.

By connecting to the spiritual elements in our life and understanding there is something far greater and far more important,
we gain access to release the bonds of materialism. We connect
to that thing that we are used by, that thing that is ourselves
in full expression, that thing that drives our passion and our
power. That is what I am inviting you all to join me in, and it
is a journey that never ends, and it is a marvelous journey. Let's
play this game.

## CHAPTER 6

# The Impact of Not Listening

*"...nobody can stand truth if it is told to him. Truth can be tolerated only if you discover it yourself because then, the pride of discovery makes the truth palatable."*

—*Fritz Perls*

Ultimately this book is about leadership. I would not say it is an exportable resource at this moment, and as I said, men have often abdicated their role. Leadership has two functions: the first is to create the vision, purpose, and mission for the enterprise, group, organization, or team; the second is to create and manage the environment where the vision, mission, and purpose can be fulfilled.

Leadership's job is to create the why and then enroll people in it. I did not say manipulate, coerce, or force. I said enroll. Enrollment is about their choosing. (We will get way more into this distinction in Part III.) It is the leaders' responsibility to communicate in such a way that people will choose to be in. One important element of communication is listening. I think I heard someplace that a common complaint about men is their selective listening, but I am not sure. (That's supposed to be really funny.)

Listening is important because it requires us to be present with the person we are engaging with in that moment. You cannot be distracted when you are listening. You can't be on your phone and listen. You cannot listen and be preoccupied because of a problem with your kids. Listening occurs in a relationship, and that relationship is generated by the person listening. Listening also opens us up to see beyond the immediate. As leaders we are responsible for the status of the environment we occupy. If we are not listening, we will not notice the shifts and changes in that environment.

If your son comes to you and says he wants to change his pronouns, I can assure you, you have not been listening. If you find out your partner/wife/girlfriend is canoodling with her twenty-four-year-old personal trainer, for sure you were not listening. If your company comes to you with a severance package and parting gifts, I promise you, you were not listening. When we see buildings burning under the guise of "peaceful protests," we have not been listening. Likewise, when a few planes fly into buildings, the economy collapses because lending institutions are making loans that probably won't be paid back, or, say, a global pandemic comes out of China, maybe we were not paying attention and not listening to what was being said. When we fail to listen, there is a break in communication.

When there is a breakdown in communication, I promise you there is a gap or absence of listening. One of the challenges in a results-only focus—a "damn the torpedoes" approach—is after the decision of where we are going is made, listening is no longer valued. The focus is on expedience, accomplishment, success, "git 'er done," winning, and efficiency. All that is good except there is no place for feedback. The opportunity with listening is that you can achieve all you want and have the folks on your team experience the achievement as well.

The second role of leadership is to create the environment where the vision, mission, and purpose can be fulfilled. When we create an environment, we must also create structure to maintain the environment. Part of the job of a leader in the world today is to operate much like a gardener would; you till and prepare the area to create the environment. You then plant the seeds; you develop the vision, mission, and purpose. You must maintain the environment to ensure fulfillment. This is the most challenging and difficult part. This is also where the leader is "cause in the matter" of bringing the creation to fulfillment. This is the art of leadership. You are like a gardener of people and ideas.

The impact of not listening is like the impact of not maintaining the garden. The weeds will overtake it, the absence of pruning will cause even the best plants to break bad, and the overall neglect will result in much of what you desire dying. That is what happens when there is an absence of leadership.

In the world today where diversity and inclusion are such a huge part of the environment, listening is essential. I don't mean the listening where we pretend like those speaking have something important to say. I mean people actually having the experience of being heard and understood. One of the challenges today with so much data, information, and noise in the space is that subjectivity and opinion are far more present than ever before. When you have a diverse group there will be diverse ideas. Not all of these ideas are great—as a matter of fact some are downright stupid. That is OK. When we listen to the variety of ideas, the leader is given the opportunity to build his team, group, or organization. When we engage with their ideas and people have the experience of being heard, there is the opportunity to create alignment and share the vision in such a way that it can be heard. When we appease or don't even respond, people feel and have the experience that they do not matter. That is where the break begins.

That is what has happened to men in the last twenty years or so. We have not shifted and listened at the level required to build strong and cohesive groups. People want to belong, and they want to be in relationships. When we put things ahead of people, that creates distance. The way to build trust and restore relationships begins with communication, and the most important part of communication is listening. I did not say hearing, and I did not say hearing verbatim; I said listening. Listening is a skill, and it is a skill we are not taught how to do. Listening is more than hearing what someone is saying. Real listening is getting what they are communicating, understanding not only their intention but also getting their desire.

This level of listening is powerful. In an environment of complexity, ambiguity, uncertainty, and, especially now, volatility, this level of listening is required. Throw in the shifts in demographics and the differences in gender, sexual preference, values, age, nation of origin, culture, and beliefs, what was once simple is now much more complex. Now put in leadership style that is focused on results with little regard to how it impacts people, add in the transactional nature of much of what we do, and throw in the agenda of fear and distrust—is it any wonder where the comments about patriarchy, systemic racism, and bias come from? It begins to get self-evident. This does not make it true, but the experience of many can make it appear to be that way.

In addition the amount of information, data, and disinformation is growing exponentially (see Chart B). There was a time when we could manage all the information that came at us. That time has since passed. We are lost in a sea of data that establishes an environment of confusion, overwhelm, and stress.

Add in the pressure to generate results due to a myriad of factors, not the least of which is global competition, and you can see how leadership in the world today is nothing like they taught us in the MBA programs in the '90s. Consider the biggest thing missing was the human connection part. Listening is how we connect with people, how we get them, how we begin to understand them, and how they begin to see us. It is how we get feedback to make sure we are on course to fulfill our commitments. Human connection is essential to leadership today, and listening is essential to human connection.

I used to sail a bit. I sailed on the Great Lakes for a couple of years, and I sailed in the Caribbean once. I am no Admiral Halsey, just a guy who knocked around a bit. I often sailed from Michigan City, Indiana, to New Buffalo, Michigan, a distance of about six nautical miles. When I left, I plotted a course and took off. I always left from the same slip, and I always ended in the right place, every time, 100 percent. I was super reliable to do that. I even got caught in a waterspout once. For those of you who have never experienced one, consider yourself lucky. Regardless of that circumstance, even at that time, shredded main sail and all, I made it back to the slip.

The reason I share this story is I made that sail many times, always successfully, and never once did I go the same way. When I checked my GPS, I was actually on course less than 3 percent of the time. Yet I was always successful and always arrived at my destination. Why I am I telling you this? In commanding that boat, I needed feedback; it did not take long to get into open water and not see the shore anymore. I needed to rely on data, on my compass, and on my instruments; this data allowed me to feel the boat and guide it where I was going. I never took that trip alone, so I was not only responsible for me, but for the other three to five people on the boat. I was responsible not only for their safety, but I was also responsible for their experience.

When we lead, it is our job to maintain the experience. We will do a much deeper dive on how to do this later in the book, but as a leader we must have knowledge, understanding, and belief in ourselves and our commitment, and we must then also be "other-focused." That is the gift of leadership. We need to make sure we have a powerful relationship with ourselves, so that we can fully serve and be of service to others. Somewhere along the way we have lost that.

When we are the leader and we don't listen in an organization, enterprise, team, family, or group, people will get scared and question their trust in us. Their fear will show up as fight, flight, freeze, or appease. Look at the people you hang out with most. Are they arguing, yelling, disrupting, sabotaging, or (my favorite) being passively aggressive? Or are they disappearing, absent, dismissive? Or how about quiet, agreeable, confused, or chaotic? These are all examples of people's reaction to fear. The source of that fear is often the absence of leadership. If you really want to turn the event into a complete shit show, add in mandates, compliance, and penalties, and you have just created a formula for complete unworkability.

When we look around we are in a time of incredible uncertainty: COVID-19, the election, and the political changes; the issue with China and the Middle East; and economic instability. People are afraid. When people get afraid, they get crazy and only focus on their survival. They seek comfort, they seek certainty, they seek belonging, and they are very susceptible to a narrative that calms them regardless of how true it is. One way to reduce people's fears is to listen to them. Our biggest fear is that we are alone and no one cares.

People have a need to be heard, and they have a need to be gotten, especially when they enroll into a vision. As leaders, we have a great opportunity of being in a position to fill that need. We can give people the gift of being heard, of being gotten, of letting them know that they matter. If we fail, we can clean it up and recommit. It is that easy if we are straight about it. The practice of leadership is not about being perfect; it is about being engaged. It is an ongoing process of movement, failure, course correction, and reengagement. We cannot enroll people into a vision, into investing their time, their souls, and their skills, and not think when we fail they will not be disappointed. We need to listen.

The reason there is so much animosity focused on men, alpha men in particular, is we have powered through it, without listening and without communicating with those who are different than us. For twenty-plus years, people have been expressing the desire to build teams, incorporating the importance of inclusion and the need for diversity, and we have not listened at the level that was required. The result is a group of humans have gotten upset. Whom are they upset at? The ones they see as leaders: men, mostly white men. From that comes the current cultural narrative in which we are engaged. They have not had the experience of being heard and gotten, and they are blaming leadership, as they should. This is a breakdown in the structure and practice of leadership.

It is our problem, which was created by not listening fully. I get it. We were putting our attention on results, and results are important. But as the environment changes, we can see how relationships are even more important. When listening is not present, there is a concern whether the relationship is really there. It is also our problem to solve, and the first step in solving it is through listening. We must listen to all of it. It will not all be true, but we must listen to everyone. People must be heard and gotten to restore any semblance of civility and respect. We must include them and partner with them so that we can make this work. Our lives depend on it, as do the lives of our children.

We must own the fuck-up, but not from shame. Romans 8:1 says, "There is no condemnation for those who are in Christ Jesus." Basically there is no reason to make a big deal out of our fuck-ups, just get it back on track. Believe me, when I was off course sailing, I did not beat myself up, nor did I deny it. I just got my ass back on course. That is what we must do, and we begin by listening. We also can begin by viewing the world through the eyes of others. Plus, listening is a simple solution— it does not cost much, it barely hurts, and on occasion we can learn something.

## CHAPTER 7

# Narcissism and Fear (What's Running the Show)

*"Since [narcissists] deep down, feel themselves to be faultless, it is inevitable that when they are in conflict with the world they will invariably perceive the conflict as the world's fault. Since they must deny their own badness, they must perceive others as bad. They project their own evil onto the world. They never think of themselves as evil, on the other hand, they consequently see much evil in others."*
—*M. Scott Peck*

The first part of this book, *Documentation of Existing Conditions,* is just that. We are looking at the current narrative of masculinity and the state of manhood in our country. You cannot begin any project unless you have a powerful relationship to the situation at hand. That is just what is needed. You cannot make up stuff about it either. The best results come from being as objective as possible, and I realize that can be a challenge. If you hear any of the stuff up to this point as blame, wrong-making, or an indictment or accusation of any kind, then this chapter is really for you.

If that is what you are hearing, then you have a "blind spot." Blind spots only become weaknesses if they are illuminated to you and you choose to do nothing. That is willful ignorance, and that is a symptom of narcissism. This chapter will be an opportunity for you to look and see, and then choose for yourself. W. Keith Campbell, PhD, an expert on narcissism, says we are all a bit narcissistic and it only becomes a problem if it interferes in our lives. The level of interference is your call, and that is foundational to your choosing and owning your life fully. That level of ownership is what this book is about.

Understanding the current condition is required before we can address it. It is also required if we want to look at these issues as a thing to deal with vs. being victimized by them. Nothing in this book is coming from the position of victimization. There may be things I see or a context I have that is completely subjective, and it is subjective for a reason. It is my "as lived" experience; it is my expression of living. (That is why this is a manifesto.) It is not *the* truth, and it *is* my truth. My perspective is one of millions of others. I offer this not because I am right, but as a commitment to others. It is my offer to provide a perspective others may not see. Do I do this because I think I am omnipotent, because I am arrogant, or because I think you are stupid? Absolutely not. I share this because I have looked, I have done a shit ton of work, and I have weathered the storms that would've choked others. Am I a narcissist? I am sure Dr. Campbell would say I have some of those characteristics but none that will take away from making my life work.

What I will say is whatever elements of narcissism I may have, they have allowed me to step through the gate of being self-focused to being other-focused. That perspective, being self-focused vs. other-focused is at the core of what narcissism impacts. We all need to take care of ourselves. When we are on an airplane and the attendant is going through the safety instructions, you are instructed to "put your mask on first, then assist others with theirs." Without us caring for ourselves, we would have no ability to help or support others. I think every adult begins to understand that. I hope all parents do. That is the balance that is required to have a healthy understanding of what we need to be fully supported so we are prepared to live the life we choose. It is how great athletes work. They train hard and practice to develop their skills so when game time comes they can contribute to their team. That is the nature of development. We spend time developing so we can get to a point where we can be of service, and that service becomes a powerful expression of who we are. At the core of that is understanding exactly who we are and what is that thing that gives us purpose, that supplies us with the passion and the understanding that defines who we are and calls us to action to fulfill that intention. That is what a healthy, happy, successful adult looks like.

We live in a time of considerable uncertainty, volatility, and ambiguity. Senator Corey Booker (D-NJ) recently said we live in a time that is "not normal." I am not sure what "normal" is, and I get what he means. Shit is weird, I think we can all agree. So what? Well, when times are uncertain, complex, and weird, we can get scared. When we get scared, fear drives the show. The title of this chapter is "Fear and Narcissism (What's Running the Show)." When we look at the question of masculinity, there seems to be even more questions and uncertainty around that. What does masculinity even mean? Am I supposed to be an ally? What if what I say offends someone? Am I being toxic; am I a misogynist? Am I practicing anti-racism? These are very uncomfortable times—what is predictable when we get scared and uncomfortable? We will seek shelter and comfort. We will weather the storm. It is the flight-and-freeze part of the amygdala hijack; we will seek safe harbor.

John A. Shedd once said, "A ship is safe in harbor, but that is not what ships are for." I believe the same can be said for men. It is not our highest and best expression when we succumb to fear. When there is this much uncertainty, some may even call it chaos, it is predictable that we seek safety. In our search for safety we can begin to look into our needs, wants, and fears, not from a place of greater understanding but from a place of survival. That survival can look like the seeking of comfort, safety, and insulation.

One of the concerns I have in the ever-increasing gynocentric paradigm that we are operating under is that we have lost the basic masculine traits of courage, strength, and freedom in order to gain safety, comfort, and acceptance. One of the primary values of the gynocentric paradigm is this need for safety and acceptance. It becomes an overriding concern for a near hypersensitive reaction to the impact of the environment. That mindset can lead to a near narcissistic perspective on life. When we are triggered or living in fear, the concern for survival is what drives each and every decision.

From this position of constant and ongoing fear for survival, all that matters are my needs and wants at this moment: an almost obsessive need for safety, acceptance, and to be liked and, of course, noticed. Those feelings will have us blend into the herd, give up our voice, and, most of all, accept the narrative of safety. Those needs and wants are often based on feelings, and our feelings change often. I know for me, if I eat a pepperoni pizza, in twenty minutes I will have an entirely new set of feelings, wants, and desires. Please don't get me wrong: feelings are very important—they are how we experience life—yet feelings should not be the only outstanding feature we use to make decisions. That is another challenge with living in the current gynocentric paradigm: feelings and opinions are valued, expressed, and utilized more than rational thinking, logic, and reason.

From this position of narcissism, especially as men, our decision-making process begins to decline. With all decisions and mindsets informed by what I feel, want, or need, it is easy to reject systems, processes, or order—or over rely on them. We lose sight of being present and being in the moment because we are consumed by our feelings and our need to get our itch scratched at that moment.

As leaders we have now entered a very dangerous place. It becomes nearly impossible to be other-focused if we are operating out of a narcissistic mindset with a constant need for approval and positive feedback. This is where the "win at all costs" mentality jumps in, and from here not much good comes of it. From the perspective of survival and narcissism, irresponsibility is everywhere. Not only do we make bad decisions, but when the results are disastrous, instead of seeking the source of the breakdown, we look for people to blame and throw under the bus. That activity of leadership, to seek to blame and punish the innocent, is the exact behavior that is most destructive and creates incredible levels of distrust.

That behavior from someone in a leadership role—blaming and punishing the innocent, no matter what it looks like—can trigger everyone's core wounds of shame, abandonment, and betrayal. At the core of the expression of toxic masculinity is just that, leaving people shamed, abandoned, and betrayed. *That* is not what masculinity is about. *That* is anti-masculine. *That* is "being a bitch." Too often in our world, especially (but not exclusively) in corporate America, that behavior of anti-masculine actions, of being a bitch, has been rewarded. The impact it has had is immeasurable. Whenever I see or hear of behavior by men as an example of "toxic masculinity," most often this behavior falls into that bucket.

Fear and narcissism happen and are part of all of us. The challenge we have as men and leaders is becoming aware when it begins to run the show and then making the adjustments needed. The adjustments required are those to core masculine roles or providing, protecting, and legacy building. In the gynocentric paradigm that is informing the current cultural narrative, there are no structures that pull for those actions. So unfortunately, the anti-masculine or bitch behavior then becomes the default. Our job is to interrupt that and shift to what is authentically us. Hang in there, brothers. We will get there.

CHAPTER 8

# Shifts in Corporations and the Unspoken Impact

*"There is one and only one social responsibility of business—to use its resources and engage in activities designed to increase its profits so long as it stays within the rules of the game, which is to say, engages in open and free competition without deception or fraud."*

—*Milton Friedman*

The greatest source of complaints about "toxic masculinity" and the "patriarchy" exists in the workplace. The phrase "mansplaining" (is that not one of the most sexist comments ever made?) is a direct reference to the failed attempt of senior-level male managers who are attempting to provide clear direction and understanding to their junior-level female leaders. Why does this environment exist in this way? The simplest answer is we were not listening, and we were not paying attention. (The other answer is the hypersensitivity that is trademarked in the gynocentric paradigm; but if we claim this we would not be owning the issue, so let's stick with *not listening*.) The terra firma shifted, and we did not adjust to it. We know now. Or I hope so.

The call for organizational cultural transformation is not new. I am old enough to not only remember but to also have been part of the last time organizations transformed and recovered from the failure of poor leadership. In the early '80s America was a mess. Our products were not only inferior, they were also expensive. The laws around organizations were archaic and not only interfered with companies bringing great products to market, but also taxed them at rates that made no sense. The complacency of management, along with stupid government regulations, created an environment where managers justified doing even more stupid stuff just to survive.

Some of the stupid practices looked like taking shortcuts in environmental protection and disposing of waste and garbage. Other practices were the reduction in quality materials and the purchase of subcontracted goods on lowest price regardless of value or quality. The other amazingly short-sighted practice was looking at workers not as assets to one's business but rather as a cost that must be reduced or eliminated. I am a huge fan of Ronald Reagan, and he, like all men, was flawed and made mistakes. One of President Reagan's biggest mistakes was his response to decertify the Professional Air Traffic Controllers Organization (PATCO) in response to its strike. The result of that action created an open season on all unions. This event occurred less than a year after the devastation of the UAW International Harvester (IH) strike that basically destroy IH. Somehow, by the decertification of PATCO and the destruction of IH, unions became the villains.

The truth is, whenever two parties reach an impasse, the root cause is usually ego and the absence of listening. There were issues on both sides, and neither side was listening. There was also a larger event occurring at the same time. In the late '70s and early '80s, the baby boomers were entering the work force. This baby boomer generation was a completely different group than ever before. They were not interested in complying, conforming, or especially being controlled. In the early 1980s, America was in a world of hurt. We had inflation rates of upwards of 13 percent and unemployment of over 10 percent. Some parts of the country, like Michigan, fared far worse. At this time just about all leaders were old white men. These men suffered from many of the maladies that men today are accused of: arrogance, pursuit of status, emotional control and protection, winning at all costs, not listening, and, worst of all, the insider business notion that if the idea did not come from us it was not good. They thought the problem was caused by something other than them, yet they were blessed with the wisdom and omnipotence to get them out of the jam, and do so behind closed doors. Most of all, they would never admit defeat or failure.

Business was failing, leadership was failing, and America was failing. At that time, quality-management consultant W. Edwards Deming advocated for a system of leadership to empower workers, drive decisions down to the operations floor, and speed up the process of making things, all while improving the quality to world-class standards. What was so exceptional about this was through empowering workers, the pride of workmanship was restored. People took delight in the work they did because they knew their work mattered and, most of all, *they* mattered. We went from complete failure to profound success. A decade that began in near depression ended in near limitless success.

Also at this time, new products and new applications for the products had begun to emerge. The explosion of the microchip and technology was a game changer. The idea of a home computer was just beginning. These were not market-driven ideas. No one said (with the exception of a few geeky math majors), "I need a home computer." Innovation, creativity, and the freedom of thought were brought on by this new generation. IBM had been making computers for years, and it was not until computer geeks from the West Coast began to dig in and utilize this technology that things shifted. Those guys were Bill Gates, Steve Jobs, Steve Wozniak, and Paul Allen.

As this expansion was occurring, the face of the workplace was also changing. Far more women held positions of leadership or in higher levels of finance, law, and engineering—long bastions of male dominance. Also taking part in the expansion were Blacks, Asians, and Latinos. This was no longer just white folks. C suites no longer looked like the exclusive country clubs that they had been in the past. There was also for the first time an understanding that being a white dude was not a requirement for being successful in an important position—or at least people were starting to question this previously held assumption.

Though this idea of a diverse workplace was a great idea, the application still had not fully set in. I wish I could say that I was never challenged extensively whenever I wanted to hire a Black guy for a sales position or a woman for an engineering position. I was. When asked, "Why do you want to hire them?" I simply said, "They are the best people for the jobs." The response was always, "If they fail it's your ass." My response was, "Cool." They never failed.

That is how the barriers of oppression are broken. This is how paradigms are shifted. You stand face to face with the false narrative and take action to disprove it, and there is no longer a false narrative. Action, not debate, is the source of change.

I will never forget when I was, as part of the strategic planning committee of a sizable organization, to select a new human resource vice president from two internal candidates. One candidate, who was a brilliant man, had a PhD in organizational development from an excellent university and actually had taken a step back in his career to move home near his ailing mother. He performed well in the exact position we had open and had the requisite skills we were searching for (or at least we said we were). He was not selected. The person who got the promotion was a savvy political operative inside the organization. She was competent but not outstanding. The biggest issue with her was trust. I expressed that I thought trustworthiness was a foundational element for this role. I was then asked about the candidate that I supported. "Do you know he is a faggot?" I was stunned, and my response was, "If you mean he is gay, yes I knew. So what?" The woman was selected under the guise of expanding the female presence on the executive team. She found out I was opposed to her hiring, and within six months both the candidate I supported and I were gone.

I bring this up because that was when I first saw the erosion of the lessons learned from coming back from near economic extinction. This company had been near dead, and as a result of the work of a great team and some new and innovative leadership, it had risen from the ashes. We were growing twice as fast as our competition. What I also saw was the established leadership got afraid of the growth and innovation because it was not coming from them. The innovation, per Deming, was being driven from the field and the shop floor. The idea of command and control was proven unnecessary. They had achieved success, and because of their ego and low-grade narcissism, they were afraid. The idea of leading and empowering was lost on those who could not release control.

Not long after that the business was sold. That company, with its rich history and the thousands of jobs it created, no longer exists. The issues with every business I have ever worked with always begin at the top. The quote that begins this chapter is from a much longer paper written by Milton Friedman and Mike Jenson. I consider Mike to be one of the greatest teachers I have ever experienced and one of the biggest influences on me and my career. In their paper they basically said that business exists for the purpose of increasing shareholder value.

In the '70s, businesses ran on the idea of management by objective. Short-term goals, often in conflict, based on political compromise of the powers that be, were what drove decisions. The results were long decision-making processes, inconsistent direction and policy, and compromised quality and investment based on short-term financial goals. As I shared earlier, by 1980, America was nearly destroyed economically. Throughout the '80s and '90s we had unparalleled productivity and profitability. Through changes in pension programs and the advent of 401(k) s, more people than ever were engaged with the buying and selling of stocks. America and Americans got wealthy. With that wealth we got comfortable. The Deming mantra of "constancy of purpose" was replaced with quarterly results and increased share price. How quickly we forgot.

Our standard of living rose, and we were winning. Consumerism became the standard to judge success. Leaders were rewarded on results. Culture and employees became secondary. Businesses were on a roll, and, of course, it made no sense to "rock the boat." Everyone was getting paid. CEOs graced magazine covers, and now wealth was cool. Wealth got you laid. With the new comfort and convenience that the consumer products provide, whatever itch you had, a scratch was available. Most importantly, you made sure you were getting paid.

As we entered the 2000s, the brakes were hit a bit on the party. The advent of global competition was beginning to show. Competition from Japan already existed, so we could figure that out. The competition was now coming from China and India. With this increase in competition also came the advent of breakthroughs in logistics. Because of technology we were able to not only move stuff more quickly than ever, more importantly we were also able to know where it was en route. That may not seem like a big deal, but it was huge because we were no longer limited by geography. The ability to source goods and services from anywhere in the world was now available. With that came the ability to buy a widget from Malaysia for four dollars when our cost to make it was more than twenty dollars. Bingo, out-source that shit!

The problem was that someone here lost their job. Or if the part was being sourced here, the old supplier lost its contract or was forced to meet the price. I will not go into the macroeconomics of the cost of goods sold, but I hope you can see this began to create a ripple effect. The success we had gained through worker empowerment and empowered leadership was now being compromised by the purchase of cheap goods from overseas or in this country. To the guys on top it seemed like a no-brainer. Bring in the consultants from Deloitte or McKinsey and they will supply you with brilliantly constructed and written reports to support the decisions. What could go wrong?

What went wrong was leaders were making decisions because they were choosing from fear and greed, which are two big drivers of the stock market. As the stock market went, so did our business. What the leaders did not look at was the connection between their business and people. All people. The first point in Dr. Deming's management system was: create constancy of purpose toward improvement of product and service, with the aim to become competitive and to stay in business, and to provide jobs.

What went wrong? Leaders put their egos, their fears, and their greed above people. Unfortunately, these leaders and this behavior can often be tied to men. Ego, fear, and greed. You can see it everywhere: from the sycophants who inhabit the executive suites to the corps of consultants who were hired to justify the most idiotic of decisions to the growing disparity in compensation between executives and workers. You see it in the unwillingness to take any risk and the insulation of the business practices. Throw in a world that is growing evermore diverse, complex, and uncertain; add in ambiguity and volatility, both economic and cultural; and you've got to ask yourself, wouldn't you be afraid?

The result of that fear, along with the incredible amounts of money being made, not only impacted leadership, it also impacted the rank and file. The "put your head down and do a good job" mentality of the '50s has returned. The fear of losing one's job, and all that comes with it, is real; the result is a level of compliance that is unhealthy. You comply, or you're gone. We are generating a culture of corporate titty suckers. The CTSs, as they will be referred to, come in of all genders, races, and ethnicities. The unfortunate thing is throughout history white men have never made great slaves, and yet the fear, money, and interruption of the lifestyle of consumerism seem to be winning.

That fear is how the fishing trips, nights at the strip clubs, or time drinking in the cigar bars are both generated and justified.

Those who do not enjoy these activities are often excluded from very important decisions and processes. Frightened leaders employ these activities to build trust, assemble their "teams," and create the loyalty oaths. It is also how they build insulation and division between them and the things they need to engage with. That structure is also how CEOs remain so uninformed.

That insulation and that fear are what drives some of the most aberrant behaviors. It does not matter if it is a sexual scandal or a misappropriation of funds; the root is always some version of fear. The biggest issue is we do not allow leaders to express fear or to even acknowledge it. To some degree I get it: leaders are there to lead, and if they are freaking out, what does that do to the people they are leading? That is why a solid understanding of oneself and the ability to be transparent and authentic is what is required in leadership today.

One place where institutional fear is so prevalent is in sales and business development. I am forever amazed when I see that the organizational strategy for growth is formed by merger and acquisition. There was a time when growth was developed by the effort of sales and marketing teams. These teams would engage in the market, understand their customers, uncover their challenges, and then offer a solution unique to the customer that would build a relationship and often create a customer for life. To the fear-based, results-oriented-only manager, that process represents too long a process. They would prefer the more expensive yet more predictable model of merger or acquisition.

The issues with mergers and acquisitions are that although there is a significant revenue gain, the integration of the merging entities almost never goes smoothly. There is always the hidden cost of the impact on culture and the political upheaval that is created by the integration. I think the biggest impact that occurs is the impact on customers. I have never once seen a merger or acquisition increase the level of service or the value proposition to the customer. That impact has a devastating long-term impact to the culture of the company, and I assert it has an impact on the quality of life for all of us.

I have been in organizations where leaders do not express their fear and operate on top of it. It is weird, and it creates division within the ranks. I have also worked with leaders who addressed the fear and have been transparent about it. I have seen them demonstrate the courage to inquire. I have witnessed their heartache when they both saw and learned that the issues in their organizations were a result of their actions and decisions. I have listened to them as they go through the space of fear and terror, and when they lost control because they realized they never really had it.

I was also there when they began to inquire, when they began to trust and believe, and I saw the triumph when they understood that they could get through it. I was with them when their first attempt failed and they continued because the power of their conviction and commitment was greater than their fear and concern. This is the power of the human spirit. This is the power of courage. The gate from fear and frustration to making things right is courage.

The challenge we face today, and the immediate challenge to establish responsible masculine leadership, is choosing the right thing over the expedient. Choosing courage over comfort. Choosing something greater over the easy. The road to establishing responsible masculine leadership, manhood, and honor runs through the gate of courage. What is so amazing and beautiful, when we look at masculinity, courage and vulnerability are synonymous. Being vulnerable is what is required to listen and gain new knowledge. Let's go!

CHAPTER 9

# Multiculturalism and Identity Politics

*"The problem is that it has become politically awkward to draw attention to absolutes of bad and good. In place of manners, we now have doctrines of political correctness, against which one offends at one's peril: by means of a considerable circular logic, such offenses mark you as reactionary and therefore a bad person. Therefore if you say people are bad, you are bad."*

—*Lynne Truss*

There is no greater evidence of the abdication of responsible masculine leadership than the growth of multiculturalism/identity politics. Multiculturalism or identity politics is the politics of differences. Identity politics has become the way the "disadvantaged" have identified themselves. It began with Black people and the LGBTQ community; it now includes indigenous people and people with disabilities. Given the constant complaint about the "patriarchy," victimized women, like the #MeToo movement, will often identify with the pull of multiculturalism. Basically anyone who identifies as a victim of any kind is lumped into this group. There are even some men—straight, white, able-bodied men—who identify with this group. They are called allies. (I just threw up in my mouth a little, fully understanding how our language has been ripped off and purloined by this mindset.)

Since we have such a large population of victims, we must have a monstrous villain to keep the drama alive. The villain in the drama of multiculturalism is any able-bodied, straight, white guy who does not claim allied-ship. As we build this drama, with our huge population of victims, and our clearly identified villains, we need a hero or heroes. The heroes in this story are the feminized males, media people, and the militant liberal women. Welcome to the United States of America, circa 2012 and beyond.

Yes, we are the villains, and our tool of oppression has been capitalism. It does not matter that most major social gains or cultural improvements in the history of Western civilization have been the result of the hard work and innovation of men. Never let the facts interfere with the narrative. We must understand that what we are guilty of is not listening and not being aware of the changes that were occurring around us. By ignoring the changing landscape and thinking those small changes were nothing to be concerned about, we missed the shift in context and the changing values that were occurring under our noses. The biggest changes are the ones in communication and manipulation of our fellow men.

> *"I would risk violence a thousand times rather than risk the emasculation of a whole race."*
> —*Mahatma Gandhi*

In times of change, uncertainty, ambiguity, and complexity it is easy to lose sight of where we are going and why we are doing what we do. The failure of masculine leadership over the last thirty years or so was our thinking everything was fine (the other four-letter "F" word). We failed to communicate what was important, thinking that leading by example was all we needed to do. We made the ultimate mistake; we viewed the world through the lens of our experiences and commitments. In doing so, because it is kind of automatic, we failed to operate in a way that was seen as transparent and showed the intention of our actions. We were just being us. The world was changing, and we did not see the change.

In an environment of rapid change, leading by example is not enough. What is required is the communication of the vision—that is, where we are going and why we are going there. This communication must be done so in a way that garners the acceptance of the forthcoming change by those affected. They must be enrolled in the idea for it to happen. That's why leadership is such a bitch.

The world has changed. There are new forces, ideas, intentions, and direction. Some of these have agendas and ambitions, and those ambitions can often be at our expense. While we were working, creating wealth, and engaging to make things better, we were not paying attention to what was going on around us. That absence of awareness was seen as us being sexist, racist, xenophobic, and homophobic by those who felt as if they were not included.

America is an idea, an exceptional idea. From the beginning of time, men have attempted to command and control their fellow man. They did so to provide some form of order so we would do more than just kill each other. For the most part, what this command and control did was just create more effective ways to kill more men and, in doing so, scare the rest of us so we were more easily controlled. Throughout the years, the idea of command and control has played out within the structures of empires and kingdoms.

The idea of America, a self-governing nation, ruled by the people and for the people had never been done before. Add in that the rights of every man and woman were not only equal, they were inalienable and bestowed upon us by our creator. The idea of a creator, a deity, a divine source, something greater than man, something uncontrollable and something inarguable, can be seen as dangerous and unworkable for those who must control all things around them. That idea flies in the face of any monarch, tyrant, or dictator. The idea of freedom flies in the face of those who desire power and control.

You can see that anyone who has an agenda to control, dictate, or operate in an authoritarian way would view America as an ideological threat that must be destroyed. That is why currently fundamental Islamists are so driven to destroy America. The idea of freedom, equality, and choices flies in the face of their rigid doctrine and need for control. Freedom and the idea of freedom are at odds with the various forms of Marxism, be it communism, socialism, or the current version that is alive and well in America today, Democratic socialism, or the Democrat Party. If America exists as constructed, if people have the ability to live in freedom and sovereignty, those beliefs are in direct conflict with the ideologies of Islam, monarchies, or any form of totalitarianism. The ideas of individual freedom, individual choice, and expression, away from approval by the state or leader, are completely unacceptable by those ideologies and represent a grave threat to them.

Multiculturalism is the false substitute for that freedom. It is used to support a form of totalitarianism in which the party or the government is the supplier of everything, including your rights, and in return you are provided safety and survival. All that is required from you is to give up your identity and not ask too many questions. This is great for you because you no longer have to worry about anything. The government will provide you with free health care, cell phone, food, education, and place to stay to ensure that you are not homeless—plus a guaranteed minimum income. Everything you need or want is provided by the government except your freedom. The only thing they want is your alliance and, of course, that you let them know of anyone who is not aligned. We must call out the noncompliers.

The idea of "multiculturalism" is not a new one. It is the way the world is organized. What do we have when a number of disengaged diverse cultures are all seeking what they want with no interconnection? The answer is a world of war. That is how we have lived throughout the ages: countries battling countries, ideas fighting ideas, all with the desire to win. Inevitably we have seen, in times of stress, this conflict will turn into "winning at all costs," which means nobody wins and the real losers are those on the sidelines—the innocent, the truly marginalized and disenfranchised. It is about *power* not harmony, it becomes about *ego* not people, and mostly it become about the leaders getting what they want: power, riches, and control. Multiculturalism is a ruse and a quest for a shift in the power dynamic.

Now we have the multicultural mindset leading the way in our country. It is the relinquishing of individualism to belong to a greater collective. As it is structured in the West today, it has become this loosely linked alliance of "disenfranchised" and "oppressed" people with no common thread or connection other than their blaming of able-bodied white men and the idea of freedom for all that ails them. The question I have is, what is the endgame? What is the desired outcome? All I see is a desire for power. Like most things that come from this mentality, it is based in emotion, and that emotion is fear and anger.

What we are dealing with is an ongoing, constant complaint from this gynocentric paradigm. Reasoning is not the answer to this insanity. The experience they have, regardless of its legitimacy, is real. They are not making this up. They feel what they feel, and feelings are the leading indicator of what is true. Add in the press and media support for their feelings, with the never-ending bombardment of information, stories, and news feeds, and it brings the fear and anger to near panic levels and a state of constant and perpetual victimization. Now please add in (running to the rescue) solutions that provide one thing, safety. Welcome to America, again, and welcome to the political structure we are currently facing.

Have a concern about gun violence? Beto has a solution—they will confiscate all the guns. Are you are concerned with climate change? The passionate rants of seventeen-year-old Greta Thunberg will deepen those fears yet make you feel like you are part of a bigger community. No worries though, Alexandria Ocasio-Cortez (AOC) and Kamala Harris have the Green New Deal, and we will end the use of fossil fuels immediately and save the world. Do you have a problem with your school loans? No worries, Bernie and good old Uncle Joe will make them go away. Do you need money? No problem, Andrew Yang has basic minimum income. Are you worried about health care? Done! Barack Obama, Nancy, and Bernie all have ideas for free health care for all. Just vote for them; the government can solve all your problems.

Sound great, doesn't it? There are just three things wrong with this idea. First is that the idea of multiculturalism—a group of groups without a shared purpose—has never worked in the history of mankind and will end in mutually shared destruction. Next, what they are spelling out is economic socialism or social Marxism, which again has never worked in the history of mankind. The most recent nightmare example is playing out in Venezuela, a once thriving nation rich in oil and natural resources that is now in the midst of economic depression and staggering inflation, not to mention limitless corruption. Finally, every solution is external to the citizen. It requires dependency on the government. That is not what the government of the USA was designed for.

This country was founded on the idea of freedom, personal sovereignty, and individuality. There is nothing in multiculturalism/identity politics that is even close to being American. That is why the role of BLM and the 1619 Project is so sinister. These two organizations, one that is openly Marxist, have instilled in our thoughts that America is inherently and structurally racist. Racist—there is no word as emotionally charged, more damning and more triggering than that. There is no idea that will instill shame and anger and an immediate call to action than that word. Why? Because America is inherently good, and Americans are inherently good people. It was not that long ago that America was a land divided by race. We fought a war over it, and that war does not seem to have ended.

As young boy I remember when Dr. Martin Luther King was going to march through my town of Cicero, Illinois. He was stopped because the National Guard and the Illinois State Police did not feel they could keep him safe. It was the only planned march he did not fulfill, and this was after Selma. This idea of racism is highly personal to me.

Dr. King's dream of having white children and black children living together has been realized. Is there work to do? Of course. The ground taken since his death has been remarkable, and there is still work to do. No other work expresses the grounds taken more than the book *We Have Overcome* by my dear friend and colleague, Jason D. Hill, PhD. Dr. King's dream is not being realized because of government policies, and I can actually argue that the policies have interfered with the completion of the dream, thus causing racial division to exist longer than necessary. The racial divide is being closed because it is the right thing to do. Because as it states in the Constitution, all men are created equal. The structure is there, and it works. There is no greater evidence of that than what occurred on that chilly November evening in 2008, when we as one nation, under God, indivisible, with liberty and justice for all, America elected a Black man to the highest position in the land. That man was Barack Hussein Obama, and that position was president of the United States of America.

So if that is the case, why is there such a divide now? Two reasons: money and power. It is that simple. Let's start with the money. As I said there has always been this pull against our independence. If you are independent, then you are hard to control. America is still the richest country in the world, and to control that would be a big win. (Consider the commission on that deal.) Being independent also means we are a bit more difficult to corrupt, because even if you pay off the "big guys," like, say, Joe Biden or Barack Obama, we still have three hundred million humans who are independent thinking and acting. (Have you ever wondered why Barack Obama is only good at getting himself elected and no one else?) Certain large global entities—primarily big tech, big pharma, and large financial institutions—want free access to these markets so they can control them and make more money. How do they do it? As with any deal, you win by gaining access to decision makers and by creating barriers for the competition—that is, small and midsize independent businesses. You must then ask the question, who has the influence to create those policies and influence access points? Again this is a high-level overview. There are more dots to connect, and it would take a book in and of itself to do that, so please look at this as the strategy.

The second piece is where it fits together: power. As wealthy and successful as these large companies and the elites have become, they have been less than successful in getting a political toehold on the US markets. We will buy their stuff; just don't tell us what to think. Even recently, you saw the failed attempt by Nike and the NBA to cram Black Lives Matter down our throats. They attempted to influence social policy in the marketplace, and the customers rejected it. Nike and the NBA lost millions if not billions in revenue. Never forget about reason number one, money. Always follow the money. If there is one truth to take from this book, it is that. In America, follow the money if you want to find the truth. So how does multiculturalism fit in with the money? Simple, votes.

To gain political power you need votes. There are not enough folks in the 1 percent to gain that. They don't have enough money to buy the votes—just ask Michael Bloomberg. They need people. Bingo, we merge large corporate global interests with the disenfranchised and marginalized, and we may have something. Politics do make strange bedfellows. (See Exhibit 1.) The issue is, are there enough disenfranchised, oppressed, and marginalized people? The real answer is no, but thank God for the elites. This is why there is an ever expanding subsection of victims. Creating victimization as a position of empowerment is essential for this agenda to succeed. They have the mainstream media to carry their water, and we had Donald Trump as our president. He was the perfect villain for their narrative. Remember—the villains are straight, white, able-bodied men. Throw in his combative nature, his wealth, and the, at least perceived, ruthlessness and privilege he enjoys, and the legend grew. Please add his sexual prowess, his less than politically correct comments, and his bravado, along with his unwillingness to ever apologize, and we had the super villain for their drama. Hollywood could not have created a better character! All that was left to do was recruit.

The first target was women. Less than a week after his inauguration, across the nation there were protests organized against his presidency. Millions of women in the bright pink pussy hats protested a president who had been in office for five days. What in God's name could they be protesting? In addition, we then had the Russian investigation. How much more anti-American could a person be than to collude with the Russians to steal an election? Only a super villain would collude with the evil Russians. My God, who would do such a thing? Someone who said, "I grab them by their pussy"—that's who. Not only was the super villain created, we had the perfect person to play that character.

That was followed with the impeachment (the first impeachment of Donald Trump, that is) and all that went with that. We have had forty-six presidents in our history, and Trump was only the third to be impeached (and the first to be impeached twice). Even Nixon avoided impeachment. The narrative around

Clinton's impeachment was that it was all political, so that one does not count either. Trump must really be a bad guy. Orange Man bad. Orange Man wanted to drain the swamp and create some balance again.

Orange Man was also a complete stand for the sovereignty and independence of America. He was an advocate for all peoples living great lives. He was a stand for the Constitution and the freedom it represents. He was an advocate for energy independence and personal sovereignty. The economy was expanding. Job growth, especially in the sectors identified by the elites as being marginalized, were growing. Standards of living were increasing, and then there was the stock market. People in the middle class whose 401(k)s were thriving after about ten years of economic stagnation could see forward movement and access to their dreams. Orange Man was a threat to the elites.

Then COVID hit, and though we don't want to get into that here because there will be hundreds of books written on this, and let's just say this was a true defining point, on the most gynocentric issue of all, safety. Never mind that the original estimate of deaths caused by the pandemic was between two million and three million Americans. We freaked out. Please don't be concerned that the actual deaths were about 16 to 25 percent of the estimate. Out of an abundance of caution, we took drastic measures and shut down our country, and as of this writing some shutdowns still remain. I am not arguing the validity of the pandemic; what I am saying is that when history looks at this, if we still teach history then, we will find that almost every action we took was in error, including our attempts to "flatten the curve."

As a result of these events (and some fairly obnoxious tweets Mr. Trump became famous for), the foundation for building a coalition of the marginalized, oppressed, perpetually offended, and morally righteous had begun to grow to create a real foundation. Now add in the video of the white police officer kneeling on the neck of George Floyd, a convicted felon, high on fentanyl, and the narrative that went with that—white policemen killing black people—we were getting closer. Orange Man really bad. White men bad. America is systemically racist. Please don't forget the media standing in front of burning buildings and proclaiming they were the result of "mostly peaceful protests." We successfully created the white guilt needed by suburban women and their cuckolded men to join in. We had a winner. From that position and emotional state, defunding the police made perfect sense. So did voting for Joe Biden and his crime family and Kamala Harris and her radical ideas and limitless ambition.

It is not lost on me that Mr. Trump is an acquired taste. A dear friend of mine described him as odious. What he also is, is a complete alpha male. He loves his family, he loves God, and he loves his country, and I believe he will do everything within his power, including pledging his life, his fortune, and his sacred honor, to support this great nation. That is why I have supported and defended him, flaws and all. All men have flaws; he is no different. Nor are you and me. If you do not believe that, you have work to do my friend.

This is where we come in. If you are having a WTF moment right now, I don't blame you. I am too. We cannot indulge in that though. It is time for us to reestablish masculine leadership to its foundational reason for existing. As men we need to get straight with what is going on and ask ourselves, is this working? My guess is, like me, you see it is not. Before we take action, we need to get our minds right. First and foremost, the relationship we must first establish is the one with ourselves. There is no one to blame here—who could see it coming? Certainly, I did not. When some folks tried to explain it to me, it occurred as wacky conspiracy theory stuff, which was more dangerous than these wacky socialists. *How bad could it get?* I thought. I am not sure I want to see.

The process of establishing honorable manhood and re-sponsible masculine leadership in America is not something we should do because we are under attack. It is something to do because it is the right thing to do. It is something for us to begin because it brings access to our own self-expression and self-knowledge. Jay Niblick, the author of *What's Your Genius?*, says that self-awareness plus authenticity equals success. I don't know what the future holds. I have no control over that. What I do have control over are my choices, my attitude, and how I respond to my feelings. That is where we are going. That is the promise of this book.

Hang in there; this keeps building. Thank you for the gift of your time, attention, mind, and heart. That is the greatest gift anyone can give another, and I am most appreciative.

## CHAPTER 10

# Clash of Ideology

*"Those who profess to favor freedom and yet depreciate agitation, are people who want crops without ploughing the ground; they want rain without thunder and lightning; they want the ocean without the roar of its many waters. The struggle may be a moral one, or it may be a physical one, or it may be both. But it must be a struggle. Power concedes nothing without a demand. It never did and it never will."*

*—Frederick Douglass*

We are ending the first part of this book, and I think I can put it pretty simply. This attack on men, this gender war, this cultural war we are in the midst of, is a result of simple miscommunication. Men and woman are different, very different, and we have not acknowledged that difference. We have made the differences wrong, and we have assigned words to it like sexism, racism, or xenophobia.

From the beginning, men have built the systems, built the processes, written the laws, and, for the most part, constructed the world. Western civilization is the combination of Greek rationalism and the Judeo-Christian ethic. That is the traditional expression of men, masculinity, and manhood. That is the way it has existed for millennia. We have accepted that the way we constructed it was "right." Wars have been fought, and these structures have survived. In many ways they thrived. There was little inquiry as to the "why" or the mindset of this way of operating. It worked, so get busy. The system was designed to produce results, and to do so effectively and efficiently. There was little thought given to diversity, equality, or inclusion. The system was structured, for the most part, for survival. Fit in or risk not surviving.

Success was dependent upon fitting in. Those who did not fit in were not treated well. Others who have not "fit in" have revolted. As our culture has developed, we have included a more diverse population into the roles of leadership, and high-level contributors. The question being asked more often is, how do we balance the need for inclusion, greater participation, and expansion of ideas without reducing the results produced and lowering the standards? The issue is, *what is the mindset that is asking the questions?* For the most part, the question is not pure inquiry, but a question informed from shame, abandonment, and the experience of betrayal. The result of the question, at least by some, is currently that America is a patriarchal nation that was founded on the principles of hate, sexism, racism, xenophobia, and greed. That sounds a bit funny if you remember America was about escaping the reign of King George and discovering something entirely new and exciting.

To quote the warden from *Cool Hand Luke,* I assert, "What we've got here is failure to communicate." That is no small problem, and if you can define the problem, you are on your way. The real problem is we (men) are looking at the issue through our lens and our lens only. The other issue is that those opposed to men are currently looking at the world through their lens and their lens only and thinking that is the truth. Insert multiculturalism, while continuing to look at the problem through those unique perspectives, and you can have a mess. Add in the media that is rewarded for drama, upset, and fear, and we have a pretty wild situation. Throw in the conflict that has existed since the Garden of Eden, and the existential question of "What is freedom and what price is to be paid for it?"

As dudes we have to own that we have not been paying a lot of attention. Come on—own it; it's OK. We have been busy building stuff and doing shit. The complexity of the world has gotten to the point where we need to significantly up our game. With freedom comes responsibility, and it is time we increase the level of responsibility at which we operate. That begins with really getting to know who we are: understanding ourselves, our passions, our strengths, our blind spots, and, most of all, our purpose. To quote Dean Wormer, going through life fat, drunk, and stupid is no longer acceptable, no matter how fun it is. It's OK for recreational purposes, but it's a no pass as a default.

Steve Zaffron and Dave Logan wrote a most excellent book several years ago called *The Three Laws of Performance.* In that book, the third law states "future based conversations transform how situations occur." That is what this book is about. It is time we men transform how this thing we call *life* will occur. It is time for us to lead from a position of responsibility and, from that position, begin with the foundational elements of masculinity to provide, protect, and leave a legacy. It is time we reestablish and reconfigure what being a man is and what manhood looks like.

Here is how the next section will go. We are going to look at root causes. We just finished looking at some of the issues; now we will be looking at how those issues got to be issues. If you are a hypersensitive beta boy or ally, it may be rough for you. What I want you to know is I love you, I understand, and we have to end the bullshit. I have limitless compassion for imperfection and timeless patience for growth, development, and learning. I have zero tolerance for bullshit. The challenge is knowing where that line is. I get it wrong often, and I will clean it up when I do. But if you are a skinny-jean-wearing, neck-beard-having, soy latte hair-bun kind of guy, this will be an in-your-face experience because you are a man and I am a stand that you experience your masculinity and manhood in the most empowered way. To do that you must tap into what your authentic expression is. To do that you must have the courage to confront your fears and any inauthentic structures you have created, including being a feminist dance therapy major at Oberlin College.

Also, if you are some clueless alpha male bully who has been running around being a jag bag, you too will be confronted but in a much different way. You will just need to put your ego and possibly your dick in check. Yep, I said it. Sexual irresponsibility is one of the violations we need to get super responsible about. This is a nonnegotiable.

Calling out or holding people "to account" can sometime be code for shaming or making people wrong, or blaming them. That is not the intention. Communicating with candor and directness, knowing you have courage and integrity, and we have the level of trust and acceptance of one another that we can be unambiguous yet respectful with one another is a way to begin to develop a deeper connection when the current may be a divide. I have found that direct, frank, bold, and loving communication can move mountains. Challenge from love, and seeing the best in you is foundational to growth. That is why we are here.

One other point I want to make. In our quest for freedom, self-governing, and personal sovereignty, we must realize we will never eliminate the threat, the noise, or the opposition or the cries of "America is bad." We must understand the resistance to freedom and the opposition to it. This is required for it to exist in its most powerful state. I know it is crazy; one can say it is fucking nuts. The truth is, for freedom to exist we must allow the Bernies, the AOCs, and even the Barack Hussein Obamas access to the public sphere. Our freedom is dependent upon it. What our freedom is also dependent upon is for free men like you and me, to stand up to the opposition: to learn, to grow, and develop into the leaders this great nations needs and desires. That is why we are here.

That is what is in store. Thanks for being in this ride. Let's rock!

# PART II

## ROOT CAUSE ANALYSIS

How We Got This Way
(Why the Shit Hit the Fan)
The Abdication of Masculine Leadership
And Its Adverse Impact

"Maybe we are searching amongst the branches,
for what only appears in the roots"

—Rumi

CHAPTER 11

# The Loss of the Matriarchy

*"The female, not the male, determines all the conditions of the animal family. Where the female can derive no benefit from association with the male, no such association takes place."*
—*Robert Briffault*

I may be wrong here, but I will assert one of the biggest costs of the radicalized feminist movement is the loss of matriarchy. Before we've gone too far, let me explain what I mean by the radicalized feminist movement. Originally, feminism was the suffrage movement: women rightfully achieving the right to vote and being seen as equal citizens under the law. Beyond the unquestionable right to vote, women now hold elected offices across the land. As of this writing, women held 24 of the seats of the US Senate and 119 of the 435 House seats. The mayors of twenty-seven of the 100 largest cities across the United States, including the great city of Chicago, are women.

The second wave of feminism was a call for social equality and control of their reproductive rights. *Roe v. Wade* is settled law, and women have the right to choose or not in all fifty states. Wage difference has been improved across all aspects of work. In executive pay as of 2019, women earned $0.98 for every dollar a man earned. Not quite equal, but a big improvement on the $0.60 of the '80s. If we look at measures like law school, women make up 52.4 percent of enrollment. Medical schools have a similar result: 50.5 percent of humans enrolled in medical school are women. I think it is safe to say that women working with men have achieved measurable equality of both social status, say, and influence in our country.

Never let the facts interfere with the narrative, though. Across social media and mainstream media, especially on MSNBC and CNN, the narrative is not that. The narrative is that America is a sexist, patriarchal, racist, xenophobic, oppressive culture and that the feminist agenda and the gynocentric cure of multiculturalism is the only solution to end the patriarchy and create true equality, inclusion, diversity, and justice for all. As long as that diversity excludes able-bodied white men. This narrative is the radical feminist agenda.

This radical feminist gynocentric agenda, which is shaping most every narrative we see or hear, is ardently anti-man and anti-masculinity. It is also anti-American, anti-tradition, and strangely anti-feminine. The impact of that is the impact on matriarchal expression.

If we look at history there are very few, if any, identified matriarchal cultures found. I

Here is the definition by the *American Heritage Dictionary.*
ma·tri·arch (mā′trē-ärk′)
*n.*
1. A woman who rules a family, clan, or tribe.
2. A woman who dominates a group or an activity.
3. A highly respected woman who is a mother.

was blessed to have been raised in one. Not only was my family matriarchal, the town I lived in was led by women. They did not hold many official positions, but if you lived there you knew who ran the show. My grandmother. This is not about my grandmother's leadership. What I am speaking of is the loss of the matriarch.

It's a difficult position. Leading from a completely feminine mindset and expression is challenging in a world constructed primarily through a masculine paradigm. I look at some who have been successful: Ruth Bader Ginsburg, Golda Meir, and Margaret Thatcher come to mind. Currently Mary Barra, the CEO of General Motors, and Kristi Noem, the governor of South Dakota, are examples of matriarchal leadership who are powerful, effective, and feminine. I believe Princess Diana was one of the last great matriarchs. Princess Di fully embraced her divine femininity and yet asserted her position and her power on causes she felt worthy of her attention all—while not losing her identity and authentic expression.

I believe the greatest characteristic of outstanding matriarchal leadership is the ability for the leader to release her personal position, knowing full well she can always return to it, to garner an understanding of the other position. Said another way, matriarchal leaders don't view issues through their own bias and prejudice. They actually get as close to an objective viewpoint as possible while understanding the relevance of the issue, yet remaining connected enough to act. This skill is what made Ruth Bader Ginsburg a legend and allowed her to have a close personal relationship with fellow Supreme Court Justice Anton Scalia. I think a great way to see the difference is to look at how different Meghan Markle is as compared to Princess Diana. The best way to demonstrate this is through Ms. Markle's tendency to personalize every event and often makes herself the victim. Princess Diana seemed to take a leadership position where she would use her place and power to forward an agenda in service of people. It seemed to never be about her, yet her identity and personality were ever present.

An extremely powerful leadership skill is the ability to release one's position in order to see the position of someone else. It is essential to root cause analysis, and it is essential to be able to reach across any aisle to create a consensus agreement. In the world of radicalized feminism, the tie to the group identity and gynocentric agenda does not allow for that. From that position, all that is left is power, control, and compliance. No one demonstrates that better than the aforementioned mayor of Chicago, Lori Lightfoot. She is a passionate and, I am sure, committed woman, who, until recently, I believed was beyond corruptible. She is also incredibly unsuccessful in her role and creates more divides every day. Her failure is her unwillingness to see and accept anything other than her own position.

Having been blessed by the experience of matriarchal leadership, I long for the warmth and clarity it provided. One of the challenges of matriarchal leadership is the need for partnership with men. Men must provide the environment so that women can lead. What that looks like is making sure the skills, resources, and elements for success are available. Men must also protect that environment so women feel secure—more than secure, they must feel free to express themselves in a way that takes the entire community into consideration. One of the challenges men face is the tendency to be myopic and see only one issue at a time. Women have the ability to see multiple fields at one time and understand the interplay between each component far better than we do. (I understand this is a generalization, but it is used to make a point.) This level of complexity can only occur in a secure space. The last thing that men provide for the matriarchal leader is the idea of legacy. A long-term vision is oftentimes multidimensional. Men are outstanding at creating plans; women are great at the execution of the complexity of them. That is why the partnerships I will explore later is so essential for the growth and prosperity of our communities.

The problem with radical feminization is they have no interest in partnership. Their perspective and narrative are that men, primarily abled-bodied white men, have abused and pillaged the land and the culture, and need to comply with the new gynocentric agenda or be cancelled. What I find most curious is that the rage, anger, violence, and destruction radical feminists blame men for are the exact tactics they are using against men. The only men who survive are the emasculated ones. They are creating a culture of men who are eunuchs and cuckolds. It is a culture of zero discourse and less opposition. It is a culture of obedience, of falling in line and, of course, compliance. It is a culture that abhors individuality, personal expression, freedom, free speech, and self-expression. The oppression they claim to despise is a product of the system they are creating.

The question is, where are we men responsible? If we are to change this we must be responsible for it. If not, it will only lead to some type of war. The truth is war solves nothing, because it is really difficult to change ideas, thoughts, and beliefs. It is nearly impossible to shift someone's truth in any way other them helping them to discover a different truth. That is a lot of work, and work worthy of doing. The truth is always discovered; it is never told.

What do we need to do? First and foremost, do the work that will allow us to listen. Clean our own house. Develop ourselves so we can be with the anger, the rage, and the upset. We need to listen to the complaints without resorting to a defensive position. This is what listening is about. Behind every complaint is usually a commitment, and that is what we must listen for. It does not matter if it is true to us; it is true to them. And if it is true to them, it is true. This is hard work, and we will want it to be over before it is, so we must continue to listen. For us to create a world that works, each person must have the experience of being heard, of being gotten, and of being understood. People, all people, must know that they matter. That is a big lift. That is the work for us to do. If you do nothing else but get someone, really listen to them so that they are heard, shit changes. And that is the beginning, my friend.

## CHAPTER 12

# The Day Things Changed; We Peed Ourselves

*"You never want a serious crisis to go to waste. I mean, it's an opportunity to do things that you think you could not do before."*
—*Rahm Emanuel*

Tuesday, September 11, 2001, everything changed. It was a beautiful morning throughout most of the eastern part of America. Clear, sunny, and warm, yet one could sense that fall was arriving. The day began with business as usual; life in the States was pretty good. We were in the beginning of a new millennium, which began much like the last one had ended: everything was cool—"It's all good, man."

We had a bit of a contentious election, in the sense that we did not know which of the two guys running was going to be the new president. In 2001, as much as Newt Gingrich wanted to express a differing opinion, there was little difference between the Democrats and the Republicans. We had been engaged in a time of constant growth and economic good times. America was rocking, and no one really paid attention to the politicians. The GOP did get pissed at President Clinton because he was kind of a party guy—I mean he did get a blowjob in the Oval Office by an intern. I guess that showed poor judgment. The truth is, at the time, which one of us dudes did not think that Billy was the cool president?

Unlike the most recent election that showed we have two distinctly different visions for America, in 2001 we pretty much could not tell the difference between George Bush and Al Gore. They were kind of the same guy. Al Gore was the son of a former US Senator and the vice president to Clinton, and George Bush was the son of the president before Clinton. Al Gore had his global warming issue that mattered to him, and Bush was really about maintaining the status quo that had been going on since the middle of the Reagan administration. It was all about the money. We were comfortable, wealthy (or at least it seemed that way), and without real issues. It seemed the Bush administration's mantra was much like that of the Joe Maddon–led Cubs team in 2016: "Try Not to Suck." America seemed to have achieved that "shining city on the hill" status, or so we thought. The job of the president was "don't fuck it up."

That morning in September, it all changed. A plane crashed into the north tower of the World Trade Center in New York City. People were stunned. They literally could not believe or understand what had happened. Then a few minutes later, another one crashed into the south tower. A few minutes later, a third plane crashed into the Pentagon in Washington, DC. We began to realize we were under attack, but by whom? And why? There was a fourth plane, which, depending on what report you choose to believe, was on its way to attack either the US Capitol or the White House. In an act of selfless heroism, several passengers acted to take the plane down to avoid further damage to America. In retrospect, I find that to be a bit too convenient, and it really does not matter. This day changed the course of America.

We now have the benefit of nearly twenty years of perspective to view this event. What I will share was not possible then because the nature of the attacks was so surprising and so unforeseen by most of us. We responded in a way that was consistent with who we were, our values, and the vision we were living into. We viewed this attack as a shocking and vulgar interruption in the status quo. In retrospect, it marked a coming of age and an understanding that who we thought we were, maybe wasn't *really* who we were.

The immediate response was one of unrivaled patriotism, or at least that is how it played in the media. Chants of "USA" could be heard throughout the land. Lee Greenwood's song "God Bless the U.S.A." celebrated the love of the USA and our pride of being American. Toby Keith sang a song about how the USA was gonna kick your ass if you messed with us. The love that sprang out to the police and firefighters who responded was beyond measure. We were injured, and we were appreciative.

We got cheapshotted, and our response was like that from a typical guy. We puffed out our collective chests and made big promises. George Bush did what we expected from him: he cowboyed up. He talked tough and made big promises. He acknowledged the loss yet refused to show it hurt. It the early days we were all together, loving America, standing for America, and being strong for America. The reality was, it was a bit different than that. I look back and see this was the beginning of the loss of masculine leadership in America. This was the beginning of our national embrace of victimization. This is when we chose safety over freedom. We failed the test of exiting adolescence to enter manhood, and we bullshitted ourselves about that.

This was not across the board. There were tens of thousands of young men and women who flooded recruiting centers to fight for their country. The flying of the American flag was everywhere, and the support for the police departments across the country was unparalleled. We said the right things, yet something was missing. We were freaked out, and we did not own that we were freaked out. What was missing was leadership. What we got was appeasement, performance, and manipulation. We were tested, and we failed.

The immediate impact was that the stock market was shut down for about a week, and when markets opened up again there was a drop of nearly 15 percent. Panic selling set in, and some folks lost a bunch of money. Please remember we had been moving from pensions to 401(k)s and tons of folks were in the market who never had been before, causing much of the sell-off. Funny thing, within about thirty days the markets were back to the pre-9/11 levels. Again, funny how that happened. Some people made fortunes.

Almost instantly we learned who was responsible: Osama bin Laden and al-Qaeda. They represented a radical fundamentalist Islamic ideology that chanted "death to America." Al-Qaeda was an anti-American terrorist group based throughout the Middle East. They were responsible for attacks on the USS *Cole* and on two US embassies in Africa. Al-Qaeda had previously bombed the World Trade Center in 1993. There were at least a half a dozen attacks by al-Qaeda on America throughout the world during the Clinton administration, and yet we did very little about it. We failed in providing and protecting our country. Our obsession with wealth, comfort, and maintaining control had us abdicate our role of truly protecting our country. The leaders of our country were not leading. They were managing; they were more focused on what was in it for themselves and keeping things "cool" than in leading our nation and maintaining an environment of freedom and liberty. This is what complacent arrogance looks like.

President Bush's response was to create the largest bureaucracy in the history of our country with the Department of Homeland Security. He also suspended the Constitution to ensure our safety. He mobilized some forces to capture Osama bin Laden, or at least that is what was reported. The result was bombing the shit out of some mountains in Afghanistan. We did not capture bin Laden for ten more years. We did get the Transportation Security Administration (TSA) out of it, so now we have to take off our shoes and our belts to get on a plane. I guess that is nice.

The government is the government, and our forefathers knew the solutions to our issues were not going to come from them. Our forefathers knew that the real solutions and the true expression of American exceptionalism would come from the people. For the most part, the population did not question what was going on. There was a time before 9/11 when we were in a world of hurt, and a strong cowboy type, Ronnie Reagan, had come in and righted the ship. Now we had another cowboy (Bush), and we were sure he would get it right. We were America dammit! and we deserved to get it right.

We had become very comfortable and very corporate. Greed was good, the stock market was our friend, and the government seemed to be working. As men we were very driven to succeed; success was our god, and success was measured by money, stock options, Rolex watches, and BMWs. We all dressed alike: blue and gray suits, white and powder-blue shirts—we were allowed some leeway to express ourselves through our ties. Yellow and pink power ties should just about say it all. It was OK to express your authenticity as long as it was in line with the corporate message. Fitting in was really important.

This could have been a time of inquiry, of questioning, and of understanding. There was no reason to inquire because the results were our target. The results were all that mattered. I remember I was shocked, and my first thought was *This is gonna cost me sixty grand.* Yep, that was my first thought when I saw the plane hit the tower. Not—*We are under attack!* Not—*Those poor people!* Not even—*Why would someone do this?* No, my first thought was that this was gonna cost me money, a lot of it. What I said earlier about not being able to see what was going on—I was a poster child for it. I was the typical alpha male at the time: shallow, money-driven, arrogant, narcissistic, and obsessed with my own comfort and pleasure, and to hell with anyone else. The patriotism, the love of country, the "upset" was mostly performance—a type of looking good. The real drive was, let's get back to normal. The challenge would be that the old normal had been removed.

Looking back on that day, we were ill prepared. It did not matter that we had the warning signs and there had been at least six previous attacks. We were the USA, and you'd have to be crazy to fuck with us—especially a pissant Arab country. We were tight with the Saudis, so they would keep their folks cool. Hell, the Bushes had a long history with the Saudi Kingdom. There was no way they would turn on us. What would be demonstrated over the next seven years or so was every behavior labeled as "toxic" by men throughout our culture, especially men in leadership positions. The items identified by Brené Brown as "toxic behaviors" were on display. The biggest one that I saw was the willingness to take very high risks.

What I discovered about risk is interesting. High-risk behavior is not generated by a sense of thrill or invincibility. It is not created by the presence of courage or even power. What I have learned about high-risk behavior is it is typically reactive. As mentioned earlier, Einstein said if he had sixty minutes to solve a problem he would spend fifty-five of it defining what the problem was. In 2001, men were very reactive. We were reactive because we operated from a sense of "cocksure ignorance"—"Don't bother me with the details; I know what I am doing." We had a bias for action and a desire to "git 'er done." One of the real powers of masculinity—rational and critical thinking—had been replaced by force to deliver results. We became addicted to results, and how we got there did not matter. Remember, 9/11 occurred in the shadow of Enron, Tyco, and WorldCom. These companies existed for one reason only: to get the primary shareholders big, short-term monetary results. Greed was good, and that was driving everything. The events of 9/11 interrupted the parade.

What was also present and never spoken of was fear. America was operating on top of a real fear. Why would someone do this to us? We did not like someone messing with our good times. Instead of inquiring, instead of looking at what had changed here, we assigned blame to an external force. Radical Islam was the problem, clearly that was the issue, and we were cool. Our unwillingness as a nation to self-assess was (and still is) truly stunning. Our unwillingness to seek any responsibility was the beginning of the attack on America and the attack on masculinity. Our ability to plow forward without addressing the breakdowns that existed in America and continuing to marshal forward, was both very dude-like and at the source of the issues we see today.

Yes, the progressive left gynocentric paradigm is a problem in our nation and our culture. I believe it is an existential threat not just for our country but for the world. America has a role in global politics, and that role is one of strength, stability, and a stand for freedom and liberty. The threat to end America and its core value of independence, and to become a global citizen would change civilization as we know it. To address the threat we need to address the root cause. The root cause is that we men abdicated our roles—we sold out.

We chose greed over liberty, we chose comfort over freedom, and we chose safety over independence. We were more concerned with not disrupting the flow of cash and the good times than we were willing to quell the unworkable. We lost ourselves. We were focused on the feel-goods of the external: the money, power, and comfort. More than being concerned with the future, we were creating for our children and their children. We suffered from arrogance and narcissism. We became Bluto. Fat, drunk, and stupid.

Fast-forward. Throughout history there has always been a pull for arbitrary groups of elites and people to rule over the mass of humanity. The idea of America and self-government with rights bestowed upon us by our creator is a truly unique idea. Throughout history that idea of self-government and individual liberty is also a fragile one. Freedom must be fragile. We are currently involved in another attack on freedom and masculinity. It is up to us to step up. Dare I say, "Man the fuck up!"

What I mean by stating that freedom must be fragile: to be truly free you must allow for every expression including the ones of antifreedom, hate, and oppression. That is the idea of freedom, and the goal is for us to make it anti-fragile. The purpose of this book is to have us, men, reestablish what manhood and masculine leadership are. Manhood and masculinity are at the core of what America is and was constructed upon: strength, independence, and tolerance. Here is the good news. It is OK to fuck up. As dudes we fuck up a lot. The secret is to clean it up and keep on moving. Before we do that we must get our thinking right: *Manhood Manifesto: A Call for Men to Lead at Home, at Work, and in the Public Sphere.* We must own that our actions, behavior, and mindset gave those who are opposed to the idea of freedom the fuel for their fire.

Saul Alinsky's *Rules for Radicals* is the blueprint being used against men, the "patriarchy," and freedom today. To defeat your enemy you must defeat their strategy. Here are the three rules I believe most apply at this time:

> *#4:"Make the enemy live up to its own book of rules."*
>
> *#12:"The price of a successful attack is a constructive alternative."*
>
> *#13:"Pick the target, freeze it, personalize it, and polarize it."*

If we just look at these three rules, #4 is just holding us to account for our words and intentions. That is actually a structure that we should install ourselves. This simply has us operate and be present to the second leadership distinction of integrity.

Rule #12 shows they have no real goal other than anarchy. I believe the gynocentric objective is actually one of safety. The gynocentric paradigm is obsessed with safety and security. Rule #13 is where we have work to do. We cannot take things personally. When we do that, we become upset, scared, and lose sight of our purpose and our reason. From there we are susceptible to influences and ideas that will "save" us and not serve our long-term vision. It is a setup for manipulation.

The only way we can withstand that type of pressure is to truly develop a very strong relationship with our self. Leadership begins with self-awareness and self-understanding. As Clint Eastwood said, "A man has to know his limitations." We need to know who we are. We need to know our darkness so we can understand our brilliance. When we get there we are then in position to achieve self-love. Really accepting all that we are and all that we are not. This is not about channeling Chris Farley interviewing Paul McCartney, beating ourselves up, nor is it being arrogant and obnoxious. It is having a profound sense of *knowing* that is connected to something beyond us, that allows us to stand in the face of tough times. It is the source of our independence and self-reliance. It is also what allows us to band with brothers to create something far greater than any one of us could do alone. That is what this work is about. That is why I am here.

Thank you for reading this. I hope this is just the beginning of our relationship and together we will join forces to build a community of men and women who create something awesome. Let's roll.

CHAPTER 13

# The Perversion of Spirituality

*"Political Correctness is communist propaganda writ small. In my study of communist societies, I came to the conclusion that the purpose of communist propaganda was not to persuade or convince, nor to inform, but to humiliate; and therefore, the less it corresponded to reality the better.*

*"When people are forced to remain silent when they are being told the most obvious lies, or even worse when they are forced to repeat the lies themselves, they lose once and for all their sense of probity. To assent to obvious lies is to co-operate with evil, and in some small way to become evil oneself. One's standing to resist anything is thus eroded, and even destroyed.*

*"A society of emasculated liars is easy to control. I think if you examine Political Correctness, it has the same effect and is intended to."*

—Anthony Daniels

It is not politically correct to speak about God. If you listen to the media, people who have faith and believe in God are typically viewed as right wing hate groups or some sort of wacko science deniers. I am not sure that is true, but who am I to have the facts interfere with the current narrative? Truth be told, our nation was created by divine inspiration. Our Constitution and our Declaration of Independence are unique because they spell out that our rights are bestowed upon us by our creator, not by man. Therefore, if our rights are not given to us by man, they cannot be taken away from us by man. That is the source of our freedom and our sovereignty. It is what makes our individual rights, spelled out in the Bill of Rights, foundational to our freedom and beyond the scope of democracy. Our forefathers understood the dangers of mob rule and the possible perversions of democracy.

The First Amendment of the Bill of Rights ensures our right of free speech. Political correctness challenges that right every day. Political correctness, as stated in the opening quote, is a tool to control language. Daniels speaks of it as it relates to communism. I say it is a tool used by any group or ideology that wants to control expression and create an environment of compliance. Foundational to freedom is free will. Free will is granted to us by our creator. Free will and free speech are in direct opposition to political correctness. Political correctness is a direct attack on our freedom and is at the battle line of our current cultural war. Let there be no misunderstanding: we *are* in the midst of a culture war.

Like most conflicts, the fog of war can make things somewhat unclear. Here is what the cultural war is about: our freedom, our liberty, the Constitution, and the American idea vs. globalism, one-world government, and centralized control of our lives. That is the deal. The people "selling" the globalist agenda are very clever in the packaging of it. Barack Hussein Obama has many times expressed the need to soften the message so more people can accept it. Most recently, he softened it as it related to defunding the police. He has used that same marketing approach with many other subjects. The globalist salespeople are advocates for world citizenship, for the prevention of destructive global climate change, and for the need for health care for all. You will see the signs outside churches and civic buildings that say things like, We Believe; Black Lives Matter; Love Is Love; No Human Is Illegal; Kindness Is Everything.

These ideologues are quite skilled in coded language and perverting most everything they say or believe. For example, the phrase, *We Believe* is code for "You must accept, or you are a racist." *Black Lives Matter* is code for "white guilt and alignment with Marxist ideology." *Love Is Love* is acceptance of sexual relationship between anyone who consents regardless of age, gender, gender identity, or level of commitment. If the relationship generates an unwanted pregnancy, it is our right to dispose of that child. *No Human Is Illegal* is an outright defiance of any immigration law or citizenry requirement. It is a call for open borders and global citizenship. *Kindness Is Everything* is the demand to comply in the most passive-aggressive way possible. Noncompliance is an indication of intolerance of this agenda and a sign you are a racist, sexist, misogynist, homophobe, xenophobe, blah, blah, blah.

At the core of political correctness is the belief that the collective knows what is better for individuals than the individuals themselves. Political correctness stands in the face of individual rights or expression. Through some level of magical collectivism, "they" have determined what is best for the greater good. Who "they" are is always unknown because at the center of political correctness is always an absentee leader, and it is the *idea* that most of the politically correct hide behind. With no leadership, it is challenging to have any accountability. Political correctness is famous for the absence of any real accountability other than mob rule. With political correctness, the masses are always more important than the individual.

This flies in the face of one of the core tenets that I believe in concerning leadership. In leadership there is a distinction, "Being given being and action by something greater than oneself." The idea of this distinction is, "Source of the serene passion (charisma) required to lead and to develop others as leaders and the source of persistence (joy in the labor of) when the going gets tough." That source of serene passion required to lead is often some version of a spiritual connection. That connection is personal, and that connection is individual. It could be a connection to Jesus Christ; it could be a belief in some other version of a higher power. It is beyond you, bigger than you; it is something that sources you and provides you, the leader, with inspiration, charisma, and power to face the challenges that leadership inevitably will be called upon to face. That is the power of leadership. In this distinction, our purpose, our why, the thing that ultimately motivates us, is located. Freedom is required for the connection and the access to our personal mission and purpose. It is why political correctness is so harmful to freedom and to leadership.

Throughout the remainder of the book we will be dealing with the three foundational elements of masculinity; they are to provide, protect, and leave a legacy. We will go through them several times in great detail. We will share and dive into the four core distinctions of leadership, why they are important, and how they are applied and accessed. The four distinctions are: (1) being given being and action by something greater than ourselves, (2) integrity, (3) authenticity, and (4) being cause in the matter. We will also inquire into the two primary reasons and deliverables of leadership: creating a clear future to live into, and creating and maintaining an environment for your people to operate in freely.

These distinctions, foundational blocks, and reasons are how we will restore responsible masculine leadership and establish manhood in America, and we will begin today. Thank you for the honor of joining me on this most powerful and essential journey.

## CHAPTER 14

# Great White Woke: Privilege and Guilt

*"Any group arrogant enough to believe that it has the exclusive ability to 'Save the Planet' will inevitably conclude that any crimes are justified in pursuit of its 'higher purpose.'"*
*—Edward M. Wolfe*

The Urban Dictionary defines "wokeness" as "a postmodern version of being 'born-again' where an individual is hyper-vigilant of the magic transgressions in human dignity because they're painfully unaware of secretly being deeply ashamed of how life is not fucking them hard enough."

Other descriptors are being constantly offended or self-righteous and masquerading as enlightened. No matter how you put it, wokeness and social justice warriors are advocates of victimization. They celebrate victimization. Without victimization I am not sure we would have a population of woke. There clearly would be no social justice warriors, and without the SJW, how could we as a culture survive without their wisdom and guidance? In addition, the perpetual state of victimization and being offended has created a very convenient villain.

That villain is white people, especially successful, able-bodied, straight white men.

What is wokeness really? Wokeness is the fundamental belief that Western civilization is inherently racist, sexist, and misogynistic. If you do not accept that premise, then you are personally racist, sexist, and a misogynist. Focusing on America and American men, which is what this book is about, wokeness is a belief that America was fundamentally flawed in its creation. The woke perspective also believes the men who created this country were flawed humans (of course they were), and they were racist, sexist, and misogynistic. The evidence they cite is the way we treated the indigenous people and that the founding fathers were slave owners. Therefore, if you have achieved success in anyway, it did not happen through hard work, investment, and tenacity. No! In the woke world, success is the result of racism, sexism, oppression, and cheating those who are weaker and less fortunate.

At the core of the issue for the Great White Woke (GWW) is their own guilt. Most of the members of the GWW are people who grew up in a time of participation awards and seventh-place trophies. These are the same people who were raised to believe that their self-esteem was the most important element of their life. They lived in constant states of affirmation, while at the same time being insulated from reality. These are the people who were raised by parents who arranged play dates and made sure they wore helmets when they rode their bicycles and skateboards. This is the generation where comfort, convenience, and most of all, safety supersede any experience or breakthrough in performance. This is a group of people trained in control, compliance, and protection. It is a group robbed of curiosity and uninterested in discovery with little access to true inquiry. They are obsessed with collecting evidence and data to support their positions so they can be right, look good, and gain acceptance and acknowledgment. They do so because they are devoid of any access to self awareness, responsibility, or means of true contribution. Greg Lukianoff and Jonathan Haidt have written extensively on the creation of this generation, and their book, *The Coddling of the American Mind,* explains it very well.

The Great White Woke generation expects perfection and has very few, if any, problem-solving skills. Its members also believe that if there is a problem, someone else should take care of it. They have no causal relationship to success. Their "go to" tactics are creating safe spaces, denouncing hate speech, assigning blame to someone other than themselves when things don't go their way, and being allies with whoever is labeled as the most oppressed and marginalized at the moment. Recently there was a protest in San Francisco over the oppression of the farmers in India. The oppression and challenge of *one* is the oppression of *all.* This mindset is required to remain in a state of perpetual offense.

It is that awakening to their own shortcomings and personal disappointments that generates this unusual perspective. A curious example of the GWW is Rachel Dolezal, a woman who was born in Montana, lived in the state of Washington, and posed as a Black person. I assert that this act of posing as a Black person, to the point where she was elected as president of her local chapter of the NAACP, was the result of her own guilt and self-loathing.

There is nothing wrong with being White and being a member of the NAACP. As a matter of fact, of the original sixty members of the organization, only seven were Black, and the first president was White. This was one of the first civil rights organizations, and who cares what color people are, as long as they are forwarding civility and social alliance? I guess Rachel Dolezal *did* care—so much that she lied and deceived the world about who she really was. Who she most lied to was herself.

The idea of guilt and self-loathing is really the issue. America is a great place, and we have been granted many opportunities. I have seen men born in the projects go on to become very successful and wealthy business owners. I have also met men who grew up in the most pampered of suburbs yet ended up being junkies and complete fuck-ups. Life is what you make it. It is much easier to not be responsible, to sit and judge and assess the actions and deeds of others, than it is to fully engage and risk yourself and challenge yourself to accomplish something that is not guaranteed. That takes courage, that take a willingness to "git some on ya." What I mean by that is to challenge your own limiting beliefs and live in service of an idea, a commitment to something bigger than just *your* wants.

I have a friend who is terminally woke to the point of being one of the most annoying and self-righteous people I know. He is also brilliant and compassionate. His self-loathing stems from his family of origin, who were from the South Side of Chicago and experienced "white flight" in the late 1960s. They were angry and upset, and the result of that upset was overtly expressed racism. For my friend to accept his family and accept their racism, he would actually have to attempt to understand what created it. That type of inquiry is difficult and confronting. It is way more easy to blame—plus it makes you look good to the woke.

*"The most striking irony of the age of white guilt is that racism suddenly became valuable to the people who had suffered it."*
—Shelby Steele, White Guilt

Shelby Steele is dead-on. The white guilt that is being expressed, especially by the media, has created victimization as an asset. Racism is now a valuable tool for the acquisition of power. As stated in an earlier chapter, the real game we are playing as Americans is that we are the stand for freedom in the world. America is a unique idea and a continual work in process. The idea of freedom is and will forever be under attack. The forces against it will come in all shapes and sizes. But it is ultimately about supplanting individual liberty, self-governance, and freedom with some sort of centralized government.

We see it all the time in organizations. At the core of most mergers and acquisitions is the centralization of leadership and services. It's OK for big multinational organizations because it creates cost reductions, eliminates redundancy, and is intended to improve efficiencies. That is OK for business organizations that are profit-focused and meeting market demands. For governments that are designed to protect people's inalienable rights, it's not great. That structure can be a death knell for freedom, liberty, and individual liberties.

Organizations and ideologies like communism, monarchies, and empires are all that structure. Neo-Marxist organizations like Black Lives Matter and Antifa are also out to reduce individual liberties for the "greater good." The newly developed Socialist Democrats like Senator Bernie Sanders (I-VT), Representatives Alexandria Ocasio-Cortez (D-NY) and Ilhan Omar (D-MN), and Minnesota's Attorney General Keith Ellison are part of that ideology. That mindset is very prevalent in large urban centers. Mayors Bill DeBlasio of New York City, Lori Lightfoot of Chicago, and Ted Wheeler of Portland, Oregon, all share that ideology of centralized power. The truth is, these organizations are really about the shifting and acquisition of power.

As men and leaders we must realize we have created the fertile ground for this movement to grow. Leadership is responsible for creating the environment people live in. Inside that environment, inspiration is found. The environment the GWW seems to live in is one of constant and never-ending offense and upset. The inspiration seems to be utilizing the white guilt and persistent victimization as a cudgel to bang on the current system of freedom.

Our system, one that is in support of freedom, is also the source of racism, sexism, and misogyny. Their narrative states that the system is inherently flawed and needs to be torn down and rebuilt. To do that, the progressives need to gain power to create the solution. The solution is, the government should fix it! And it seems like the Socialist Democrats have created a narrative that will address that issue. The only problem is there has never been a solution created by socialists that has ever worked or delivered on the promise. That is OK. Per their narrative, install them in power *this* time and it will work; they will share their plan *later.*

This is the impact of us, able-bodied men; not only have we not addressed these issues, we have also missed the boat on providing adequate leadership and addressing the issues at hand. The truth is, many of these complaints seem weird and stupid. That was our error. While we were working, watching sports, and working on our golf game, our children were becoming indoctrinated into a world of expectation and blame. It is time for us to wake up.

When I say it is time to wake up, I mean it is time to get real about where we are and take ownership in it. As Jocko Willink says, "There are no bad teams, only bad leaders." As men, we have abdicated our leadership. I am calling for us to step up, now. Leadership is not a position; it is a way of being. This does not call for an attack. This calls for the being a bulwark.

The time is now for men to get clear on our foundational role as leaders and members of our society. As leaders we must provide. Providing used to mean to ensure that the financial resources were available for the family, organization, and community. The problem was, we stopped there. Providing is bigger. As leaders, providing means not only providing the space to grow but also holding and maintaining the space for those in your charge, as well as providing access to the resources, available skills, and tools they need to grow, learn, and develop.

The next essential role as leaders that we as men must deliver is to protect. Of course, this can look like cleaning your shotgun on the front porch when your daughter's special friend arrives to take her on her first date. It is way more than that. Protecting is taking that space you created for your people to grow, learn, and develop, and making that space sacred. That sacredness is there so there is no fear in the space for them to develop. Protection is different than safety. Protection is proactive. It requires knowledge, training, empowerment, and clarity. Safety is fear based. If people have the experience of protection, the concern for safety disappears, so they can move forward and begin the process of creation and innovation.

This brings us to the third foundational element of masculinity: leaving a legacy. That means creating a future not only for you but also for generations to come. A legacy is a process by which the environment you construct is not only healthy, it is also inviting to future generations. From the mindset of legacy creation, there would be little concern for detrimental environmental issues, because it would just not make sense. It would create a practice of stewardship and responsibility built into whatever environment you are creating. Respect and honor would become a core value, and the need for forced identity and equality agendas would be moot. Freedom, liberty, and personal sovereignty are baked into the cake of a community focus on sustainability, health, and pursuit of happiness.

When building a legacy we are able to connect the lessons learned in the stories of the past with the structure and actions of today. We can then drive all that into the fulfillment of the future. Building a legacy connects the past and its wisdom with the state of today and the vision of the future.

This is the beginning of the work we, as men, need to take on. To do that though, we must begin with ourselves. We must create a powerful relationship with who we are and what our personal purpose is. Once we understand our purpose, why we are here, what drives us, and what will fulfill us, we can then truly begin the process of restoring responsible masculine leadership in America.

## CHAPTER 15

# Gynocentric Paradigm AKA Wokeism

*"First of all understand that I get it. That there are millions and millions of women who are steely-eyed realists. And millions and millions of men who are anything but. However. For lack of a better term I would say that the feminine values are the values of America:*
*"Sensitivity is more important than Truth. Feelings are more important than Facts. Commitment is more important than Individuality. Children are more important than People. Safety is more important than Fun.*
*"I always hear women say, 'Y'know married men live longer.'*
*"Yes. And an indoor cat also lives longer."*
*—Bill Maher*

Some may already be triggered by the title of this chapter. Let's begin with the definition of gynocentric: "dominated by or emphasizing feminine interest or feminine point of view." For me, gynocentrism is simply putting the current feminine perspective, which I believe is informed by radical feminism and left wing Marxist teachings, before everything in politics, culture, and society, often to the detriment of everything else. It is just another version of "winning at all costs."

My assertion, and one of the reasons for this book, is we currently exist in a gynocentric paradigm. The reason I chose Bill Maher's quote is he is pointing to it as well. The "why" we do is a response to an overly masculine paradigm of the '50s and '60s that led to the rise of the feminist movement and women's liberation. That movement, along with the abdication of healthy male leadership, has created a shift that currently has achieved a level of unworkability and actually threatens the existence of our country.

Today you can see the gynocentric paradigm in virtually every aspect of our lives. The gynocentric narrative sets the tone for every component of the mainstream media. I invite you to objectively read the *New York Times, Washington Post, Chicago Tribune,* or *Los Angeles Times.* Notice the context, the tone, and the position of not only the reporting but, more importantly, the editorials and columnists. Listen to the narrative of MSNBC and CNN. Beyond the media, look at the policies of public education and the agenda around our schools. It goes even further. Look at the policies of human resource departments and corporate employee handbooks. We exist in the default condition of the gynocentric paradigm.

This is not part of a conspiracy theory. I don't think there is some massive feminist plot to overthrow America, although Black Lives Matter does come close. This is another of a series of examples throughout history that—although a good idea in its time—once it achieves its objective, needs to be adjusted. Equal rights for women is much more than a good idea; it is a moral imperative. Feminism and the ideas and structures of feminism have achieved their objectives. Currently, 56 percent of the managerial jobs in business belong to women, and as stated previously, 52 percent of the students currently in law school are women, and 50.5 percent of the people in medical school are women. Executive women currently earn $0.98 for every dollar earned by men. From the standpoint of measurable equality, I would declare, "Mission accomplished." It does not mean we must stop working for women's equality, it just means the condition of inequality has been overcome and we are in a new state. We have achieved a state of equity regardless of what the radical media would suggest.

Like many other great ideas that have fulfilled on their intention, the great idea becomes an ideology. When ideologies become ingrained, we can lose sight of why they ever began. The ideology takes on a persona of its own, and if you are not for it, you can then be seen as against it. That is my assertion with feminism. The objective has been achieved. It is now time to shift and look at the situation through a new lens. In the world today, to express that thought is likely to be met with a response that the speaker is misogynistic or sexist. In looking at the numbers, economic equality (which was the intention of feminism) has been achieved. The question is, what is next? I assert we are at a point where the radical feminists want cultural, economic, and social dominance. I am a stand for cultural, economic, and social balance.

This has gone so far that we have grown to unconditionally believe women and disbelieve men whenever there is a question of perspective. We have to go no further than the Supreme Court Justice Brett Kavanaugh confirmation hearings or the #MeToo movement. It actually started sooner than that: the women's marches five days after Donald Trump took the oath of office in January 2017. That ideology is expressed in the shift to a gynocentric cultural paradigm. The intention of this chapter is to honor feminism, begin the shift back to normalcy, and stop the unchecked gynocentrism. The process for the return to normalcy is to take what is working and build on that, while removing the malignant aspects of it. The process for that change will be direct, respectful, and open communication.

Before I go too much further, I want to say that I love, respect, and honor women. They play such an integral part in my life. I would not be writing this book and including this chapter if it were not true. I must also say that I accept full responsibility for how it's gone. Because of that, what I say in this chapter and the next few chapters absolutely needs to be said. I will be direct, and I fully intend to be respectful. I will also accept the impact of my failings and those of my fellow men. If this triggers you, it is not my intent, but I understand it may. In that case, all we can do is work it out. At the end of the book there are a number of ways to contact me and interact with me about what we are creating. I must also say that I will no longer be held hostage and thwart my communication because of the fear of your response and reaction. The hypersensitive, perpetual offense and use of personal attacks have been weaponized toward any opposition or critical response to gynocentric tactics.

If you choose to cancel me, that will be your choice. Please know the act of cancelling someone or some idea only grows the divide. Finally, this book is not an argument for anything or a technical work to prove anything. It is a position, a point of view, based on an "as lived" experience and coming from a commitment that I have. It is an idea. I have a stand that the divide that exists in the world today, specifically between sexes, comes to an end. I have a commitment that the cultural wars we have should also end. I believe that if we men are going to be leaders in our organizations, families, and communities, we need to take 100 percent ownership in how it has gone and how it will go. Ownership does not mean blame; it means owning the problem and the solution.

This preamble is necessary because of the vital nature of this topic and the sensitivity around it. I want to create a context in which I view women as complete equals yet different. We are complements to one another, not competitors. I believe the ultimate design of humans was for men and women to work in equal partnership, each possessing unique skills, talents, and attributes. Foundational to that partnership to work and thrive, there must be a condition of acceptance and trust that exists. The premise of this book is men, we dudes, have not held up our end of the bargain, and the result of that has been profound disappointment, hurt, distrust, and rage by women. I am sorry for that. Though we cannot go back and undo the past, you have my solemn oath that I am committed that men operate in a way that is both authentic to their nature and respectful of the human condition. That is my stand, that is my commitment, and that is the purpose of my life.

Let's get started. *Gynocentric:* "dominated by or emphasizing feminine interest or points of view." My assertion is that is the conversational environment in which we currently live. It is a context, a perspective, the lens through which we see the world. Most of all, from a cultural viewpoint, a gynocentric paradigm would be the indication of what society sees as correct. For all intents and purposes, the *gynocentric paradigm is the structure of "Wokeism."*

One of the biggest gynocentric values currently running the show is safety and the emphasis on safety. Other examples are fairness, equality, and justice (as currently constructed). From those we build into diversity and inclusion. To achieve the agenda of safety and equality we will create quotas, measures, mandates, and, when needed, compliance regulations to achieve that status. The idea of equality then justifies all actions regardless of the impact to freedom, independence of full self-expression. We could even go so far as to limit those rights and expressions for the purpose of achieving equality. The limiting or removal of rights then gets justified to achieve the agenda of safety or equality. That is what hiring quotas and programs like Minority Business Enterprise actually do.

That is also what happened with the lockdowns and the restrictions imposed on small businesses during the COVID-19/ Chinese flu pandemic. Safety became the ultimate value, with no concern for the impact across the board. The narrative was that this was about a public health issue—but there was little data and less knowledge. The mantra became an "abundance of caution" and we must "flatten the curve" to be safe and save lives. As the issue grew, you could see it became less about public health and more about ideology. The truth was that we had never dealt with anything like this and we were ill-prepared. The decision-making process, always preceded by "with an abundance of caution," is clearly oriented in fear and safety. This is the perfect example of the gynocentric paradigm informing the decision-making process and policy direction.

This is not just a liberal or Democrat issue. The Republicans and the conservatives did the same thing. After 9/11, the Constitution was, in essence, suspended. We created the bureaucratically mammoth Department of Homeland Security, we instituted TSA, and we lived in fear. The biggest issue is we abandoned the Constitution because we were fearful. Our Constitution is there for times of struggle and challenge. The mindset of fear has us retreat into concern for our own survival, in the belief that is where the solution lies. Unfortunately, our survival is only concerned with our personal survival. The gyno-centric paradigm is one that is most concerned with individual survival—that is, saving one's own ass—and not the greater good or big picture, regardless of the narrative. It goes beyond species. Think of the idea of a mama bear. There is nothing she will not do to protect herself and her family. There is no logic, no reason, no problem solving. It is pure reaction and ruthless determination for safety.

Going back to COVID-19/Chinese flu, you can see pure reactionary fear being expressed in the outrage waged upon Donald Trump, and using the death of one person as an example of his lack of empathy. COVID-19/Chinese flu is generated by an unknown source. That being said, the reactions we have taken at best were guesses. Mr. Trump took positions that were aimed at protecting our freedoms over the hyper reactions called for by many more woke/gynocentric/leftist leaders whose primary motivation was safety. He also led the initiative called "operation warp speed" which led to the creation of effective vaccines in record time. The obsession with safety and the fear of death has led to a position and belief that any deaths caused by this disease are preventable and at the fault the government. That is simply an irrational perspective based in fear. Any argument or position in contradiction to that will be felt as uncaring or inhumane. This has been the major criticism of Donald Trump, and facts or actions be damned, as Bill Maher says in the opening quote—sensitivity is what drives the show.

Other elements of the gynocentric paradigm are the emphasis on feelings, which will lead to a pull for comfort, convenience, and accessibility. None of these things are bad; it is only when they become overemphasized that they become a challenge. From here, things like sensitivity and "appropriateness" will come into play. This is where I begin to get concerned. This is the genesis of political correctness, where one's sensitivity becomes more important than one's ability to communicate, speak openly, and share. From this place of "sensitivity," rational thinking and objective reasoning take second chair to "an abundance of caution." Risk is not allowed; we then begin to skew other perspectives. My favorite one is "essential workers." What is a nonessential worker?

When sensitivity becomes a barrier to free speech, we have censorship. I am not an advocate of yelling "fire" in a crowded theater. I see the damage and the division that is created by the cancel culture and the obfuscation of language. This is not a hard, clear line, and it is my belief that we have gone too far toward the side of censorship. It takes little effort to be offended. It takes strength, courage, and vulnerability to listen to an opposing viewpoint. The only way this divide is bridged is through difficult and direct conversation. Candid conversations are difficult to have if our priorities are to ensure that all spaces are "safe" and all language "appropriate." Who became the arbiter of "safe and appropriate?" Therein lies the quest for power and control.

You can see where an emphasis on feelings and sensitivity can then open the door to sheltering people and supporting their experience of being offended. I am 100 percent in favor of people treating others with respect and honor, and no one should intentionally cause harm to another. From sensitivity though, the arbiter of being offended *becomes* the offended. That flies in the face of "innocent until proven guilty." Our newly constructed hypersensitivity has now become a tool of structural censorship and a barrier to free speech and full self-expression. What also has come from this is a sense of "appropriateness" and what is allowed and not allowed. The intent and the structure of the victim's being held responsible for also creating the offense results in an imbalance of power and skews it toward the side of the victims. Victims can then become a powerful ally in a battle for power.

One illustration of this is the idea of hate crimes and hate speech. I am not an advocate for hate speech or hate anything. I hate broccoli, but I am certainly not out to outlaw it or eliminate it; I just don't eat it. What I want to point out is a clear problem with the gynocentric paradigm; from the value of feelings and triggers of being offended, the solution becomes the removal of others' rights. This becomes a big deal when they begin to reduce the rights bestowed upon us by our creator; the rights of life, liberty, and the pursuit of happiness. This is a delicate balance and one we cannot lose sight of.

What has also happened in these last thirty years or so is the feminists organizing and using their cohesive voice to raise issues to create change. Many of the issues are just and right, and positive change has occurred. Unfortunately, we are dangerously close to making the female perspective the "right one" and the male perspective one that is almost instantly invalidated. Thus the narrative of patriarchy, structural racism, and structural sexism as being accurate without any investigation or objective testing. These are *not* truths, but they are being looked on by many as if they are. This imbalance in perspective, if allowed to go on for too long, is not good for our culture and not good for our republic. Most of all it is not good for our citizens.

Consider we live inside an ecosystem where men and women were designed to live in balance. When we are in balance, there is some stasis of harmony. When out of balance, there becomes a stasis of instability or disharmony. Look at all the programs and outlets for young girls and young women to assist them to grow and develop. Title IX is a game-changing program to bring equality in athletics. NASA has a program for young women in STEM (science, technology, engineering, and math) programs. There are other programs, such as Girl Up, to support young women in urban setting to have the support to succeed. What do we have for young men?

One of the most devastating aspects of the gynocentric paradigm is that men's lives are viewed as less valuable than women's lives. This has gone on for centuries. Who goes off and dies in war? From 2001 through July 2020, some 173 female service members had been killed in Iraq, Afghanistan, and Syria, according to the Congressional Research Service. Is this what we aspire to? And yes, 173 brave American service women have died in the line of duty. However, the numbers throughout the ages are still highly skewed toward men. History is filled with the idea of "women and children first." We have an unconscious bias in our culture that men are expendable. "Next man up" is a common theme in athletics. We do it to ourselves. We have called this behavior *chivalry*. I call it unconscious and self-destructive.

The result is ever-growing incarceration rates, growth in unemployment and under-employment, increases is mental health issues and depression, increased level of narcotic and alcohol abuse, and, most of all, a horrible self-image and self-understanding. Throw in the narrative that any masculine solution is unworkable and think of the confusion we will generate with young men. We wonder why there are questions in the area of gender identity. The world is not supportive of young men today, and the way many are raised by their mothers is to be hairy women and become indoctrinated into the gynocentric paradigm. They may survive doing that, but they certainly will not thrive.

This gynocentric mismanagement continues as it relates to raising our children. In the world today 45 percent of the children are raised in fatherless homes. In Black homes it approaches 90 percent. This occurs not because the men have abandoned the children; it occurs because the legal and social structures are set to generate that result. More evidence of the gynocentric paradigm. This narrative has reduced the value of men, and the value of biological fathers. The belief that biological fathers can be substituted for by a good stepfather has been disproven by the works of Warren Ferrell. Children need their fathers in their lives. This truth is even more important for boys. That is not how the current cultural narrative is being communicated or perceived.

There is a tremendous amount of misinformation and manipulated information out there that is in service to a cultural, social, or political agenda. In the areas of race we have Robin DiAngelo and Ibram X. Kendi. In the area of men and masculinity there are a number of authors, writers, and thought leaders whose message is one of reducing masculine expression for men to contribute to the forward movement of our culture. I disagree wholeheartedly. It is through these writings and messages that express the abdication I am speaking of. What I am calling for in this manifesto is for men to own their expression responsibly and stand for the changes that are needed. I am calling for men to step up, engage, inquire, and lead. It is through men being more "men" that we can provide the environment for women to be fully themselves and express the beauty, passion, and creativity they were intended to provide.

The truth is, the world is changing. The current narrative says the needs of the postindustrial world are more geared to skills and attributes of women than men. As men we must adapt, and that adaption will be a newer, more developed version of masculinity—not the elimination of it. To begin that adaptation we must start with understanding ourselves and coming to terms with the conditions in which we currently exist. That is step one.

Men are skilled in problem solving and building solutions. We are grounded in rational thinking and reasoning. The problems and challenges of today are more complex and ambiguous than at any time in history. We have the ability to withstand discomfort and endure through resistance and challenges. These are the gifts of masculinity and manhood. The first thing to know is men and women are fundamentally different. We see the world differently, and we experience it differently, and that is a foundational strength. We must own and honor the things that make us men, not deny or reject them. Men are not hairy women. Men are men and women are women, and we are designed as partners and complements. Understanding that is the journey we all must undertake. That is what is best for all of us.

## CHAPTER 16

# Liberal, Well-Educated, Millennial, Woke White Women

*"Feminism…I think the simplest explanation, and one that captures the idea, is a song that Marlo Thomas sang, 'Free to be You and Me.' Free to be, if you were a girl—doctor, lawyer, Indian chief. Anything you want to be. And if you're a boy, and you like teaching, you like nursing, you would like to have a doll, that's OK too. That notion that we should each be free to develop our own talents, whatever they may be, and not be held back by artificial barriers—manmade barriers, certainly not heaven sent."*

*—Ruth Bader Ginsburg*

There may be no more destructive, invasive, and dangerous creature on the planet than liberal, well-educated, millennial, woke White women (LWEMWWW). The Asian carp comes close, but I have never heard an Asian carp refer to rioting and looting as a "peaceful protest." Nor have I ever heard an Asian carp claim someone was being abusive to them because that person disagreed with them. Nor have huge hordes of the fish gathered together wearing pink pussy hats and chanting hate slogans while condemning hate speech and destroying public monuments. I am only partially joking about this because I would cry if I could not laugh at the absurdity of it.

One can only imagine the enlightening perspective of a female graduate of the gender studies program at Oberlin College. The truth is I have never met one, though I did meet and sort of spoke with a gender studies major from the University of Wisconsin—Madison. These women have taken the gynocentric paradigm to the next level. They operate from a gynonormative context. Gynonormativism prioritizes the feminine point of view hierarchically within the culture, on both a political and interpersonal level, and pressures males in particular to adopt a supposed feminine system of values as a component of one's authentic personality. That acceptance and "authentic" integration of this viewpoint is called "being an ally."

This platform, gynonormativism, is a form of totalitarianism. One must comply with the edicts and proclamations. There can be no opposition. If you are not in compliance with this doctrine, you are instantly labeled a misogynist, racist, or sexist. If there is opposition, that person is zeroed out, cancelled, or discredited. There can be no discourse, no discussion, no give and take. One must either agree or be eliminated. This is what misandry looks like. This is what is being practiced today by AOC, Black Lives Matter, and, in many ways, Nancy Pelosi. A poster child for this behavior is Lori Lightfoot, the mayor of the Great City of Chicago. Mayor Lightfoot recently rejected the Constitution of the United States of America because she is Black, female, and a lesbian. She rejected it because none of the founders represented her—a Black, female gay person. Lori, you weren't around 234 years ago. I think that level of arrogance is a glaring depiction of the unworkability of multiculturalism: no one who created the Constitution 234 years ago could ever envision the plight of poor Lori Lightfoot.

You can see the arrogance throughout the media in people like Rachel Maddow, Joy Reid, and the queen of this corrosive mindset, actress Lena Dunham. This mindset is most openly practiced by Lena Dunham's buddy, Emily Ratajkowski. The product of this brilliance is Emily, who was about eight months pregnant at the time of this writing, has decided not to "assign" a gender to her newborn, because that would be too prejudicial. She will allow the child to choose their own gender upon their eighteenth birthday. The most disturbing part of this story about Emily and her soon-to-be newborn? She is married, and her husband is aligned with this decision.

This is the breakdown in masculinity we must address. This platform of gynonormativism is somewhat new and does not have traction no matter what Joy Reid and Rachel Maddow say. It is gaining momentum because resistance is futile as a result of the zeal and energy that is unleashed against any opposition. The biggest concern for me is the men who will just go along.

These are inherently weak men. Men who are scared. Men who have no sense of self, no sense of what masculinity is, and no sense of what to do other than be a beta bitch to out-of-control women and an insane social narrative. The truth is also that these weak men are not loved in a way they want or need to be by these abusive women. They are just tools or accessories to them. They serve some useful function for now. They are completely expendable. Here is an example of what men with no boundaries and no values other than being an ally looks like.

I can go on for pages about the egocentricity of these woman and the damage that they do. I can speak about the impact of them divorcing or leaving their men for no reason and then moving away with the children, and the impact to both the children and the men. I could write about the impact of the narrative they are creating of being powerful and independent while at the same time being the victims of misogyny and the patriarchy. I could speak to the privilege and insular nature of their upbringing and yet how they identify as eloquent surrogates of the oppressed and the marginalized citizens. These humans who have virtually no understanding of anything practical and yet are experts on social justice policy. I *could* write about them, and I will choose to leave it at that. They are a distracting group who often steal resources that would be much better served elsewhere. I will leave them here. LWEMWWW are a distraction for me and really play no role in my work or my life.

Where we will go next is to begin to speak about our development. About us men establishing our manhood and masculine expression. There is no greater reason to restore than as a result of the damage done by an unexpected force. That unexpected force is the potential damage that could be caused by a gynonormative context informing all the decisions made in our country and world. One of the main reasons for the gynonormative platform to even gain a slight toehold is the absence of authentic masculine leadership. Authentic masculine leadership and authentic masculine expression are not the installation of feminist values and behaviors into a masculine construct. That is nuts!

To begin with, men need to be strong. The need for physical strength is not what it once was for us to create value and do work. Physical fitness and strength are integral to how we see ourselves and foundational to creating a positive relationship with ourselves. How we do one thing is how we do everything.

If you are able-bodied yet physically weak, you will be weak of mind and, most concerning, weak of will. The biggest issue I see with men today is they are weak of will.

You may be wondering what I mean when I say weak of will. I mean many men are lost. Too many men don't stand for much and have no idea what their purpose is. Your purpose: why you are here, what matters and who matters to you is the most important thing in a man's life. Your purpose runs the show; it sets your agenda. Your purpose is what informs your decisions. Your purpose is what sources your mindset. Without a sense of purpose, feelings will inform decisions. Feelings are what also sources most of the gynocentric paradigm. With no sense of purpose we make choices based on arbitrary wants and desires. The issue then is we can be easily manipulated. An extremely effective manipulation tool is the promise of sexual favors.

If you don't discover and create a purpose for you and your life, and then maintain it, there is still something running the show. That would be a default purpose. A default purpose is never powerful and always based in survival. It could be comfort or convenience, it could be money, it could be seeking admiration, or something as simple as not getting into trouble. No matter what your default purpose is, you must know it is running you and you have little say in it. It will leave you in a constant state of feeling like you just can't win or there is somebody else to blame. It is a setup to be constantly victimized and in a state of continual butt hurt. Discovering, owning, and living into your purpose is the access to personal freedom and authentic expression.

The leadership distinction we will go into greater depth about later is "being given being and action by something greater than oneself." One's purpose is the source of serene passion that is needed to develop oneself and others in their development as leaders. It is also the source of strength when we meet opposition. As men, and as leaders if we are doing it right, there will be resistance and opposition. You cannot care whether people are liking you or not; you gotta let your balls drop. Operating by being driven by your passion and your purpose is what the practice of giving zero fux looks like. That is a key milestone in masculine leadership. This does not mean you must be an arrogant a-hole; you just are more committed than concerned.

When we are clear on our purpose, our why, and our reason for waking up in the morning, we get to take on the three key roles of masculinity. These roles have been present for generations, and they are traditional in their purpose. This is also where we can fall into the trap of taking practices and having them become ideologies. These are *not* ideologies; these are foundational practices for being a man. They feed us and source us.

The first, *provide*. (I am approaching this from the perspective of a straight male.) In the world today the chances that a woman will need you to provide for her financially is greatly reduced from years ago. I actually think that is a good thing. Do you want a woman to want you for your money? Hell no! Men want women to love them for who they are not what they do. There is a reason the NFL has a 90 percent divorce rate for players after they retire.

What I mean by *provide* is to be the source of resources, space, encouragement, support, understanding, and listening to the women in your life. Listening is important, and we are usually not great at that. It is important because women are dynamic creative creatures, and they are ever changing. They are also far more complex emotionally, structurally, and chemically than we are. There is zero chance we will ever understand women the way we understand things. Because of that, if we want to have a woman in our life we must listen and we must understand what she is needing and requesting. This is not to say women are high maintenance. That would be grossly unfair. What they *are* is completely different from us, and we need to take 100 percent ownership in understanding what they want. To do that, we must be able to release our position and our filters to really get them.

The second foundational piece may be the most important, although I really believe they are like three sides to a triangle. This piece is *protect.* The value that drives women the most is the value of safety. If they feel protected, that safety need is greatly diminished. The obsession with safety in the narrative by both women and men is the absence of this foundational piece of masculine leadership. When people don't feel safe, they get crazy and it triggers them. All they can think of is survival. Leaders don't get how important protection is. This is not control. Protection is simply creating an environment where people no longer fear for their survival. We have operated in this country without protection for a long time. Ronald Regan was the last president who actually gave us a feeling of protection in leadership. George W. Bush, who I thought was a shitty president, did a great job of making America feel protected on the evening of 9/11. I will never forget the experience I had when he walked off Marine One and across the lawn at the White House. I had the experience that he had this and we were protected.

The final foundational piece is *leave a legacy.* That is simply creating a future that others are inspired by, that others want to join, and that others want to be part of. When we have a future that we are inspired by, engaging in the day-to-day is neither a chore nor a problem. Leaving a legacy requires us to be clear in our purpose and understand that if that purpose does not include others it will be both boring and lonely. It is our job to share it so others understand what is available to them. That is the work to do, constantly working on our legacy so others can be as inspired as we are. One cannot do that unless one is authentically believing it themselves. Sometimes that takes some work. That work usually begins with trust.

We will get into much further discussion and detail about these three foundational pieces later in the book. This is at the core of restoring manhood. I wanted to share this with you now to provide a glimpse into the future.

This is how it goes—we begin with LWEMWWW, and we end up with the three foundations of masculinity. Life is not linear, my friends, and oftentimes the biggest challenge or the most resistance is exactly what we need to be who we need to be. Life is precious and urgent; don't waste it on stupid shit...unless that stupid shit can teach you a valuable lesson.

## CHAPTER 17

# Feminized Men and Allies (Emasculation as Standard Practice)

*"This is a crisis in our culture because we have stopped raising MEN and we are raising PUSILLANIMOUS males at epidemic proportions!"*

*—S. J. Gold*

Feminized men provide such a value for me. They are the perfect foil for me to practice my ability to get untriggered. They are a gift because my first natural and primal instinct is to beat the shit out of them. That is in complete contradiction to my commitment of building bridges, improving communications between all people, listening to those who have differing ideas and ideology, and knowing that most solutions exist in the realm of relationship. Knowing my commitment and having the visceral experience of just wanting to destroy them allow me to build that muscle and detach from giving permission for my feelings and emotions to run things.

If we look at feminized men not from a place of disgust, if we can detach from our own opinions and inquire why they would choose to operate that way, what could we see? I believe feminized men operate that way because they think it is the expedient way to be. In the Chapter 2, *Winning at All Costs*, we discuss the problematic behavior that some men demonstrate when choosing the expedient over the right thing. Another way to say it is "taking the path of least resistance" or "going with the flow." This behavior shows someone who clearly lacks vision and purpose, and someone who is content with surviving. The flow we are speaking of is the gynocentric paradigm.

There is something in it for them to "just go with it" that they see as more palatable than standing for what is good or right. They may not see it that way; they may not have ever inquired. Choosing to stand against the current could seem too costly or too frightening. I have compassion for these guys. The world is changing, and the narrative is that traditional masculinity is obsolete or becoming obsolete.

There is no greater perpetrator of that than Michael Kimmel. He is a sociologist who has written a handful of books condemning traditional masculinity and calling for men to embrace more gynocentric behaviors and practices. He is a voice, along with many of the radical feminists, who believes we need to unconditionally believe women and always disbelieve men. This voice calls for compliance to the agenda and demands allied-ship. If you are not aligned, you are instantly labeled toxic, misogynistic, or sexist. The result of that can be zeroing out, cancelling, or, a favorite practice among the radical feminists, doxing.

Currently there is a tremendous amount of pressure for men to become more feminine—I believe they call it "inclusivity." This is painfully prevalent in the media and politics. The poster boy for the feminized man is none other than Canadian Prime Minister Justin Trudeau. He is, of course, Canadian.

And I do say (as an older, straight, white, crunchy male) he is a good-looking man. This kinder, gentler, more inclusive and accepting human also has his own sex scandal to deal with—something about grabbing a woman's body part without permission. That should never be done, due to the absence of respect that demonstrates, and deserves a throat punch for doing it. What I find interesting, though, is that very little is said about his indiscretion. But barely a day goes by when we don't hear about the DJT "grab them by the pussy" comment made in a locker room setting. You can see how ideology can set our perspective.

On my radio show one day, I asked Rollo Tomassi, a powerhouse in the manosphere, on why men choose to operate in a feminized way. His answer both stunned me and made perfect sense. In a way that only Rollo could, he said, "It is a strategy to maneuver through the sexual market place, it is a way to get laid." There we go again. Don't we always end up in this place? Sex, power, and money.

Our opportunity is to, as Gandhi said, *"Be the change we wish to see in the world."* Our job is to be the person we want other men to be. We must model the behavior and values we desire. We will not be perfect, and when we fail or make a misstep, we need to clean it up and keep moving forward. That is the only way this will change. If we practice this and live this, other men will see it and get curious. All there is to do is to model what we desire. *We Must Be the Change!*

We live in a time of polarization, of embattlement and alienation. There is no consensus, no listening, and no acceptance of anything different from what we believe. This leads to the dismissal of values. There is just shouting. Integrity, honesty, and truthfulness are rare commodities. We have given ourselves permission to treat others like shit. We have put barriers up between us, especially if we disagree. We see those who disagree as the "enemy." We have taken on a wartime mentality, and some people actually fear an impending civil war. That mentality allows us to dehumanize those who do not share our ideals. When we dehumanize others, all bets are off. It is the beginning of the end of a civilization and culture. War of some sort is next.

This cannot be how we live. *"If it is to be it is up to me!"* I hate slogans—I think they are jive—but if there is one to know, please own this one. It is about responsibility; it is about *being* the change. It is about owning the problem and the solution. This is a movement, because it's gonna take a metric fuck ton of us to band together to build on this idea.

To begin the process of *"Calling Men Forth to Lead at Home, at Work, and in the Public Sphere"* we need to look in the mirror. We need to own where we are and where we need to be. Don't worry if your shit is not completely together. Here is the secret: there is no end to the journey; there is no top to this mountain. There is only the pathway. Much like riding my Harley, the journey is the joy.

As it relates to our little bitch-ass girly-men feminist man friends, we have to love them. Yep, and to do so, we should probably stop calling them "little bitch-ass girly-men," and if the shoe fits, wear the damn thing. We must love them and have compassion for them. We need to model what being a responsible masculine leader looks like. We have to provide the space and the information for them to discover a different way. We need to get curious. What do they see? What has them believe what they believe? We never change anyone through telling them anything. We can only inquire and offer our support and acceptance. We love them anyway.

We also need to protect them, make sure they know they are safe. No throat punches and beating the shit out of them. As a matter of fact, we need to take on a solemn promise never to strike out in anger as the aggressor. If something happens we must *never* be on the attack unless attacked first. *We Must Be the Change* we want to see in others. In doing so, we may experience their fear, anger, rage, and hate. So what? It is theirs not ours. Be with them, listen to them, get them, and, most of all, love them anyway.

The next thing to do is share the vision, the idea, the purpose, and the legacy we are out to build. Own it; have it be yours. There are mission and vision statements in the beginning of the book. Use them. I invite you to make them your own or integrate them into your own personal purpose and share them with all you'd like.

These feminized guys I have ragged on are our brothers. Like brothers they may annoy us. (I am actually so blessed; I have the coolest brother on the planet.) So what? Love them. We will discover that as we deal with these things we view as obstacles and problems, much like when you restore a vintage house or car, you learn those "problems" are really an access point to develop the character of the project. This is our work to do.

## CHAPTER 18

# Blue Pill/Red Pill: Expertise vs. Leadership

*"This is your last chance. After this, there is no turning back. You take the blue pill—the story ends, you wake up in your bed and believe whatever you want to believe. You take the red pill— you stay in Wonderland and I show you how deep the rabbit-hole goes."*

—*Morpheus*

In the movie *The Matrix* Neo has an opportunity to awaken. We do not live in a science fiction movie with an alternate reality operating simultaneously to the one in which we exist. It is not that easy. We live in a world of our own construct and our own perception. We create our own "as lived" experience based on our values, our training and upbringing, our desires, our intellect and curiosity, and, most of all, our journey.

The blue pill/red pill choice that Neo has is a metaphor for how we choose to engage in life. We can choose the blue pill, which represents a sort of beautiful prison. We choose to remain comfortable and safe within the confines of the rules we accept. There is certainty available and predictability that comes with it. One way this could look is to remain comfortably attached suckling on the corporate teat and accepting the "good enough" scenario that it provides, being of service to their agenda, doing your time, and living for your three to four weeks of vacation each year. Inside this existence is the compliance required to maintain and progress in that environment. There is nothing wrong with this existence until the end when you realized you really did not live.

The red pill existence is not that. It is a world of uncertainty, a world of challenge, and a world of freedom. The responsibility is 100 percent on you. There is no backup; there is no safety net. Just you, your skills, your ideas, and the opportunity to live every day on your terms. There is an element of awakening that few can understand or experience. This is being alive. This is also being at risk. Your vision is keener, your sense of taste greater, your sense of smell heightened. You feel more, and you hear more. Your senses are enlivened.

You can see from these descriptions that the blue pill experience is much more aligned with the current narrative of the gynocentric paradigm. It is an experience that is based in comfort, safety, convention, and, most of all, fitting in. Given the gynocentric need for compliance and conformity, not only is the red pill experience not accepted, but it would also come across as threatening.

Gynocentric leadership, structure and organizations abhor uncertainty. The red pill experience exists in uncertainty. Not chaos, uncertainty. Nothing makes a gynocentric leader go nuts more than something that is unpredictable and beyond their control. You can tell one by, when the going gets rocky, the draconian measures they employ to control the situation and then their demands for compliance. The most recent pronounced representation of this was observed by watching the various responses to the Chinese virus by the differing governors of the states in the USA.

The gynocentric leaders, like the governors of Illinois, Michigan, and California, had completely different responses and policies than the governors of South Dakota, Florida, and Arizona. In both groups, members were of both genders. Gynocentricity does not mean female.

The really interesting thing is that the results were just about the same. The truth is, empirically speaking, nothing they did really changed the outcome. What they did do was influence the experience of the people living in the state and the rest of us who observed it. Notice how the results had little impact on our experience at times? That is because we often want to believe what we want to believe.

People who see the world through the blue pill experience are constantly seeking certainty and assuredness. It does not matter what the result is, they just want to have their actions justified and beliefs verified. These are the people who seek out experts and will look for data to corroborate their findings. They want everything to be OK, to be safe, and they are good with waiting for things to change.

They really love "experts" who provide the "specialized knowledge" that will make them feel good about their positions, beliefs, and decisions. These decisions are often made with much deliberation and made in committees. Assuring that decisions are a collaborative experience creates a process to assure that the decision is the fairest and demonstrates the most equity. Notice how this process begins to negate the results. The result is secondary as long as everyone is OK with how it came about. The result could be destructive and expensive, and miss the promised date, but that is OK as long as it is inclusive. This is a common example of gynocentric decision making. You can also see how an organization will begin its descent with this way of operating.

The red pill decision-making process is much different. Not only does it look at the result, but because of the heightened sense of awareness, it also takes into account the ripple effect of the result—the interaction between what is decided and what ends up occurring down the line. Data, science, and information are important, but in a different way. The decision is not to justify and minimize risk, the decision is based on forward movement and fulfilling on a commitment. The red pill experience is foundational to leadership in the twenty-first century.

Expertise is the expansion and development of specialized knowledge. It is the development of one's subjective reality. In essence, it is a solution looking for a problem. Expertise relies on the known and the proven to solve the issue at hand. Therefore it is the application of historical data to apply to current conditions.

The narrative determines if the expertise is valuable. The results can be secondary to the narrative.

Leadership is the ability to look at a problem and set it to the side for a moment—one's own subjective reality. That allows you to see the problem from a new light, a new perspective, and develop a new pathway to solve that problem. Leadership is the ability to see things as objectively as possible yet apply the specialized knowledge, skills, and abilities they have developed to address the issue at hand. It is essential for innovation and creativity. The results determine if the action was successful or not, and the results are not as important as the lessons learned and the pathway that gets expanded.

One of the biggest realizations we need to accept is that life occurs in the realm of uncertainty, and no matter what we want or desire, that is what is so. We have little control of what is going on around us. We can control our response and our reaction. If we practice, we can learn to control our thoughts and our perceptions. The leadership distinction "being cause in the matter" is that. We have little say in what goes on around us. We have 100 percent say in how we see it and how we respond, what we make it mean, and our actions. That is what Jocko Willink refers to as *Extreme Ownership*. We own every aspect of our life. I don't feel good, good. That task is hard, good. It's not fair, very good. So what? That is where we begin.

Please look at the "Manhood Manifesto Graph" in the Appendix. What this chart shows is that for the longest time, our intellectual ability was a match to the environmental stimulus that we had to deal with. This ability led to a huge effort to control and manage things. It was also our approach to people and how we would attempt to manage and control them. The reason was, if we could manage and control things and people, we could create some element of certainty or predictability, which would make us feel safe. God knows we love to feel safe and comfortable.

This condition and ability were kind of the way things went from the beginning of recorded history until just recently. Now look at the red line again, where it crosses the blue line is literally where the shit hits the fan. I am not sure when that was. I will assert it was not before the year 2000. It could have been in 2000 when Y2K was a non-event and the tech bubble crashed. It could have been in 2001, when the Twin Towers fell. It could have been in 2004 with the advent of the tech explosion like social media, or it could have been in 2008 when we elected Barack

Obama and the economy collapsed. I also believe it happened before the Occupy Wall Street movement occurred, and the beginning of Antifa and similar organizations. For the sake of perspective let's agree it was somewhere between 2000 and 2011. My personal belief it is very near 2007 or 2008.

This is important because it signifies a new domain for the human experience. My assertion is this signifies a time when humanity went from a need and response to being managed, to a time that requires leadership. The challenge is that there is nothing we have ever done that has prepared us for this. We talk about leadership a lot, and we know so little. Here is the good news, leadership is *not* a practice of knowing or doing; leadership is a practice of being and being with. Management requires control and leverage. Leadership requires inspiration, communication, and understanding. Understanding is way different than knowing. Management is about fitting inside a box, leadership is belonging to an idea, a movement, a commitment.

Management is about having it all figured out. Leadership is understanding that *knowing* makes little difference. Leadership is solving as we go, being present and utilizing the resources you have at hand. Management requires expertise and experts. Leadership requires inspiration, courage, and if you have a sense of humor, that comes into play pretty well. Leadership is about engagement. Leadership is a contact sport. It requires you "git some on ya."

The role of leadership is to provide the vision, the purpose, and the inspiration for why we are gathered together. Leadership is also responsible for creating and maintaining the environment, space, and culture the group operates within. Leadership, when done best, is about getting out of the way and empowering the folks who have joined you to be the change you desire. That way of being exists to change, build, and fulfill on the commitment you have created.

I know it seems I have been a bit rough on the folks who are aligned with the gynocentric paradigm. I am only rough on them because they are so hunkered in and I have failed to enroll them in a new way of seeing the world. I have yet to have them see that we are living in a new realm of human experience and that obsession with safety can be our demise. My intention is not to be rough on them at all; it is to be a bulwark to stop the progress of the unworkable.

What is also predictable is, as we get near the end of the functionality of a system, there is always extreme opposition to its extinction. This is why I am so critical of Michael Kimmel's criticism of masculinity. He is so off it is crazy. Have you ever witnessed an animal or human when they are dying? They do not go quietly. They fight. They struggle until their very last breath. That is our desire to survive. We are passionate and vital beings that love life and want to cling to it and squeeze every drop out of it that we can get. This trained passivity and addiction to comforts through indoctrination are complete and utter bullshit. It is not who we were designed to be.

We are entering a new age of masculinity, one where our creativity and leadership will be needed more than ever. We will also need the skills and talents of women. That is why this book is ultimately about partnership. Thanks for being on this journey with me; it is my honor. We are jumping into leadership and what it means. Hang in there, brothers (and I hope a few sisters).

CHAPTER 19

# Barack Obama and the Loss of Masculine Leadership

*"You can't make people listen to you. You can't make them execute. That might be a temporary solution for a simple task. But to implement real change, to drive people to accomplish something truly complex or difficult or dangerous—you can't make people do those things. You have to lead them."*
—*Jocko Willink*

Barack Obama was our first gynocentric president. It is possible Woodrow Wilson may have been, but that was before my time. During my lifetime Barack Hussein Obama is the only gynocentric president we have ever had. The impact of that leadership platform has been devastating and world-altering. His leadership, or lack thereof, was also awakening and presented the perfect arrogant stubbornness to prepare us for the future.

To me, Barack Hussein Obama is a con man, a street hustler, or an entertainer. His hustle is to appear nice, safe, and cuddly. He learned if he were a well-mannered, polite young man, he could play on the underlying racial tension that has existed in this country since the end of slavery. There is no worse accusation from 2008 through today than to be a white person and be called a racist. Barack Obama knew that, and he has used it to his advantage throughout his entire life.

Obama's primary strategy was to fit in, appear nonthreatening, and utilize the underlying concern of white people being perceived as possible racists to his advantage. The truth is, if there were actual structural racism in this country, there is no way he would have gotten elected and definitely no way he would have been reelected. However, there has never been a national conversation about race, racism, and the impact of slavery, so it is our dirty little secret that no one talks about in the American family. Much like drunk Uncle Ed and his pervy behavior, it is nothing for polite people to deal with. So we allow the tension to exist. Like any good hustler, Obama knew how to read the room and take advantage of the situation. His chief of staff, Rahm Emanuel, famously said, "You never want a serious crisis to go to waste." All that was needed was a crisis of race; so Barack Hussein Obama created one.

The situation was changing, we were entering an election year, and people were tiring of George W. Bush and his clumsy leadership. We still had not captured or brought to justice Osama bin Laden, we were fighting wars in multiple countries, and his cabinet looked like a bunch of old, stupid white guys who were full of shit. The country had just shifted the House and Senate to Democratic control, and Hillary Clinton had declared herself a candidate for president and was presumed to be the front runner. Were the American people going to accept the fourth in the line of the Bush-Clinton-Bush-Clinton succession in the Oval Office? That was the question. But if not them, who else?

Nancy Pelosi had just been named Speaker of the House. She was the first woman to hold that position in the history of the United States. Hillary Rodham Clinton, senator from New York and former first lady, was the presumptive Democratic candidate. It seemed the time had come for female leadership—the gynocentric paradigm was clearly installed. Whoever challenged HRC had to be someone trustworthy, nonthreatening, and, most of all, appealing to the gynocentric tendencies that were clearly being cultivated and exhibited. Yes, the time was ripe for Barack Hussein Obama. The only issue was no one really knew him.

Of course we did! He spoke at the 2004 Democratic Convention and gave probably the most inspiring speech of the convention. "There is not a Black America, or a White America, or a Latino America, there is only the United States of America." Obama channeled the skills and charisma of JFK; he not only won a seat in the US Senate, he was now a known identity. This unknown Illinois state senator was now a national figure. He was charming, articulate, passionate, kind, and, most of all, as Joe Biden said, "clean." Hey, if Joe, an old school, documented card-carrying racist and longtime cracker, was OK with Barack, he must pass the test. Gaining Biden's buy-in was a sign that he could be trusted by the political establishment. Throw in the JFK-esque "all for America and unity" speech, and this guy was America's darling. Plus, he was good looking and had a lovely family with an amazing and powerful woman as his partner, along with two adorable girls. What was not to love?

Barack Obama was not a candidate; he was a brand. As part of that branding he published a huge-selling book, *Dreams from My Father*. His brand message was a simple one, Hope and Change. Hope is a great message for the developing gynocentric paradigm because it makes us feel good. Who does not want to feel hope, especially after a bunch of old white guys who have just been fighting wars, ruining the world, and excluding people? Those guys were bad, and they made us feel icky. All you had to do was ask the Dixie Chicks—oh I'm sorry—The Chicks. This all-American gynocentric country group was no longer proud to be American. Can you imagine, a country group espousing comments against our president?

We wanted to feel hope, and with hope we wanted change. Change to *what* was the question. Of course, based on Obama's 2004 Democratic Convention speech, the change would be one America, a unified America. Who could not want that? No one questioned his agenda; it seemed so clear. So on November 4, 2008, in what seemed to be one of the most unifying events in the history of our county, we elected Barack Hussein Obama the forty-fourth president of the United States of America. The hustle had just been set.

Obama's biggest ideological influencers were not Washington, Jefferson, and Franklin. The fact was, Obama was not really raised in America. He was born in Hawaii during the early stages of statehood. He was raised by his mother and grandparents. He spent a significant amount of time in his childhood in Indonesia. That ain't Kansas. His true influences were some unusual people. His mother shared with him the anti-colonialist views of his father. Her father had some interesting socialist viewpoints. One of Barack's early mentors was Frank Marshall Davis, well known by the FBI, because of his pro-Soviet and communist beliefs.

When Barack was in Chicago, one of his close friends was Bill Ayers. As a member of the Weather Underground, an anti-government radical group, Ayers was convicted of several bombings. During Barack Obama's campaign, Ayers let it be known he regretted bombing those buildings. Barack was also very influenced by Edward Said, a former advisor to the Palestine Liberation Organization, and a somewhat radical anti-Zionist. Closer to home, his spiritual advisor was the Reverend Jeremiah Wright, famous for his anti-Semitic remarks and the phrase, "Not God Bless America, God damn America."

One other huge influence on Obama was Emil Jones. Emil was a big swinging dick in the regular Chicago Democrat organization—that is, he was one of the mayor's guys. He delivered what the mayor needed in the Illinois Senate. He was also a get-out-the-vote guy for "Hizzoner da Mayor." He was the one who taught Barack how Chicago politics work. He was also a huge promoter for Obama to gain the Senate seat. One of Emil's best political buddies was none other than Rod Blagojevich. He was the guy who was sent to federal prison for attempting to sell/influence peddle Barack Obama's Senate seat. I'm sure that was a coincidence.

What I am hoping you are seeing are the prodigious inconsistencies of Barack Hussein Obama. Inconsistency is a trademark of a con man and a hustler. It is also a trademark of someone who is constantly in survival mode and focused only on what is in it for them. Here is a man who was proclaimed to be a constitutional scholar, yet he was raised by a radicalized mother and influenced by the teachings of an absent father that were based in socialism and anti-colonialism. He was speaking of a United States of America, yet people close to him were convicted terrorists and known anti-American race baiters. He claimed to love America, yet was highly influenced by Saul Alinsky.

Barack Obama was wildly inconsistent except in one way. His anti-colonialist background is the fuel for what seemed to be his commitment to end the idea of American exceptionalism. He was notorious for going around and apologizing for things

America did. He was a stand for the poor; all the while the economic gap between the top 1 percent and the rest of America grew. Barack claimed to be a man of peace and many saw him as that, yet he had more drone attacks on more different countries than any president before him. He claimed to be for peace and positive change, and yet during his eight years in office, America experienced forty-one mass shootings and growing racial divide and unrest.

It seemed like the results that were created by Obama's time in office were incredible tension, uncertainty, and chaos. The man who was brought to office by a coalition of Whites, Blacks, and Hispanics had created what seemed to be a bigger racial divide than we had in the '60s. The evening of his reelection in 2012, I remember Karen Finney, a Democrat Party operative, going on the Rachel Maddow show, and saying what the 2012 election showed was that older, straight white men were obsolete. I was not able to foretell what would come of that statement; I just knew it was dumb.

I could generate another two to three more pages of information on the failings of Barack Obama, but it would not serve the purpose of this book; it would simply be an indulgence. Barack Hussein Obama represents the highest level of the failing of masculinity and the trend in our culture of a gynocentric paradigm. The issue is feelings were more important than results, and if those feelings could be supported by a narrative regardless of what the facts were, that works. Barack Obama was a great storyteller, and he was a master of telling us bovine excrement smelled like peppermint. No greater story was told than the Affordable Care Act.

Most recently this bullshitting skill of Barack Hussein Obama was expressed in the agenda to defund the police. Mr.

Obama was speaking to a group of leaders in the Democratic Party about their messaging. He warned them of being "too direct" and "too incendiary" for the "average person" to understand. Obama, ever the master of the coded language, being too direct and incendiary meant expressing the truth was not acceptable. The average person, of course, meant white people. Obama is ever the deceitful, indirect, and disingenuous racially dividing con man.

Barack Hussein Obama was a horrible leader. He was a horrible campaigner. The only person Barack Obama is good at getting elected is Barack Obama. A hustler will always have a great story and a cool narrative, and provide a charming experience. And the only one who gets anything is the hustler. Barack Obama did gain one skill during his rise to power. He learned how to get paid.

Having been raised modestly, when Barack was in the US Senate, his net worth was a modest $600,000. He did own a beautiful home in the Kenwood neighborhood of Chicago. There were questions of how he got that—again another story. His net worth today is a reported $70 million. I believe that is a somewhat underreported number based on his real estate holdings. The house in Chicago is worth more than a million, he has a place in Martha's Vineyard that he purchased for $15 million, and the crib in DC is worth more than $7 million. If you look, he accrued a tremendous about of wealth while he was earning $400,000 a year as president. He must have one hell of a financial planner. I have raised this question to many of my friends who are Obama apologists/supporters. Everyone has the same answer: "He wrote books; he's an author." This is an area in which I have some subject matter understanding, because I too write books. I am very thankful for my publisher and the arrangement we have, but it is really difficult to get to $70 million.

The issue with Barack Hussein Obama is not his wealth, although his ability to get paid is prolific. The issue was that this man represented leadership, change, and hope. He failed, and in doing so he attacked the traditions of America, he attacked masculinity, and he attacked our freedom. It is my opinion that the Barack Hussein Obama presidency was the biggest hustle that has ever befallen the American public, and it is a hustle based on fear and guilt.

Mr. Obama pressed on the most sensitive nerve of our American culture. Mr. Obama earned our trust by claiming unity while all the while he was feeding the divide. He had an opportunity to heal and an opportunity to bring us together as a country, but he did the opposite. He ignited the fear, the upset, and the anger that I am not sure is even real. We saw with him that the facts do not need to be present for his narrative to be accepted. Mr. Obama drove a wedge into our nation, a wedge between Blacks and Whites, a wedge between gay and straight, and a wedge between men and women.

In my opinion, Barack Hussein Obama is fundamentally untrustworthy. I think there is no greater failing in a man than that. Mr. Obama created his brand by saying, "There is no Black America, or White America, or Hispanic America, there is the United States of America." That is an empowering and uniting statement that brings "folks" together. Yet my experience of him is that here is a man who uses race as a tool to create power, influence, and personal wealth. He came into office under a coalition of Americans and left office with an America more divided than at any time in my lifetime. We were divided not only by race, we were also divided by religion and spiritual beliefs;

we were divided by sexual orientation, and the widest abyss he created was with gender. Men, particularly able-bodied, straight white men, especially of a particular age, were the target of his indignation.

What Mr. Obama says and what he does are seldom the same thing. He is the master of misdirection, of deceit and the con. Mr. Obama demonstrates all the characteristics of Hillary Clinton: righteous indignation, intellectual elitism, and intolerance for ideas other than their own. But he is far more visually appealing and shrouds his narrative with a folksy charm. Mr. Obama operates with the same racially divisive ambition as the Reverend Al, yet he does so in a much warmer and less angry way, so he can be more appealing to white folks, especial white women. Mr. Obama is the consummate performer. Because of that, I believe we never really got to know him or his agenda. That is dangerous and reckless behavior for a leader.

Mr. Obama represented the most nonmasculine expression of any male leader that I have ever seen. He saw appeasement and apology as a way of operating when courage and stand would create opening for engagement. He saw deflection and distortion when direct communication would have been the access to creating and renewing relationships. He refused to negotiate, only to rule through dictates and executive order. He did not see opposition and resistance as opportunity, only as something to be victimized by. Mr. Obama was a problem to which Donald Trump became the solution.

I am actually not sure Mr. Trump was the solution, but what I think he provided was the bulwark to cease the trend and flow of the Obama narrative. What is needed is solid, conscious masculine leadership to be installed. I am calling for manhood to be present. It is up to us men to pick up the reigns and begin the practice of leadership. One practice area we must address is the unspoken racial divide. There is no way we can make the history of slavery disappear. It is a part of who we are. What I believe is that in addressing it openly and honestly, the resilience and antifragility of the American experience will shine through. It is tough work and work worthy of doing. That is the opportunity we have, and the gift of Barack Obama is that he was the catalyst to bring it to the forefront.

# CHAPTER 20

## Chinese Virus and Peaceful Protest

*"No matter how bad things are, you can always make things worse."*

*—Randy Pausch*

America is an idea. Yes, it is a country with fifty states, all of which have a number of unique attributes and characteristics that express their individual distinctions. Yet first and foremost, America is an idea. It is an idea of freedom, individualism, personal sovereignty, and individual responsibility. The idea of freedom is not easy; it is not intended to be easy. The idea of America is a distinctly masculine idea; America is an expression of manhood. It is an expression created by men through divine influence. It is an idea that calls for men to operate at their highest and most powerful way of expression. It is an idea where men can practice honor, respect, creativity, and chivalry. Chivalry is the idea that the more men are men, the more women can be women.

One can argue that the idea of America was intentionally designed to be difficult. That is why I say it is an expression of manhood, because men learn most effectively by trial and tribulation. That is also why America will never be perfect and the idea will never be totally realized (it's OK to insert your man jokes here). Imperfection is evident everywhere, and failure is required to achieve the idea of freedom and self-governance. That idea is a worthy pursuit, and therein lies the value of vision. When we connect to our purpose, it is not so much to achieve it as it is to inform us of the pathway on which we need to be. Freedom is far more a journey than a destination. The idea of freedom must be earned through not only our actions, but also our mindset, our attitude, our vision, and our purpose. Our actions are an outpouring of those. That is how we can know if we got our minds right.

The Chinese virus has been a test to challenge our beliefs around freedom, personal sovereignty, and individual liberty. We have failed that test. We abandoned independent thinking in service of "remaining safe." Those few who did question and stand up were instantly subjected to the ridicule and condemnation of the left-leaning gynocentric media. The messaging was so deceitful that any inquiry as to its legitimacy was instantly attacked as inhumane and not valuing our fellow man. Individuality was attacked and replaced with a call for the "greater good" and "together we are better." I am a huge fan of teamwork, community, and organizational cohesiveness. I also understand for those systems to work they must be constructed on a foundation of personal and individual integrity.

The Chinese virus has tested our willingness to operate with courage. We have chosen to conform to the idea of comfort, safety, and convenience while accepting the narrative as truth. Mandatory mask-wearing (is there any way to better remove individual identity than that of wearing a mask?), government-sanctioned lockdowns, contact tracing, and compulsory vaccines have become ways to test our resolve and desire for freedom. The results are alarmingly obvious. Government officials will never forget how easy it was for them to seize control of our lives. We don't have to go too far back in time to realize this is the second time in this century this has occurred. When 9/11 occurred, we complied. We fell into line, and we leaned into the government to protect us. That did not work out too well, and I don't expect much different from the result of the Chinese virus protections.

All this is the preconditioning for the biggest attack on the idea of America, the new world order. The idea of the new world order goes back to Roman times. The Roman Empire, followed by the Holy Roman Empire, followed by the Ottoman Empire, and later the Third Reich. I am sure there are others you can insert here, along with a number of monarchies and dictatorships. The idea is that a few should manage and lead the many. The idea of self-governing and sovereignty is a radical idea and one I feel is worthy of pursuing because it is a structure that allows for individual freedom and authenticity to be expressed. It is also one that holds individuals responsible for how their lives go.

One of my heroes, Walter E. Williams, spoke of the idea of America as not only a unique idea, but also as one that had not been historically prevalent. Ronald Reagan spoke of the fragile nature of our freedom. The event of the Chinese virus demonstrates how fragile that freedom is, how unique it is, and, most concerning, how easily we give it up. We give it up because we are afraid, and the fearmongering and daily death counts by the likes of MSNBC, along with the infections rates, keep us in that state of fear. Let's not be concerned that the Center for Disease Control's own numbers say that 81 percent of those diagnosed will be asymptomatic. (If you have no signs of the disease, how do you know you have it? Because the government says so?)

As men we have failed. We have sat back and watched. The two behavioral expressions I have seen are: quivering like a little bitch and buying into the obvious phony narrative, or getting angry. The deception, the fraud, and the hypocrisy are unprecedented. This includes the possible stealing of a presidential election. I only use the word *possible* because I really don't know, and the idea of having half the population vote by mail to avoid spreading the Chinese virus is only one example of the manipulation. Sure, there are states who have effectively used mail-in ballots for years; Colorado is one that does well with it. There are others, though, who effectively slapped together an unproven system for the collection of ballots. In viewing the irregularities associated with them, we can definitely question the security and validity of their process. States like Michigan, Pennsylvania, Wisconsin, Georgia, and Illinois quickly expanded their mail-in voting as a direct response to their "fear of the spread." I don't think it is a coincidence that four of those five had very close outcomes and were instrumental in pushing the result toward a Joe Biden win.

As men we have failed because we have been passive. We have allowed nonsense to go on for too long. Men have also been part of the nonsense. A fantastic illustration of this occurred during the George Floyd riots, when MSNBC's own Ali Velshi was reporting on the protest said, "I want to be clear on how I characterize this. This is mostly a protest. It is not, generally speaking, unruly but fires have been started." He said this while standing in front of a burning building. Ali Velshi, you have achieved a lifetime revocation of your man card. Ali Velshi "who you crappin'?" We can no longer allow for this. We must stand and speak truth to the false narrative. We must be a bulwark for freedom. Our role as men is to provide, protect, and create the future needed. The first thing we must accept is the irrational fear that has been driving the show. That fear is described, in part, in the chapter on narcissism. The perfect antidote for narcissism and irrational fear is the first distinction of leadership: "being given being and action by something greater than oneself."

We failed in doing so because we fell into the belief that the government would take care of us and had our best interests in mind. Bureaucracies only operate with *their* best interests in mind. The purpose of a bureaucracy is to survive. Plain and simple. Bureaucracies exist only for their own self-preservation, and they cannibalize the constituencies they claim to be serving. The truth is that bureaucracies only exist for the good of those within them. If you ever looked at the perks and benefits of state and federal workers, you would puke.

When we connect to our purpose, the thing that gives us being and actions, it all begins to get clear. We realize everything to this point has prepared us for this, we just need to demonstrate the courage to own that realization. We need to accept the deception and ask ourselves why we allowed ourselves to be deceived. What were we afraid of? We need to inquire. What made us OK with the fraud? What was the quid pro quo for me? What had me look the other way? We need to really look at what the payoff is for buying the hypocrisy. What itch are we getting scratched? The answers don't matter, except now you can begin to understand your own level of where you will sell out, where you will quit on you and your family. We have to know this so we can create the structures to support us when the going gets tough. If you are sitting there saying, "You know,

Mike, I will never sell out," I get it, brother, and I love you, but everyone will sell out, denies, or betrays at least once. You will too; you just don't know when. Even Saint Peter denied Jesus. Unfortunately, the not knowing is what makes you both dangerous and untrustworthy.

The gift of uncovering your purpose, connecting to it, and understanding the conditions of when you will sell out is the beginning of self-awareness. We must know and own our darkness. That understanding of self is how we prepare ourselves to be leaders. Some will call this experience a spiritual awakening, and some will say the understanding of all this a process of sanctification. If that experience fits you, praise God and welcome brother. If not yet, stay on the path.

It is at this point of discovering of one's purpose that reality sets in. I know it sounds great, but it is usually not good news. Some get frightened and stop; the most common response is anger and agitation. Anger is a masking emotion; it allows us to power through. Oftentimes it's cool, and we can get through what we must. Keeping anger in his toolbox is one of the most valuable resources a man can have, but if he doesn't understand it and gain facility with it, then it can be destructive.

When anger shows up, I have learned it is an indicator for other less practiced emotions. Sadness is one I have most recently discovered. Sadness allows me to be with more of the unworkability, to understand more and have more compassion. It allows me to inquire deeper. This is especially important in times of deception. One of the things I have noticed about dudes is we are easily deceived. Women have known this about us for millennia. The story of Adam and Eve is basically the story of a man being deceived by a woman. The fact that women get triggered by that story is more evidence of women's, and especially the gynocentric paradigm's, utilization of deception as a tactic (see the chapter on Barack Obama). We need to begin to take on the practice of accepting reality as is, without judgment and upset. What other choice do we have?

Make no mistake about this, the Chinese virus was an act of war. If the virus was not, the response was. (Maybe that is why it took about six months from when the virus was first discovered to the mass shutdowns in March 2020.) It is an attack on our freedom and our way of life. The biggest challenge is people in our own country and in our own families are against our country and, more importantly, the idea of freedom. We are a house divided, as Lincoln said, and I do not believe war is the answer. I believe that calling forth manhood and masculine leadership is the answer. The process is the development and installation of courageous, responsible masculine leadership in partnership with women who share our vision. The enemy at this time is more an idea than people, but there are some people who cannot be trusted.

In Sun Tzu's *The Art of War,* he states that to defeat your enemy you must defeat your enemy's strategy. The enemy is the gynocentric paradigm, which is fed by the radical teachings of Saul Alinsky, Karl Marx, and Vladimir Lenin. The processes of Marx and Lenin have both been proven not to work. Saul Alinsky has created a simple operating system for adherents of the gynocentric paradigm to follow. Barack Hussein Obama is the chief marketing officer of the global new world order. When one reads the thirteen *Rules for Radicals,* what the opponents of freedom are counting on is that we cannot withstand the pressure of their misbehavior. Anyone who has raised a teenager, especially a teenage daughter, understands this strategy and, if they tell the truth, has been marginalized by it.

Remember to defeat our enemies we must defeat their strategy. The way to defeat their strategy is to not lose our shit. That is easier said than done. One only has to engage in one conversation about transsexualism to understand the complete insanity of their mindset. That is OK; engage in actions. Standing our ground is a powerful action, and to do that we must really become self-aware at a completely new level. The best access to self-awareness is connecting with our purpose. If you take anything from this book, please connect to and discover your purpose. If you decide not to follow the calling, that is your choice, but please get who you are and why you are here.

Closing up on the China virus: my guess is it will be years before we know what it really is or was. At this time it does not matter. As with most things in life, it is seldom the event and almost always how we respond and who we "be" about the event. It is from that experience of witnessing our being to an event that we can become very informed as to how we are doing this thing called life. We have not done so well; that is the good news. The better news is we can shift that and restore our manhood. The best news is there is no time like the present. Can I get an AMEN?

## CHAPTER 21

# Errors in Application and the Absence of Systemic Thinking

*"When there is no enemy within, the enemies out-side cannot hurt you."*
—*Winston Churchill*

When we listen to the complaints from the great white woke globalist gynocentric perspective, there is the never-ending finger-pointing to the abuse and issues generated by white supremacy, patriarch, white privilege, misogyny, xenophobia, and, above all, systemic racism. There is a never-ending call for social and racial justice. At the core of the complaint is really straight, white, able-bodied, successful men. We are the villains in their drama. I get it, and to some degree we have provided them the evidence for this novella.

Why these constant and never-ending attacks on men and masculinity? The simple answer is fear. I was recently shopping in my neighborhood Whole Foods. I purposely chose to wear a camouflage Trump 45 trucker hat. I wore it as a type of social experiment. I wanted to see if I would get a reaction and, if so, what would occur. I am a pretty-laid back dude and often interact with those around me in small talk and banter. I enjoy

Whole Foods because the baked goods are outstanding and the people there are a bit different than me. As I was walking to the bread racks, a young Black woman was staring at her screen. I stopped as she accidentally bumped into me. It's what happens at times when people are looking down and someone else enters into their preplanned route. She was walking around a corner, and I did not see her coming.

What I also did not see coming was her reaction. Her response to me was first shock as she was distracted and did not know I was there, and then she looked up. The first thing she looked at was my hat. The look in her eyes was complete terror. She looked at me as if I wanted to only cause her harm. The fear was impactful, and I also realized my social experiment generated an unexpected result, terror in the eyes of a young woman. I realized we, as a culture, as a country, as a community, are severely broken.

As the second section of this manifesto is completing, we must understand that if any of this is to change, it must begin with us. The cavalry ain't coming, and the folks on the other side are scared and righteous. As men and leaders we must get responsible. We must be the change we want to see in the world. That change cannot be reducing our masculine expression, giving up our beliefs or appeasing the fearful. We must be the change. That begins with understanding what the change we want is and then living in accordance with that.

It would be easy for me to say, "I will never wear a MAGA hat again in public." That is just more of the same, and that is not getting at the root cause. Where we must begin is in realizing behind *every* complaint there lives a commitment. If we listen to the people represented and living inside the gynocentric paradigm, we must inquire, "What is their commitment?" If we observe what they practice, it is clear they want power and the authority to eliminate any expression that is not aligned with their own. That is also the strategy that is generated from fear and is based in killing off humanity that one does not know or understand. The result is the censoring, the cancel culture, and the constant and never-ending attacks on all things different. If we listen to them and what they say, they say they want diversity, they desire inclusion, they want their voice to be heard. I am willing to trust what they say they want is what they want. For that to occur there must be a structure for it to happen. The structure they are proposing is not one that is acceptable to most men, so we need to negotiate. As men and leaders we must provide and build the structure for the environment to occur for them to be heard and included. We must create a structure to have them be our partners and fellow citizens.

Structures determine outcomes. The structure of a contract determines the outcome of the transaction. The structure of a facility determines the output of a factory. The structure of an organization determines the service and value created by that organization. As a country, one based in freedom, our structure is the government, and the services must provide that (freedom). Those structures are determined by the Constitution and the three branches of that government. In the United States, we can never forget that we are a government "of the people, by the people, and for the people." We are a country that is self-governed. We are a country that is based in freedom. When there is freedom, there will be failure and error. There will also be corrective action, learning, and growth. That is what justice is.

When we look at structure for the desires of the people of the gynocentric agenda, we see diversity, inclusion, having their voices heard, and equality. I look to the Declaration of

Independence, one of the foundation blocks upon which the structure of this country was built:

> *We hold these truths to be self-evident: that all men are created equal; that they are endowed by their Creator with certain unalienable rights; that among these are life, liberty, and the pursuit of happiness.*

All men are created equal with certain unalienable rights... life, liberty, and the pursuit of happiness.

Another foundational block is the Constitution:

> *We the People of the United States, in Order to form a more perfect Union, establish Justice, insure domestic Tranquility, provide for the common defense, promote the general Welfare, and secure the Blessings of Liberty to ourselves and our Posterity....*

We the people (self-governing), in Order to form (work in process, understanding we have not yet arrived), a more perfect Union (future condition, an aspiration), establish Justice (a legal system to insure personal *individual* rights regardless of race, creed, or ethnicity), insure domestic Tranquility (the establishment of law and order while ensuring rights), provide common defense (create an army and military that protects *all* citizens and our borders), promote the general Welfare (please notice the word "promote" not *ensure*), and secure the Blessings of Liberty to ourselves and our Posterity (this speaks to the legacy piece of the masculine role.)

I look at those two structures, and I am clear it is divinely inspired. I am also clear it is an idea to be pursued. It is *not* guaranteed. For freedom to truly exist, there can be very few guarantees. What is not guaranteed here is your safety, your well-being, your success, your financial independence, your education, your diet, your medical care, or your student loans to be paid off. What is guaranteed are freedom, access to opportunity, and, most of all, one's liberty and one's voice.

I have asked myself that if liberty is so clearly spelled out, why is there so much intention on limiting it? I sought the answer in many places, but the only place we can go to get the real answer is within. Why would someone want to limit another person's liberty? Simple—fear. There is fear. So I have to ask, why does that fear exist? Again, I can go to all the crazy places, and, again, the answer really resides in the mirror. Fear exists when trust is violated.

As men we have been blessed with the opportunity to live free and to have prospered to some degree. That is what is guaranteed to us by the Constitution. Since the beginning of this project I have been really looking at the complaints of "privilege, white supremacy, patriarchy, racial justice, and equality." I must say when I hear many of these complaints I want to just tell people to shut the hell up. That response only amplifies the noise.

John F. Kennedy once said, "To whom much is given, much is required." That is a take from a biblical verse—Luke 12:48: "For unto whomsoever much is given, of him shall be much required." I believe therein lies the issue. America is a great country, and it has been, and is, structured to provide an opportunity for success and prosperity. People have traveled across the world to achieve that. Yet there are people in our country who have not shared in the prosperity. We have done little to understand that.

My concern is the structure of the left-leaning gynocentric paradigm is to attack the system of America and to tear it down because portions of our citizenry have not enjoyed the success that others have had. That narrative has created a story that America is an evil place; that it is inherently racist and biased; that it is structurally created to abuse certain citizens and use an oppressed group to prop up the greedy, the wealthy, and primarily the white men. I have looked in my heart, and I have looked around, and I see no evidence of systemic or structural racism and systemic injustice. What I have seen is misapplication and abuse of the existing structures.

To some that may sound like semantics; I can assure you that is not what I mean.

I am a former engineer. I worked in both the manufacturing and construction industries. To accomplish anything you need to create a process to get it done. A process simply creates order and constraints that ensure that the inputs generated the desired outcome. Process engineering is pretty easy once you understand what it is about. You will then see that for every result there is a perfect process that generates that result. We need to really look at the process.

Let's look at injustice as an outcome. It is an undesired outcome but an outcome nonetheless. What are the inputs to it? If we look at poverty as an output, what is the process that leads to it? You can see how easily our mindset can devolve into having the results be guaranteed, thus the equality of outcome argument. The real issue exists in the equality of opportunity and what gets in the way of that.

One of the biggest challenges we have culturally is we over-value results. In doing so we pay winners too much and others too little. The inequity is not systemic; it is cultural. It is based in our belief that to the winner go the spoils. Culturally, we love winners. Culturally, we are an aggressive and competitive culture. That is what freedom allows. The problem with competition is it generates winners and losers. The gift of competition is that it is the perfect structure of resistance to grow and develop. The challenge with competition is when people value winning too much they will cheat to achieve victory. We have become accustomed to cheating and allowing others around us to cheat too. We may have lost sight of what cheating really is. If winning is all that matters, is cheating a problem? Only if you get caught. If we get caught or someone calls us out, then we will just bribe them. If it gets too bad, we will just pay the fine. See, in America, justice is served in one of two ways: money or time. If you are a very wealthy guy or a large corporation and you get caught cheating. you pay a fine. What is a few million if you are making tens of millions? If you are a poor kid and you get busted for stealing something out of a convenience store, and you have no money and a bunch of time, well—you pay with time. Money or time, it's the same damn thing, right? Maybe not.

This section is about root cause analysis; this chapter is about error in applications of processes and the absence of systemic thinking. When you have a culture that is constantly changing and shifting, the system needs to change and shift accordingly. As the inputs in the process change, the outputs will change, or we will need to adjust. That fine-tuning, that adjustment, is where leadership is required. Those changes exist in the area of structural integrity. It takes courage to address the issue of integrity. People get very sensitive when you question their integrity. They get sensitive because they have not questioned their integrity first and they tend to get defensive. What people don't understand is that for most, integrity is not a natural state. Survival is. Our integrity is always going out—meaning it is getting worn down and slipping away. Think of it like changing the oil in your car. As soon as you turn your car on, that oil is beginning to wear. Integrity is a wear item, and we always need to be reinstall it. The blind spot is when folks think they have "arrived." There is no arrival; there is just the journey. That false sense of arrival is not problematic until you deny you must replace that which is worn. Continuous maintenance is required to keep us in good working order. If we don't adjust as the components of our system change, the system will break down. That is where we are culturally—we are broken down.

As men we must own the breakdown. We have not. For much of the greater part of this century, we have continued on as the cultural and ontological "check engine" light has been flashing. Most people ignore the light because they don't know what to do, so they keep on going on and pretending it will go away. Sorry—the magic wand is not an option. What is even worse is that some of us have become male feminists and allies and have done the Pontius Pilate/Judas/St. Peter combo platter. We have washed our hands, betrayed our brothers, and denied we had anything to do with it. We are just human.

Systems cannot be biased or racist. Those are human characteristics. We will never end racism or prejudice no matter how many sidelines we spray with that message. The reality of spray-painted sidelines is they reduce real issues to mottos and slogans. These, then, become a structure to support the perpetually offended and the permanently victimized. I don't think that is what why our forefathers created the Constitution.

What is needed is courageous, value-based leadership. That is why it is incumbent upon men to lead again. We must first get responsible for the breaches of trust, the abuses of power, the exploitation of wealth, and the damage we have done. I am not calling for a Barack Obama apology tour. No, the great deceiver went around and apologized for all of the bad things we have done. In some ways some of that was necessary because he followed eight years of a shit show and an administration that lied and started a war. If Obama had been at all sincere, I would have been OK with it. But it was just another of the many deceitful acts of Kabuki theater that punctuated his presidency. What I am calling for is purpose, integrity, and authenticity aligned with the intention of the Constitution and the reason the United States of America was founded. So people can live freely, experience liberty, and pursue happiness. I am calling for us to end the nonsense, lead intentionally, and develop our environment so that all people can live to the best of their ability.

To do that, men must provide, protect, and share the legacy and future vision. To do that we must end the practice of abuses we have allowed to continue. We must end the abuse of women, children, and other men. The abuses I am speaking of are physical, sexual, emotional, and financial. We must walk our talk, no more deceitful half-truths. We must ensure that our businesses are operating ethically and honorably and that we have healthy environments for our workers. We must create government in a way that restores the public trust—especially trust in our elections. We must have the courage to stand up to tyrants, despots, crazed mobs, and any country, organization, or ideal whose aim is control and the elimination of freedom. We must be willing to sacrifice luxury to ensure the sustainability of this nation and the people who live in it. We must be willing to speak truth to bullshit no matter who is spewing it. This is just the beginning. There is much to do.

We have had a good run. It is time to tighten it up a bit. Our future and the future of our children and their children require that. I know we are more than capable of delivering.

# PART III

## DOING THE WORK

(Gittin' Some on Ya)
Shifting Mindset, Engagement and Next Steps

"Be the change you wish to see in the world."
—Mahatma Gandhi

## CHAPTER 22

# Masculine Leadership: Building Brotherhood

*"Extreme Ownership. Leaders must own every-thing in their world. There is no one else to blame."*
—*Jocko Willink*

In every construction project you begin with a set of plans. They used to be called "blueprints," but I have not seen a set of actual blueprints in forty years. We will just call them plans. The plan for *Manhood Manifesto* has three sections and one practice. In this chapter we are going to discuss the first section, one part of the second section, and the practice. I am going to invite you to begin the practice today.

## The Plan

1) **Two Duties of Leadership**
   A) To provide a future vision for all people to join in and live into
   B) Cultivate and maintain the environment such that the vision can be realized

2) **Four Core Distinctions of Leadership (distinctions, not skills)**
   A) Being given being and action by something greater than oneself
   B) Integrity
   C) Authenticity
   D) Being cause in the matter

3) **Three Foundational Roles of Masculinity**
   A) Provide
   B) Protect
   C) Leave a legacy

4) **Practice: Love Your Brother; Unconditional Love**

That is the plan. Easy peasy, right? Before we can engage in any plan we must connect with our purpose. As Simon Sinek calls it, our "Why." Begin with Why!

The first of the four core distinctions of leadership is: *"Being given being and action by something greater than oneself."*

I learned this distinction in the Being a Leader Program, at Clemson University. This program was developed by Werner Erhard, Mike Jenson, and two other brilliant people. Their definition of this distinction is as follows: *"Source of the serene passion (charisma) required to lead and to develop others as leaders and the source of persistence (joy in the labor of) when the going gets tough."*

I believe they expressed this distinction really well, and I want to share with you what I have learned since experiencing this course and integrating these distinctions into my mindset. This distinction is beyond motivation. It is actually what calls you forth when you remove your fears, concerns, ego, training, cultural indoctrination, degrees, and professional credentials.

For me, it is access to my soul and the thing that makes life make sense, even when it seems really weird. It is sourced by love; it is where I can access God and the divine. By connecting to this, my relationship with God has gotten far stronger, and it is not about religion. This is where one discovers their purpose and their reason for being. This is where your soul sings, and every minute is a Chappelle concert. (Let's say most minutes.)

My why, my purpose: "To be the space where authentic leadership is created." What I got out of this distinction is that the really important part of leadership is building new and more leaders. Think of leadership as a form of multilevel marketing (I am only partially joking). The why for the book: "*To begin the process of awakening American men to their role, their contribution, and their leadership, regardless of their position, needed to have America be the bastion of freedom and possibility in the world.*" If you are a barista at Starbucks, lead from that place and join in this purpose.

If you are unclear as to what your purpose is—sometimes it is really hard to know—reach out to me. We'll get it done. This is where we must begin. Without knowing, understanding, and fully owning our purpose, it gets really tough to begin the process of discovering who we truly are. If one does not understand who they truly are, our strengths, weakness, blind spots, triggers, talents, and gifts, we are destined to live in a state of continuous aimless frustration.

Living a "red pill" life, a life that is truly free, requires acceptance of discomfort and challenge. It is knowing that discovery, challenge, and opposition are the field in which we are permitted to grow, develop, and become ourselves. The discomfort and challenge provide the resistance required for lift and the resistance required to build mass and strength. It is the context that causes us to reframe things to one of ownership, responsibility, freedom, and full self-expression. Discovering, creating, and owning your purpose is the beginning of the journey of leadership, of contribution, and having a say in your destiny. It is the gateway to freedom and true agency in one's life.

The two duties of leadership are required only if change is desired. If the status quo works, no leadership is required. If you are in a static condition, no leadership is required. Freedom is a dynamic condition and requires massive amounts of leadership to exist. Socialism, communism, totalitarianism, and monarchies are static states. They intentionally do not change. Their focus is on control and compliance. The condition of safety is a static state. When we are in a static condition no leadership is required, only control and management. Remember, safety exists in the gynocentric paradigm. Though well intended, a long-term commitment to safety can be highly destructive. It can lead to stagnation and atrophy.

Sun Tzu has *delay* as a strategy. Delay is often used as a transition tool to resupply, to garner information, or to reformulate a plan when conditions change unexpectedly. A beneficial use of the delay strategy occurred when most of the world went on a two-week shutdown in March 2020 due to the COVID-19/ Chinese flu pandemic. We had no idea what it was, and the delay was required to gain an understanding and reduce the perceived risk. It was the prudent thing to do.

You could see when things began to get tense between the gynocentric paradigm (when fear and concern for safety took precedence) and those concerned about freedom, economic impact, and viability. That tension continued because both sides were convinced they were right, regardless of the evidence to the contrary. The position of safety went from being one of public health to a political one. If you did not "wear a mask," "social distance," and practice an "abundance of caution," you were needlessly putting "lives at risk." What was a good and prudent idea shifted into one of control, driven by fear and panic. This is another beacon of the impact of a gynonormative perspective.

One of the challenges of a gynocentric paradigm, which shifts into a gynonormative platform, is that the fear becomes so powerful that is all anyone can see. There is no discussion, no discovery. The only input allowed is to support the position that is being taken. It really becomes a totalitarian model. The impact is the loss of, or at least the hindrance to, any creativity. Problem-solving is limited to really narrow bands of acceptance. The solution lies in enduring the current condition until the cavalry comes or there is some external force that changes the situation.

Leadership is a practice based in courage. It is one of vitality and engagement. It is not foolhardy risk-taking. It is engaging with the issues and understanding that failure may occur. It is also having an understanding that failure is not fatal, and it is always an opportunity to learn. Through that learning, break-throughs and results can be generated.

Capitalism is a dynamic process, filled with risk, and re-quires leadership. With freedom there is also the opportunity for corruption. The nature of freedom is that things will occur because humans are involved. Leadership is responsible to mit-igate the possibility of those bad things. We lead humans; we manage things.

The first duty of leadership: *"Provide a future vision for people to join in and live into."*

This sets the picture, allows people to see what is possible beyond what they know or have now. Donald Trump inspired

189

with his idea of Making America Great Again. For many it was a sense of inspiration, but for an equal number it was a source of fear and concern. His breakdown was, instead of listening to those who opposed him and inviting them to join through communicating what that future meant for them, he dismissed them and used them as opposition and resistance to build his message. The problem was he was attacking the people and not the idea. The opposing idea was a rich target; we will chalk that up as an opportunity lost.

The key skill in this duty is enrollment, one of the most difficult skills there are. Enrollment is sharing yourself and your vision in such a way that others are moved, touched, and inspired by you and what you are up to. When enrollment works, it is actually a catalyst for action. People begin doing things in alignment with what you are committed to, people you don't even know. It is the single most powerful tool in creating change. This is not *convincing*, and it is not *manipulation*, though some have done so and called it enrollment. I caution you, please do not do that. The truth will reveal itself, and when it does the people who were at one time very close to you will reject you and become mortal enemies. To abuse the skill of enrollment is one of the cruelest, most evil, most perverted acts anyone can do. It is why I hate Barack Obama, and I do not use that word frivolously.

The second duty of leadership: *"Cultivate and maintain the environment so that vision can be realized."*

This is essential to any leadership assignment. As we said earlier, leadership exists in dynamic environments. Those environments are ever changing. There are constant challenges and never-ending forces around it—not always attacking, but seldom assisting, in moving in the direction you are going. Anyone who has ever sailed learns to uses those forces to move forward. Anyone who has ever gardened knows there is a constantly changing environment, and cultivating is required for fulfillment. One needs to gain facility in being with impermanence and uncertainty to excel in leadership. The Buddhist practice of being unattached is a useful skill. One of Don Miguel Ruiz's agreements in his book *The Four Agreements* is "Don't Assume Anything."

The essential skill in this duty of leadership is coaching. Coaching is truly about ensuring the environment is set up to supply the resources and skills for the vision to be fulfilled. A man I know and respect, Christopher D. McAuliffe, has said, "Coaches lead, and leaders coach." In the world today, leadership and coaching are often synonymous. My favorite quote on coaching is from the Hall of Fame coach of the Dallas Cowboys, Tom Landry, who points to one of the greatest values a coach can provide: get the person to see who he or she really is. A coach unleashes greatness Tom Landry said:

> *A coach is someone who tells you what you don't want to hear, who has you see what you don't want to see, so you can be who you have always known you could be.*

One of the most powerful tactics in leadership is curiosity. No matter how seasoned and experienced you are, every day is a new day filled with new challenges and people. The trap that managers fall into is finding a problem for the solution they have. Leaders address the problem at hand with either existing skills or new skills and processes that fit the need at the time.

The other skill set that is required for leadership and a thriving environment is where multiculturalism fails. You must address each person you are leading as a unique child of God, not as a unit in a subset. Our politically correct, identity politics, pluralistic, anti-racist, and cultural diversity people love to do just that. Joe Biden clearly demonstrated this in his "If you don't vote for me you ain't Black" statement. Leadership is about people and individuals, regardless of their ethnicity, race, color, gender, gender preference, or any other category that is used to divide and separate. People are people. It's that simple. Really.

Those are the two duties of leadership, and we will refer to them throughout the remainder of the book. The last thing in this chapter I want to discuss is the practice:

*"Practice: Love Your Brother; Unconditional Love."*

This can look a lot of different ways, and I said this is *not a how-to book*; the practice of unconditional love is ending the practice of speaking, acting, and thinking in a dehumanizing way. It is understanding that every person is a child of God (this includes the humans reading this book). This means you are *not* going to be a wimp about stuff and look the other way when atrocities occur. The opposite is true: opposition sourced from love is the most powerful expression we can have. It is opposition sourced by our soul.

Unconditional love is loving everything you are and everything you are not. It begins with us, loving and accepting ourselves. We will be addressing this in most of the upcoming chapters. What I mean by acceptance is not agreement. What I mean by acceptance is, it exists. I find Kamala Harris to be a profoundly objectionable human. I accept she is the vice president. (By the time you are reading this—hell, she may be president). I will not reject her legitimacy. I will only oppose it and hold her to account, not from a position of being right, but from my stand for freedom, for American exceptionalism and for a world that works. My opposition will look like inquiry. For Harris, my opposition may be bit of "prove it to me," and that is a result of the prior actions and communications she has delivered. Though I am fundamentally opposed to her, I must be responsible and never stop the inquiry.

Your assignment is to practice unconditional love, especially with the other men in your life. Get curious with them. Instead of judging them, inquire into why they do that thing that makes you upset. Inquire how they see the world, what is important to them, what inspires them, what has them see the world as they do. Take on the practice of doing no harm, end the practice of dehumanizing another, and finally practice honoring. Honor ourselves and others with our thoughts, words, and actions. While taking on these practices, make note of them, notice what is showing up. This is the source of inquiry, and this is the opportunity of connecting our actions with our soul. Let me know what shows up for you, please.

Thanks for being here. Let's keep on going.

## CHAPTER 23

# Forgiveness, Grieving, and Responsibility

*"I wanted you to see what real courage is, instead of getting the idea that courage is a man with a gun in his hand. It's when you know you're licked before you begin, but you begin anyway and see it through no matter what."*

—*Atticus Finch*

In the last chapter, the takeaway is "leadership begins with purpose." In this chapter we are going to do some gardening to ensure the purpose has a pathway to fulfillment. In Jay Niblick's book, *What's Your Genius?*, Jay shows that success in leadership and in life is a result of us discovering who we are and then practicing authenticity to achieve the results we desire.

### Self-Awareness + Authenticity = Success

As an executive coach I have administered close to a thousand IMX profiles to humans in a working environment. Most of my clients are men. The women leaders I coach, though beautiful and extremely feminine, have a lot of masculine tendencies in their management and leadership style. More than 90 percent of the people I have coached would be labeled as successful based on the role, title, compensation level, and overall impact to their organization and industries. To a person, they are all ballers.

I have noticed a very interesting trend. Most everyone had very high levels of competencies in managing what I refer to as the external world. That includes relating to others with empathy and understanding, having a high degree of competency in their role and the job they do, and possessing a solid understanding of how the work they do and their role fits into the bigger system. As I said, I have been blessed with the opportunity to work with truly amazing humans.

The challenge always arises on the side of self-awareness. Especially with men. They have a great understanding of the world around them and a far lesser understanding of the person in the mirror. The reason this occurs is equal to the number of people with whom I have interacted. Leaders are rewarded for the results they produce. Those results are measured by two things: time and money. The more money we generate in the form of results, the more value we produce. The less time we take, the more we can produce, and the more value we create. It is simple. It is also deadly.

This process can become very linear, and "produce more with less" seems to have become the mantra. This can also lead to high levels of stress, a pull for the expedient, and, at times, a violation of one's own beliefs and values in favor of delivering on the results that we've been charged to deliver. As we pointed to in Chapter 8 on corporations, the constant requirement for compliance and adherence to policy has an effect on us. It creates a sort of cognitive dissonance. We want to do good work and fulfill on our jobs, and we want to be good, kind folks who treat others with respect and honor. The pull for profit, market share, brand recognition, and success can sometimes put those two things at odds. Throw in the characteristics of the alpha male enduring hardships and powering through obstacles, and we create a dilemma. Add in the absence of personal purpose; a lack of self-understanding; and a strong identity to our career, our role, and the organization we belong to, and you have a setup for an existential personal conflict. Include the never-ending narrative of corporate HR with their diversity and inclusion programs, critical racial theory training, pronoun usage policy, and global compliance registration, and this becomes an environment festering with confusion and ambiguity. Welcome the ever-changing musical chairs of a new CEO every thirty months or so, and the spin never seems to end.

This constant change of direction and ambiguity does not just impact employees; it also impacts subcontractors, vendors, consultants, and customers. The singular purpose of corporations to drive profits with little to no value-based boundaries creates an environment of uncertainty. With the enormous level of profit and cash that it creates, people are concerned that any nonalignment with these organizations will impact them in the most adverse of ways—financially. This is the source of great stress. This is also a tinderbox of repressed emotion and upset. The repression of our emotions is one of the most damaging aspects to our development and our own self-awareness.

I use the example of corporations and the inconsistency of HR policy because it is so common. The truth is, gynocentrism, given its emotional basis, is the source of the inconsistency. Emotions and feelings are inconsistent. They are supposed to be. They are what gives us joy and has us feel pain. They are not designed to be the source of our decision-making process. The source of decision making is our purpose, our reason for being, our why. In the USA, the source of policy and decision making is the Constitution—or at least that is the design. In corporate America, the source of policy and decision making is the vision and mission statements. When the source becomes the financial statements, it is obvious how issues can occur. When fear sets in, when courage is not a value, and you have a culture based on the gynocentric paradigm, then inconsistent policies, rules, and behaviors are the obvious outcome.

The rise of gynocentrism is also at the root of the rise of upset and anger. This is why as men and leaders we must step in and create balance and bring stability to our culture and social environment. Before that we must not let our emotions run the show. To do that there is some work to do. That work begins with forgiveness. If Jesus can forgive the people who persecuted him, who are we to not to forgive those who have offended us? If God the Father has forgiven all mankind, who are we not to forgive the knucklehead who cut us off in traffic? Forgiveness is powerful, and it is difficult.

The person we must forgive first is the person in the mirror. Forgiveness does not mean forgetting or allowing more atrocities to occur. Forgiveness is just clearing the emotional slate. It is beginning again at the start. It is a view of life from where you are and looking to where you are going. Forgiveness allows us to release the pain, hurt, upset, and anger of the past. It requires us to understand that sometimes there is loss in life, and shit is not perfect. W. Edwards Deming said, "Perfection is the enemy of quality." I believe perfectionism is the killer of life, joy, and full self-expression.

A challenging aspect of forgiveness is the unpacking of the past. Taking an inventory of all the events that have occurred, the impact they have had on us, and the stories we made up about those events can seem overwhelming. Leaving them unaddressed is also not an option. Those stories are not fiction. They are real, and they are stories that had us get through a painful event ten, twenty, or thirty years ago. Those stories may not be valuable today, though we tend to keep them alive. That is why we have to go back and look. Is that thing that happened still a problem today? If so, why have we not addressed it and been responsible for that issue? If not, why is that belief still informing our mindset? This is just a small sample of the work we need to do to really grant forgiveness to ourselves and others. Things change, people change, circumstances change, but yet we can operate like they don't change, and every event is carved in stone.

A great tool for this is grieving. As dudes we don't grieve well. We are great at enduring; we are amazing at powering through situations. Without the ability to put our past in the past, we can look like Lady Gaga and Beyoncé on safari, carrying around the burdens of twenty years on our backs. The process of grieving allows us to release those burdens and to do so at our choosing and our pace.

When we begin to grieve, the first step is *denial*. With dudes it looks like, "I'm good, no problem," or "Ain't no thing." "Hey, Chuck, I heard you lost your job. You OK?" Chuck's response would be, "Fuck 'em, that job sucked." Or "Yeah, it was time to move on; this is a great opportunity." Or better yet, "I needed some time off; I am really thankful." OK, some or all of that may be true, but what is being stepped over is the pain, and the experience of shame, abandonment, and betrayal. When we step over that, the cumulative effect can be devastating. In a gynocentric world no one is even looking at that.

There is a reason men suffer from heart disease more than women, and have a higher incidence of drug and alcohol abuse and suicide. The cumulative effect of shame, abandonment, and betrayal is no laughing matter. The second step of the grieving process is *anger*, and we live in a cultural environment where anger expressed by men is not allowed. The gynocentric paradigm equates anger with violence. I'd like to say to these radicals, "*This just in.* I know it is only possible for you to see through the gynonormative lens, but not everything is about you!" When anger is suppressed, the impact is the same as the impact of denial of emotions and experience. One thing we must do is have heathy outlets for our anger—be it riding your Harley, going to the gun range, playing golf, punching a bag, or just sitting down with someone who gets you and can actually hear you. As dudes we can no longer suppress our anger. It must be expressed, and it must be expressed in a way that is responsible.

The third step in grieving is *bargaining.* This is a tricky step because much of the source of the upset that we as men have had is a result of the bad deals we have made. We have to cease the practice of bargaining and begin the practice of true negotiation. To do that we need to put all the cards on the table and connect what we are negotiating for with what we are committed to. If the deal in front of us is aligned with our purpose and is a step in the direction of fulfillment, done. If not, no deal. The shit is that easy. The difficult part is really being clear on our pathway and our purpose. Until then, *NO* is a complete sentence.

The fourth step of the grieving process is *depression.* Another way of saying that is having the experience that you are completely fucked. We spend so much time avoiding being completely fucked or denying that we are completely fucked. We can create an existence of being kinda sorta fucked for a long time.

Two examples are struggling with staggering debt and staying in a shitty relationship. We will create strategies to survive and ultimately fuck ourselves some more. There is no worse way to live than to sell out on yourself and your dreams only because you are afraid you might get completely fucked. Consider if that is how you are surviving, you may be worse off than completely fucked.

Do you want the good news? Once you are completely fucked, the process is over. There is nowhere else to go. You are free. Kris Kristofferson said it in "Me and Bobbie McGee." It is not the loss of material goods he is speaking of; it is loss of our attachment to our ego. The belief that whatever you have experienced has anything to do with who you are or what you can do in life is a false one. When you get that, that sometimes "shit happens," you can now step into a powerful place, the one of 100 percent badass.

Which brings us to the fifth step of grieving: *acceptance.* Accepting what is so. Accepting the world the way it is: no whining, no bitching, no complaining, just playing the holes as they are designed. Lose your job? Good, let's get another one! Partner cheated on you? Good! What was my part in that—including partnering with someone who would do that to me? Lost money? Great! What can I learn? Diagnosed with a disease? Awesome! What do I need to do to get well? Get a bad review on Yelp? Great! What is their commitment behind the complaint?

Werner Erhard says, *"Transformation begins with a powerful relationship to what is so." What is so* is the beginning. It is where we begin. Clear, clean, sourced, and ready to go. That is what is powerful about forgiveness and grieving.

The final piece in the chapter is responsibility. Responsibility has become this burdensome thing. It isn't. Responsibility equates to freedom. You want to be free, take on more responsibility. One of the most bizarre aspects of the gynocentric paradigm is their relationship to responsibility. They refuse to accept it and then blame those who have it and take it on as being privileged. I personally do not think there is a bigger crock of shit than that. If your perspective is completely safety-oriented, then responsibility can be scary because with responsibility comes risk. This alone, the fear of accepting and taking on responsibility, is why the gynocentric paradigm will never be a structure where leadership can live. It can only criticize, judge, and assess. It is without engagement; it resides in complete fear; it is like living in your basement for nine months.

The only way for improvement to occur, breakthroughs to be encountered, gains to be made, and changes to happen is if someone takes a risk and steps beyond their comfort zone. A side note, for all the psychobabblers out there who speak about their "zone of genius," those are just the talents you have *inside* your comfort zone. You can be productive at some level, but it is just more of the same. Also leadership, true leadership, lives outside everyone's comfort zone. Leadership requires engagement. Leadership requires you "git some on ya."

## CHAPTER 24

# Creating and Building Partnerships (Integrity: Part I)

*"In successful relationships, perfection is the acceptance of imperfection."*
—Wayne Gerard Trotman

Partnership is a bitch. I don't know of any other way to say it. The thing that makes partnerships so difficult is that power dynamics don't work in them. Power dynamics are how most people get stuff done. Power dynamics are about force, evidence, persuasion, leverage, manipulation, coercion, compliance, duress, pressure, muscle, strength, and pure horsepower to achieve results. The funny thing about power dynamics is that they can achieve results while destroying partnerships and relationships.

Partnerships are hard because they are about more than our own self-interests. They are about that thing that is bigger than us. They are about our commitment and serve as a structure to fulfill our purpose. They are difficult because they require treating another human as our equal and having them share the same commitment we do. That is big lift. When we look at the purpose of this book and the movement we are intending to create, our purpose is: *"To begin the process of awakening American men to their role, their contribution, and the leadership needed to have America be the bastion of freedom and possibility in the world."*

A partnership is a structure to fulfill the commitment that the purpose states. When we look at structure we often get confronted because people begin to look at policies, restrictions, rules, and limitations. I prefer to view structures from a construction viewpoint. Structures are frameworks from which the commitment can exist. If your commitment is football, the structure would be a football stadium. That stadium can be Hoffman Field on Harlem Avenue in Berwyn, Illinois, or it can be the "Jerry Dome" in Arlington, Texas. Both will deliver the result of the football game. They just have different expressions for that delivery. That different expression is what makes them unique and individualistic. That is why it is so important we create our purpose: so we create the structure that is right for each of us, and honor our own unique individuality.

When we use the four-core distinction model of leadership, *integrity* is the distinction associated with structure. The definition of integrity (in our model, a positive phenomenon) is "being whole and complete—achieved by honoring one's word as we define honoring (creates workability, creates trust)."

Fundamentally, integrity is honoring our word. To whom or what we give our word is a big deal. We honor our word as we would honor our self. Integrity creates workability and trust. It sets the stage to create the environment to allow for fulfillment of the commitment. When we break our word, we break our relationship with our self. Success is dependent on the level of integrity we bring. The partnership will go in direct correlation to the level of integrity we bring to it. Simple and difficult.

A partnership is a relationship, and in a relationship there is always this question: Would you rather be right or in a relationship? To make a partnership work, we must develop the skill to release our point of view in order to see the other point of view clearly. This is not about giving up our point of view, it is just releasing it to better understand where others are coming from. The ultimate success in a partnership comes from me releasing my position and you releasing yours, and then we build a completely new position that provides all of what we both want, need, and desire. Think of it as an ontological 1+1=3 type scenario.

The key point is that the relationship is what is most valuable. The relationship is in service of the purpose. Both members are committed to the purpose being fulfilled. Partnerships are not actually fifty-fifty; they are more like one hundred to one hundred. Sometimes they may feel like one hundred to ten. So what? You gave your word. Just know there will be days that will be ten to one hundred. If you get caught up in keeping score, you may be valuing being *right* over the *relationship*.

The final part of the partnership structure is with whom we partner. In the current condition of the gynocentric paradigm, I suggest we get in the practice of partnering with women. There is a balance that is available when partnering with women that can achieve a social equilibrium. To do that, we must share the three foundational roles of masculinity: *provide, protect*, and *leave a legacy*. The role of protector is truly required to enroll women into the idea of creating responsible masculine leadership. The gynocentric paradigm is centered around the idea of safety. Safety becomes even more important when there is an absence of protection.

Partnership begins with the relationship we have with ourselves. As stated, when we break our word, we begin to question if we are trustworthy. Integrity is not about being perfect. As humans we will never be perfect; therefore, we will break our word. We will break it for a bunch of reasons, and none of those reasons matter. What matters is when we do break our word, we clean it up. Over time, we will develop this muscle, and it will become much more of who we know ourselves to be.

When entering partnerships we also must be responsible for the beliefs, the fears, the taboos, and the traditions we bring with us. One of those is how we regard women. My generation was conditioned in a world that valued chivalry. Chivalry sees women as special and needing protection. Chivalry calls for the sacrifice of men so women can survive and carry on the species. Sociologists point to chivalry as the beginning of the gynocentric paradigm.

The intention of partnerships is to create true equality: one partner is not more valuable than the other. Together as partners, all are better and stronger than they are separately. In the gynocentric paradigm, the call for equality is not actually what is being asked. The call for equality is a call for power. That power is gained by taking it from someone else. This is not equality; this is bargaining. We have been bargaining for too long. Bargaining is a win/lose proposition based on scarcity and power dynamics. As men, we must get really clear about what we are intending to do. To create real equality with women, we must not be afraid to express where there is inequality. In the current gynocentric paradigm, inequality is ever present on both sides. Establishing balance within the relationship can provide the stability and workability we desire.

As you read this, one can imagine that I am anti-feminine or anti-feminist. That is not true. I am anti-gynocentric and also anti–radical feminist. To build partnerships we must partner with women. That is the only way it will work. There are many women who are strong, independent, and powerful leaders. Kristi Noem, Candace Owens, and Sydney Powell are just a few of the many powerful female leaders who operate to create workability and freedom across this land. All three of those women are inspirational leaders. There are many more than them.

As Werner Erhard has said, "Transformation begins with a powerful relationship to what is so." As we create real partnerships, a shared and accurate acceptance of what is so is required. This may require the interruption of a narrative that is popular and not accurate. To build a foundation for partnerships, we may have to call bullshit on some beliefs that are simply inaccurate. We must also endure the predictable upset that will follow the challenge of the narrative. Here is ultimately where partnerships break down. Please remember, partnerships are a structure, and a structure requires a strong foundation. That foundation is trust. Bullshit, hidden agendas, unstated concerns, and unaddressed fears are not strong foundations and will impact the structure latter. Transparency, courage, vulnerability, and honor will build trust.

We must remember that partnering is not a doctrinal approach; it is one that is co-created and one that is mutually beneficial. It is also a relationship absent of any power dynamic. When you truly begin to practice partnerships, have a sense of humor. You will see how unpracticed we are. We are not a culture that practices partnership much. We talk about it; we just don't do it. One of the things that gets in the way is our value of independence. Someone who is independent is highly functional and has creative skills. If you think about it, independence is a perfect characteristic for a partnership. The only barrier then would be trust.

Trust is a funny thing. We think of trust as something someone must earn. I see it differently. I see trust as something we give as a gift of ourselves. Just like giving someone a gift at Christmas or on birthdays, the recipient can do with it what they want. A gift of ourselves, if someone truly wants that, can be the beginning of the partnership we desire. The gift of trust is a very appropriate and powerful beginning.

## CHAPTER 25

# Fatherhood

*"If you want the experience of having complete responsibility for another human being, and to learn how to love and bond in the deepest way, then you should have children."*
— *Mitch Albom*

I can think of no greater gift than the gift of fatherhood. I can also think of no greater undertaking that guarantees failure more than fatherhood. The expression of fatherhood and the expression of masculinity are one and the same, which can explain why the institution of fatherhood is under constant attack today.

The constant cry for the elimination of the "patriarchy" is the narrative of the radicalized feminist that dominates the gynocentric paradigm. The legal system is incredibly anti-father in the way it adjudicates family law cases. Make no mistake: masculinity, fatherhood, and being a man are under attack as we speak. We are in the midst of a cultural and gender war.

There is no greater example of this than the attack most recently waged on Donald J. Trump through the media and in his run for reelection. The biggest complaint about him was that he was an alpha male. Our culture is so adamantly anti-father/

anti-masculine that America's father, Bill Cosby, was sent to jail. He symbolized fatherhood, masculine leadership, and masculinity. He was convicted of crimes that were alleged to have occurred fourteen years prior to trial. This is not to defend him as much as it is to point out how the zeal of the attack on men, fatherhood, and masculinity has no limits in time, attention, or in the narrative they are out to create. Have no doubt, fatherhood and masculinity are in the crosshairs of the gynocentric, left-leaning cultural narrative.

I get it. Men have done some bad things. Men have been guilty of abuse, sexual misconduct, and abuse of our privilege and our power. We have made mistakes, and we have resisted at times correcting those mistakes. And, may I ask, is not the vast overreaching assessments made about patriarchy, "toxic" masculinity, and systemic sexism the same mindset and actions as the very thing being condemned? There is never a solution that is the opposite of; it is the same context, the flip side of the coin. This is what we are beginning here: calling men to be responsible, authentic, and connected to their reason for being.

I have never seen a legitimate solution that requires the diminishing of another human. In a world that is faced with the challenges we are today, diminishing the role of father or the expression of masculine leadership, seems insane. Consider we have been doing that for quite some time and things are not progressing. I see the current opportunity, as well as possibly the greatest need, is one that calls men to step up and own their voice. The time is now for men to man up. It is time we generate responsible masculine leadership in America. The development and provision of a healthy model of manhood is essential for our future. No role requires that more than being a dad.

We can no longer accept our boys and young men being abandoned and left to wither in the gynocentric paradigm. We can no longer allow the girls and young women to be trained to grow into narcissistic, self-centered, arrogant, misandrist monsters. As men and fathers we must stem the slide and step in and lead. That leadership begins in our homes. Before we can correct any issues in our environment, we need to begin with ourselves. Where have we been off? Where have we been disconnected, emotionally unavailable, or removed? It does not matter what the reason; they all are valid, and we need to really look and listen.

My assertion is that most guys have done nothing wrong other than get complacent. The world has changed, and it is a far more complex and unforgiving place. The forces against men and masculine expression are more present today than at any other time in our history. We can no longer see that opposition as a problem. It has become the playing field on which we get to engage. We have had it pretty easy for a while. We would go to work, come home to our "sanctuary," and chill. It ain't that way anymore. Women have often complained, especially working women, that their days are never done. They are right, and now ours can never be done either. We must understand that their point is valid, and we must own our responsibility at home. One of the biggest reasons the gynocentric paradigm has grown in popularity is that we men abdicated our roles as men and leaders in our own homes and communities.

I am declaring we begin that process of establishing manhood now and that we begin at home. There is no better way to begin than by being fathers to our children. In Chapter 22 I lay out the three foundational roles of masculinity. Here they are in detail:

The first role is *to provide*. A few generations ago that meant simply being the breadwinner, the funder in chief, the person who provided the financial resources for the family, community, or organization. As time progressed and the value of that role became distinguished, so did the perks that came with it. Certain privileges were granted as a result of that role. Those privileges ranged from sitting at the head of the table to cutting the Thanksgiving turkey.

Those privileges might have extended to opportunities others did not have access to, or they might have been a simple perspective others did not see. That access to opportunities, social ecologies, financial investments, and social and political influence created possibilities for the acquisition of power and wealth. That growth in power and wealth then created a separation between those who provided and those who were being provided for. A power dynamic was created. As life became more complex and situations changed, the role of provider had shifted; it became less an expression and more an opportunity to manipulate, control, and dominate/oppress. If it wasn't really that, it definitely could have been perceived as that. Any time a power dynamic exists, we must be responsible for the potential of corruption and manipulation.

The point is, providers over time have done a good job of providing. In time they have also reaped the rewards of their provisions. Those rewards have delivered a return on investment (ROI), and in some cases a substantial one. When questioned about the relative fairness (gynocentric value), the provider either dismissed the question or justified the return without inquiring into the source of the question. The most important thing providers provide is an environment or a space for the recipients to grow, develop, and thrive.

There may be no greater gift than providing space for others to grow, develop, and thrive. As fathers that is our primary job. As we provide that space we also must share the intention and the vision. We must communicate what success looks like and accept feedback from those who are growing, developing, and thriving. That is what providing looks like today, creating the environment and space for others to live their lives to the fullest extent possible. That space is more than physical. It is also emotional, spiritual, intellectual, and social. The best way to create that space is by the installation of value-based boundaries. Boundaries are constraints based in beliefs that are sourced by our purpose. Constraints are not limits; they are structures that provide support, clarity, and focus. Without constraints chaos is imminent.

The most valuable way for fathers to provide the leadership required for our young people to develop into successful, contributing, happy, and fulfilled human beings is through the demonstration of the very values and beliefs that fathers have shared with their children. Nothing is more valuable than spending time with them, engaging with them, and allowing them to walk beside you. It can be fishing or hunting, a game of catch, or a walk around the block. Spending time in the shop or going to Home Depot is a valuable exercise in the development of young people. Young people learn about society by seeing their parents interact. Young men learn what being a man is by witnessing their fathers. Young women learn what being a man is by witnessing their fathers. We must walk the walk with them.

The breakdown in the area of providing is that we, as men and providers, did not answer questions or engage with the complaints and concerns about it. This is the source of the attack on "the patriarchy." The complaint about the "patriarchy" is simply a complaint about the environment. This is also the source of other nonsensical concepts like "structural racism" and "institutionalized sexism." Our unwillingness to address complaints and create and maintain value-based boundaries and structure is the source of most of the grievances of the gynocentric paradigm. We have been complacent and arrogant. We have supplied the evidence that has sourced the attack on masculinity, and when we were attacked we did not take it seriously. We have ignored the complaints, the concerns, and the outcries. Behind every complaint was a commitment, and we did not inquire as to what that was.

The next foundation is *to protect*. The definition of protect is "to keep safe from harm or injury." What a simple idea. In an ever-changing environment, that can be a challenging proposition. In an environment where there is constant opposition, it is a never-ending task. The biggest challenge to the idea of protection is complacency. To think you "have it handled" is the first crack.

In sports, when I think of protection, the first place I go is to the big left tackle who has the quarterback's back. I think of a goalie in hockey who is there for one purpose only: protect the goal. I think of the huge center in basketball who is there to protect the lane. In baseball it is the closer who comes in to protect the lead. Is he the most talented pitcher on the team? No. Usually, he is typically the most courageous. To protect is to be a bulwark, a stand, and a bastion for people to trust and really understand. The very structure under which we operate is dependent upon that protection.

When that protection is in place, it allows those within it to step beyond what is comfortable. It allows them to go beyond their limitations, take risks, and fully engage. That freedom from fear leads to access to creativity and innovation. True protection fills the greatest need of the gynocentric paradigm, the need for safety. When the gynocentric need for being safe is met, it creates access to the greatness it can create: a sense of beauty, connection, and love. When safety is provided, then women are free to bring their greatest gift: the gift of nurturing. When people feel safe, they are allowed to be free, allowed to fully be themselves. When that protection is breached, the very foundation of those relying on it is compromised. Providing safety is the role of the father.

As men we must accept this responsibility. Part of the role of protector is to defend. We must be able to defend ourselves and our families. Yes, I said it. As men we must know how to fight. It is our responsibility to be as physically fit and strong as possible. Being mentally fit and mentally strong goes without saying. Fighting includes the ability to physically and mentally defend yourself and others. To argue, to strategize, and to choose wisely. There is no limit to what is needed to protect our homes and our families.

We must understand it is our job, our expression as men, to protect those we love and for whom we are responsible. As a collective we have not lived up to that responsibility, not fully. (Shit would not be as weird as it is if we had.) We can no longer allow "not my job" as a reason to allow breaches of decency. We can no longer tolerate the number of weak, frightened, and scared men. It is our job to be there for our brothers so they can break through the barriers that have them so scared. As fathers we cannot throw up our hands and say, "It's not my problem." When we father a child, that child is ours until the day they throw dirt on our face. We do not have the luxury to walk away.

If you do, realize you are abdicating your role as a man and a father. When you abdicate, there are always consequences.

We have an issue in this country. Too many men have abdicated their role as fathers and as protectors. As outlined earlier, 45 percent of children today are growing up in fatherless households. In the Black community that number is over 70 percent. The radical feminist gynocentric narrative suggests men, masculinity, and fathers are not needed. Organizations like BLM speak about a world that removes the patriarchy. The media agrees. Unfortunately, the numbers on depression, youth suicide, school dropout rates, incarceration, and drug and alcohol abuse say otherwise. Add in the number of unwanted pregnancies and we have created a perpetual structure.

The commitment now seems to be the overthrow of the patriarchy. That is simply a desire to shift the power dynamic. There is a false belief held by the gynocentric populace that if you just put more women in charge, things will be better. Changing people is not a structural change; it is a personnel change. That is why quotas and virtue signaling hires almost always fail. These changes will not make a huge difference and may create more issues. We must understand the commitment. We must listen, we must inquire.

The third and final foundation is *to leave a legacy*. Leave a legacy—in the gynocentric paradigm this is offensive. When one's agenda is to destroy the patriarchy and end tradition, a legacy is out of the question. Leaving a legacy is foundational to building sustainability. It is foundational to passing on tradition, intelligence, and skill. Without the practice of leaving a legacy, we are destined to never develop and to continue making the same mistake over and over again.

The legacy is not about the person leaving it; it is about the future generations who will be enjoying the fruit of our labor and love. It is a way that we can continue on, build momentum, and bring connection from one generation to another. The fear and anger so associated with the gynocentric paradigm are such that its practitioners would rather cut off their own nose to spite their face. This radicalized and twisted mindset is so narcissistic that it can seldom see anything but its own point of view. Because of the fear and anger that inform that viewpoint, and its commitment to destroy the patriarchy, we must connect the dots and share with them why it may be in their own self-interest to inquire what this legacy looks like.

As dads that is often what we must do: stand and be, and allow those around us to challenge our beliefs and ideas. We must practice curiosity and grace as they test their reasons. That will be the only way for our children to learn and validate their notions. It is also a way for them to discover the folly of some of those beliefs and ideas. That is what dads are here to do. It is OK.

Regardless of the challenges and opposition, there is no greater gift and opportunity in life than that of being a dad. There is no greater opportunity to love unconditionally, to accept completely, and to learn to appreciate life better than the role of being a father. There is also nothing more humbling, nothing more confusing, and nothing more confronting than fatherhood. That is the gift. That is also our responsibility. Being a father does not mean you must be perfect. Being a father means you will screw up; you will fail, and you will make a million mistakes. That is a great opportunity to demonstrate possibly the most valuable lesson of all: overcoming setbacks, failures, and errors. What greater skill to demonstrate to kids than to show your humanity and prove to them that failing is not fatal?

We must get real about being dads. If you are a dad, you are being called to man up. Fatherhood is the ultimate expression of manhood. It does not matter how old your kids are. If you are still taking a breath, you are their dad. If your relationship is not where you want it to be, get to work making it what you desire. Your kids may not respond the way you want because trust has been broken. So what? I promise you that if you are standing for them and loving them, everything can heal. Sometimes it's tough, but that is why we are guys.

The role of father is essential for our culture. We have faced headwinds for nearly sixty years. The time is now for us to stand up as a collective and love our children. The time has come for us to stand up and love ourselves and allow our expression as men and as fathers to be seen and heard. The world needs us now more than ever.

CHAPTER 26

# A New Paradigm for Leadership: Listening

*"It takes a great man to be a good listener."*
*—Calvin Coolidge*

Brené Brown says, "If we can share our story with someone who responds with empathy and understanding, shame cannot survive." Likewise, if we can be the space where someone can share their story, the same result will occur. Shame cannot survive. In the current gender and cultural war in which we are engaged, all there is to do is listen. Another great leader, Stephen Covey, spoke often of the power of listening. We are not great at listening, mostly because we don't understand what is available by practicing it.

The purpose of listening is to give the other person the experience of being gotten, to actually know that what they say matters and their message is received fully. The purpose of listening is so the person speaking can have the experience of being heard fully. We want to understand not only what they are saying, but also why they are saying it—to fully get the intention behind what they said. The only way we can understand another human is through listening.

Here is a practical definition of listening that I find helpful: "Listening is the ability to accurately receive and interpret messages in the communication process.

Listening is key to all effective communication. Without the ability to listen effectively, messages are easily misunderstood. As a result, communication breaks down and the sender of the message can easily become frustrated or irritated.

Our culture is obsessed with messaging. Every place you go there is a new app or a new way to send communication to someone else. People spend tens if not hundreds of millions of dollars a year on "perfecting" their messages. There are countless webinars and training sessions on "how to communicate" effectively. What good does it do if no one is listening? I'm going to use "The Donald" as an example again. Mr. Trump is a highly effective communicator by every measure. Yet a little over 50 percent of the American population did not get his message as intended. The problem isn't the messaging; the problem is the listening.

The fact that there is so much misinformation and bullshit being transmitted, and we continue to traffic in it, is not a messaging problem. It is a listening problem. We also live in a time where more data, information, and messaging are being created than ever before. Part of the reason we are not listening is we are overwhelmed. We have no idea what to listen for, let alone understand, to actually listen. This is a huge breakdown in communication, and when we are not able to communicate with one another, we are in a mess. Tons of talking, tons of messaging, very little communication, less listening. The result is anger, disconnection, upset, and rage. This is completely unworkable.

Conventional wisdom suggests the issue is in the messaging and everyone needs to shift their message so others can hear it. I get the idea, but what I have seen when that happens is a loss of authenticity and a shift to performance mode. Communication becomes a form of manipulation to generate the desired result. Barack Hussein Obama is a master of that. The messaging then shifts to erroneous or false information, or lying. Guys have done this for years. It's called appeasing. It's telling you what you want to hear, and then doing what I was going to do anyway, regardless of what I said. That does not work. When we do that the foundation of trust begins to crumble.

The other way of shifting the messaging is the one currently being used in the gynocentric world: to increase the volume and demand acceptance with little to no discourse or inquiry. The outcome of this tactic is the eunuch herd of emasculated allies who now roam the surface of the earth as male feminists. This strategy is one based on force, obstinateness, and rejection of any idea that is not their own. It is based in demand and compliance. If someone disagrees or challenges the position, they are met with the automatic response of ridicule. That person is then labeled a racist, misogynist, sexist, xenophobe, or whatever the personal attack of the day is. It has become a mob mentality. Therein exists the battle lines of the current culture and gender war.

For the longest time, men took a relatively passive or surrendering approach to the false messaging. Our tactic was appeasement and indifference. That tactic has failed. It has also allowed a near infestation of the radicalized feminist way of thinking. The only way they will achieve their agenda is the complete annihilation of the masculine expression. This is why it is time for *The Manhood Manifesto*.

Unfortunately, we are in a war, a cultural and gender war, but there is no need for violence as of yet. As Sun Tzu said,

"Avoid war at all cost, and if you go, go in a way that will leave your opponent in a position they will never consider that action again." I prefer to think of it as "all bets are won at the first tee." We are in the "terms and condition" part of the war, and we must step up now. This is what DJT was so good at and why he was so maligned.

It is incumbent upon men and the masculine paradigm to solve this issue and do so in a way that honors all people. Sun Tzu also said, "To defeat your enemies you must defeat their strategy." Their strategy is one of deceit and manipulation, and it is an indirect strategy. To win with a direct strategy you must outweigh your opponent three to one. To defeat the indirect strategy, you simply must see it coming. I am not sure the gynocentric collective actually has a strategy. It seems to me they are following Saul Alinsky's *Rules for Radicals*. That strategy is an anarchistic quest for power, not real change.

Their strategy is bound to fail. Unfortunately, many unwinnable wars have been fought, and the damage created by them is profound. I don't think they desire to win. I think they desire to disrupt, to impact, and to cause harm. That is why we cannot allow it to continue; that is why we must be a bulwark. The profound damage here is on young people and the family structure.

This is a structural problem. The breakdown in communication exists in the structure in which we operate. We are not listening, and we are unwilling to listen to one another to the point we are diminishing each other. When we look at structural problems we need to look toward the leadership distinction of *integrity*. This issue between the genders exists within the distinction of integrity. The definition of integrity (in our model, a positive phenomenon) is "being whole and complete—achieved by honoring one's word as we define honoring (creates workability, creates trust)."

Listening requires integrity, and integrity requires you and me to be whole and complete with everything—that is, we cannot let our emotions and our fears get in the way of receiving the messages being sent. We don't have the luxury of allowing ourselves to get pissed by any message that attacks us or is a complete fabrication. They call us a racist—thank you! We get called a misogynist—so what? Men are pigs—OK and thanks. That is the work for us to do. The members of the gynocentric paradigm are enraged. It really does not matter anymore why they are enraged. The condition of rage seems to feed on the rage itself. Directly opposing it, as President Trump did, seemed to only throw more fuel on the fire.

I heard him in an interview give a great explanation for why he did what he did. Mr. Trump has an action bias. He assessed all the opposition and comments as misinformation. He may have been right. What is more important, being right or being in relationship? He chose being right. I agree with his position but not with his tactics. I am not sure it was his job to listen to every complaint and upset, because that work needs to be done much closer to home. The protest and rallies feed the flame. To alleviate the upset, the work of listening and understanding must be done with the people we know.

As warriors for peace, we need to begin the process of listening in our homes, offices, churches, places of play, and communities. This is a personal one-on-one type of engagement. To do that work we must have the self-assuredness (not cockiness) and the self-knowledge to withstand a huge amount of rage. We must understand the rage being expressed is not toward us; it is toward what they think we represent. We must not do this work to placate or appease them, as this is not a parlor trick or a game. This is foundational to understanding someone and really getting their view of the world. We must release our attachment to our perspective so we can understand and experience where they are. This is the practice.

This is not fun; however, it is essential to restoring responsible masculine leadership in America. This practice is actually part of the duty of protection. If folks are enraged, that is an element of fear. If we can listen to them fully, get them, and have compassion for them (please note I did not say empathy), we can begin to rebuild trust. Trust is what all relationships are built on. Relationships are the only realm in which we can operate to make change.

CHAPTER 27

# Authenticity, Courage, and Transparency

*"Courage is the most important of all the virtues because without courage, you can't practice any other virtue consistently."*
*—Maya Angelou*

When we begin to fully own the expression of manhood, we must begin with *authenticity, courage,* and *transparency.* These elements are the essence of the masculine soul. These three characteristics are essential in building trust, and trust is what is needed for the experience of protection. When I see these three elements I think of the Gandhi quote: "Be the change you wish to see in the world."

Real change begins with being (see Be/Do/Have Chart). Change must begin with us first because we cannot change anyone else. The change is a shift to being authentic. The definition of authenticity I love is "being and acting consistent with who you hold yourself to be for yourself, and who you hold yourself out to be for others (leaves you grounded and able to be straight with others without using force)."

What is so great about this definition is it is completely self-generated. It is an expression of freedom. *"Who you hold yourself to be for yourself, and who you hold yourself to be for others."* No one is assigning anything to you, you are not obliged or beholden to anyone. It is entirely your choice and no one's business but your own. The next part of the definition is powerful. By being a complete expression of who you hold yourself to be that *"leaves you grounded and able to be straight with others without using force."* No performance, no concern about fitting in, no worrying if you are liked or not. It leaves you with a sense of inner strength that connects you to the serene passion that is your purpose. It is what Brené Brown describes as standing in the wilderness. In one way you are all alone, and in another way you gain a sense of belonging to it all.

Authenticity is your purpose expressed inside the structure (integrity) that you have created to live and operate within. It is unattached and unconcerned with the judgments and assessments of others. When we are operating authentically, we are using feedback to check whether we are in alignment with our commitments. We use resistance as ways to build strength and mass. We do not avoid resistance, as resistance is often an indicator that we are on the right path. It is resistance that also provides lift.

Courage is about our relationship to fear. Courage is not the elimination of fear; it is taking action in the face of it. Fear can be the source of resistance that we need for growth and lift, and an indication that we are on track. What is so cool about courage, especially with guys, is that courage is how men express vulnerability. There is a direct connection between courage and authenticity. It is the tool to get who you are.

One of the many challenges with the gynocentric paradigm and the entire conversation about "toxic masculinity" is it diminishes the expression of masculinity. I am not sitting here arguing for guys to continue to do stupid shit. What I am calling for is men being responsible for their actions. When masculine behavior is labeled "toxic," in essence it is being shamed. The members of the gynocentric paradigm have been using shame, blame, and scolding as a tool of control. They have been using control to shame men into "behaving." It does little more than push outward expression deeper and cause it to become more camouflaged. It is how and why secrets are created and needed. That is why hate speech laws, and all the talk about hate speech and hate groups is only going to give this group more fuel. Never forget sunlight is the greatest disinfectant.

What people do not understand about men, especially alpha men, is that they require constant testing and resistance. They need something to push against to grow and develop. When that resistance or opposition is not there, they will occasionally create the opposition, the test, and the challenge to assure themselves they are who they have constituted themselves to be. I don't expect many who have not walked in these shoes to understand. I can tell you emphatically that much of what is labeled as "toxic" is men testing and challenging themselves. This is especially true in younger men (less than forty years old). Those guys are less aware about the impact of their presence than older guys. Part of their development is the "managing of their wake."

In our process of establishing manhood and responsible masculine leadership, we must look deep. We must look at our darkness; we must inquire into our hate and our anger. This inquiry is not appreciated by the gynocentric types because it causes them fear. They instantly equate their fear to environmental danger. That in and of itself explains much. It is the act of courage that allows us to look into the dark places and express that anger and hatred in a way that is responsible so we can actually see it. We want to know how dark we can go and what we are capable of. We need to know. That is the test I was speaking of. It takes courage to go there. The level to which we go dark is equal to the level we can shine brightly. It is the yin and yang of life. By thwarting our darkness and keeping it hidden we also dim our light and reduce our expression. You see this thwarting of manhood all around us. Many of our brothers who claim to be allies and feminists suffer from this. By reducing our expression we are reducing the presence of manhood in the world. Maybe that is the gynonormative agenda. The damage it is doing is causing generational harm.

Our job is not to be offended by their actions and words. It is our job to simply understand the current conditions. The current condition in the gynocentric paradigm is the reduction of masculinity and masculine expression. To create a world that works for generations to come, we must begin the practice of responsible masculine expression and the establishment of manhood as a normal. That begins with us fully understanding what that looks like for each of us. We must begin the practice of self-awareness. Not *self-centeredness;* self-awareness. That begins with discovering our true purpose and understanding who and where we belong. Brené Brown says, "True belonging doesn't require you to change who you are; it requires you to be who you are." It requires us to be courageous enough to understand who we are authentically.

If you are frustrated with this dive into self-awareness, please hang in there. At the end of the book, there are some resources for you. In addition, I want to share with you that this side of self-awareness is not a one and done. There is no arrival. To begin this process is to begin the process of lifelong learning and development. Wherever you are is cool. This is not a problem. The only way problems occur is when you are unwilling to look. The fact that you are this deep into the book tells me you are not *that* guy. You, my friend, are a badass.

That brings us to the last piece, *transparency*. I don't mean oversharing your deepest, darkest, and strangest secrets. That is both dumb and gross. I am speaking of operating out of the shadows. End the practice of shame and shaming yourself. I personally find groups to be a challenge and incubators for bullshit. And sometimes there is a real power in connecting with a number of people and understanding how similar we are and how much we share. It is not to create popularity for stupid shit; it is for us to see that what we may be so ashamed of in ourselves is actually shared by so many.

Shame and shaming are tools for control used by weak leaders. When shaming is done, there can be no inspiration, only control. One of the least effective gynocentric institutions, our public schools, use shaming as a way to control and forward their agenda. In the most recent Chinese flu event, shaming was the tool to control and gain compliance. The companion of shaming is virtue signaling. Look at any PSA about the Chinese flu. It was filled with shaming and virtue signaling; if you pointed that out on social media, the response was more of the same—shaming.

To operate with transparency requires courage. To operate courageously requires authenticity. Authenticity requires a willingness and practice of self-discovery, self-awareness, and self-acceptance. Self-acceptance, not arrogance, is based in loving oneself. To love ourselves we must honor ourselves and our word. To honor who we are, we must understand why we are here, our purpose, our reasons for being. When we have that, when we get our why, we will be propelled forward. Simple, and not easy. That is what we are doing. When we get that down, now we can go make some stuff happen.

Thank you for your willingness and courage to engage with me. Your time and attention are a gift I can never repay. Let's keep going.

CHAPTER 28

# Balance vs. Equality

*Helen Lewis: "How would your life be different if
you were born female?"*
*Jordan Peterson: "Multiple orgasms."*

I start most chapters out with a quote that speaks to the idea of
the chapter. In this chapter I took an excerpt from an interview
with Jordan Peterson. There are so many things I love about
this. First, I love Helen Lewis, because she is a poster child for
the woke, gynonormative, dysfunctional culture that abused
her. Ms. Lewis was ruthlessly attacked by other woke, gynonormative, dysfunctional cult members for questioning whether
self-identifying gender was the best way to roll. She was attacked
because she was questioning the purity of the doctrine served up
by the woke, dysfunctional, radical feminists.

The controversy that she was engaged in speaks volumes to
the inconsistent, reactionary, feelings, and fear-based perspective
of the gynonormative platform. These radical feminists will eat
their own young if they do not comply. That part is funny to me.
The really funny part of it is that followers of the gynocentric
paradigm cannot help themselves and see everything through
their own worldview.

In the world of "there are no stupid questions," to ask Jordan Peterson how life would be different if he were female meets every measure of the requirements of stupid and self-serving questions. What I loved most was that Professor Peterson's response was so quick, so simple, and so spot on. It also reflects the two completely different perspectives of the male and the female.

Another inane element of the dysfunction within the gynocentric paradigm is its obsession with equality. It is not equality of *opportunity*; it is relentless in the pursuit of the equality of *outcomes*. The gynocentric obsession goes so far as to mandate the reduction of standards to achieve equality of outcome. A petrifying example is the reduction of physical strength requirements of firefighters so that women can be "equals." As a man who weighs over 200 pounds, I hope I am never trapped in a burning building (to begin with), and I hope the brave firefighter who comes to get me out is not a 120-pound, agile, and dynamic female firefighter. I would be concerned that the 100 or so pounds I have on her could be a problem for us both.

The issue I really want to address is the idea of equality. There is no arguing about it. The idea is fantastic. So are the idea of justice for all and the idea of fairness. They all look good on paper. The issue is we do not live on paper; we live in an energetic, breathing, moving world. For equality to exist, a static or stable environment is required. One could offer that it would work best in a highly rigid environment. That is a great idea, except the world in which we live, work, and play is a dynamic one. To achieve equality you must stop all movement and reset all circumstances so equality is achieved. You can see that equality, at least equality of outcomes, is not a natural result of anything other than mandates and demands. The only way to achieve equality of outcomes is through the archaic application of laws and edicts that interfere with free expression and free enterprise. Most predictable is the reduction of standards, and with that comes the decline of quality and service. (If you want to see what equality of outcomes looks like, go to your local DMV and interact with the best and brightest who have met the standards of employment.)

When we speak about the gynocentric perspective of equality, it always begins with the assumption that there is some inequality already in existence: systemic racism, glass ceilings, or the patriarchy. Much like the idea of equality, these things look and sound great on paper. But when you get into the dynamics of it and really look at the "what is so," that dog does not really hunt. I challenge their assessment based solely on the gains that have occurred and some of the statistics I have shared earlier in the book. I don't think for one minute we have "arrived." There is, and will always be, more work to do. Our culture and the workplace environments are dynamic places.

I also reject the idea of systemic racism. If we just look over the last thirteen years, we have had a Black president and now we have a Black female vice president. I know to never let the facts interfere with the narrative, but as unpopular as it may seem, I have to call bullshit on the idea of systemic racism and the idea of a dominant patriarchy. The Speaker of the House continues to be a position held by a woman.

This quest for the equality of outcomes, and the need for mandates and so forth to achieve it, is unworkable in a dynamic and ever-changing world. The rigidity of the structure of equality and the lowering of quality and standards that are a result are actually a design for failure. I often wonder if the intended idea of political correctness, wokeness, radical liberalism, and gynocentrism is indeed failure and collapse. Clearly the intention is the collapse of the "patriarchy," if not the whole system. We can see this intent in the way the Chinese flu pandemic has been handled.

Equality is a great idea. It is very fair. It just does not work in a dynamic environment. Equality is a static phenomenon and occurs through policy. Like many policies, it seldom takes into account the environmental issues. When the policy fails, the bureaucrats operating the system demand compliance, which seldom improves performance and often increases cost and reduces effectiveness. Equality does not require leadership; it only requires policy. What does work is *balance*. Balance not only lives in a dynamic environment, it requires it. The challenge with balance is it requires skill by the operator.

A shining example of equality of outcome policy is that of Obamacare. This is the exact structure that Jocko Willink speaks of: "It's not what you preach, it's what you tolerate." The idea of Obamacare is a great and noble idea, where everyone has access to health care. Like so many things in the gynocentric paradigm, successful implementation gets impeded because of a lack of clear outcome and the attachment to how it has to look. When stressed, power and control take a senior position to the objective. Power and control are used to protect the doctrine and ideology, no matter how flawed. It is the essence of the cover-up and the double down. To put the objective first would require testing the ideology that one holds so dear and whose righteousness one is so invested in. That did not happen with Obamacare. The result was a great idea with far less than excellent execution. What we had was a bunch of people arguing for mediocrity. This is an example of the loss of standards as an acceptable result in the gynocentric paradigm. Therein lies the issue. The way it looks and who is included are more important than workability and what is produced. Inclusion is great for kindergarteners; workability is what adults do.

The practice of balance requires skill and training. The practice of balance requires leadership. The practice of balance also requires the ability to operate in an environment that is dynamic and uncertain. The practice of balance is best expressed by the leader managing the issue at hand. This is the basis of empowerment. Balance is not policy-based; it is achieved through engagement. Engagement is how we learn and move forward. Creating a vision and building and managing the environment to fulfill on the vision. To have that structure of leadership to work, transparency is required so even the staunchest of disbelievers can see. Agreement is not required; trust is. Transparency is an essential element in building trust.

Balance is not a practice toward perfection; it is a practice that provides lifelong learning. Lifelong learning is required because balance is a dynamic activity. It exists in an environment that is ever changing. Equality exists in a static environment and is used as a tool when trust is limited or missing. We must restore trust. To begin that, we must trust ourselves. I fear I am beginning to repeat myself, but repetition is necessary for learning. The ongoing lesson for this book is to establish manhood in a workable and responsible way. That process of establishing manhood begins with a strong relationship with ourselves and restoring our trust and confidence in ourselves. To build trust in ourselves we must be willing to test ourselves. We must build that internal strength because that is what is required to stand in the face of the outrageous and silly (at least how it may occur for us) and to do so from a place of compassion and unconditional love.

Not everything about the gynocentric paradigm is destructive. It does provide compassion and beauty, which adds to the experience of life. It oftentimes has a broader perspective and relieves the challenges of the myopic and binary decision-making process that can occur too often from a purely masculine perspective. The masculine role of providing along with the gynocentric perspective of equality and fairness, when working together, can create a balanced setting for remarkable workability. The masculine role of protection can reduce the obsession with safety and allow for a space of creativity and innovation. The masculine role of creating and leaving a legacy, paired with the feminine desire for community, can create a sustainable environment to build upon and nurture.

> *"In nature, Yin (feminine) and Yang (masculine) are balanced and equal. Just as in nature, if society values one over the other, it weakens both and creates an unnatural state, where harmony is lost and turbulence is created."*
>
> —*S. J. Gold*

The opportunity is for us, the masculine and the feminine, to work together. Each individual is to discover within themselves what their unique and authentic expression is, and then for us to share, learn, and grow together. We are not there yet, and if we as men own who we are and are committed to being responsible for our actions, I am extremely optimistic this challenge we have gone through the last few years will not only be useful but also needed. It is a worthy endeavor.

## CHAPTER 29

# The End of Excuses and the Double Down: Standing for Something (Integrity: Part II)

*"When there's an elephant in the room introduce him."*

—*Randy Pausch*

It is increasingly obvious we are in a gender and cultural war. We also must accept that we're not winning. We are not winning because we have not accepted the errors we have made. When we do accept them, we don't own them. If you want to understand the rule book of the gynocentric paradigm and the radical left agenda, just read the works of Saul Alinsky. He spells it out quite directly. As Sun Tzu said, "To defeat your enemy you must defeat your enemy's strategy." The strategy is clearly stated in Alinsky's *Rules for Radicals.* The attackers of masculinity have been successful at rule #4: "Make your enemies live by their own rules." As we have pointed out, especially in the Chapter 2, "Winning at All Costs," this is an area we have not been adroit at and an area they have been successful in exploiting.

It does not matter that we have mostly operated in alignment with our commitments. In the gynocentric paradigm of contemporary media and the conversational environment, there is evidence to the contrary. Examples such as the police violence on citizens or events like #MeToo provide evidence enough to support their narrative. The challenge is not *eliminating* the actions that have led to these accusations; the challenge is in *owning* them. There are two predictable responses.

The first one is the appeasing apology that you see in all the completely insincere and comical public service announcements. The leaders in this cluster are the major sports leagues. The NBA is the absolute worst offender, pandering to the extent that it nearly cost them their entire television audience. The next worse offender is the British Premiere League. The level of emasculated pandering and virtue signaling is enough to trigger a gag reflex. The one sports entity that I find the most disappointing is the NFL, and the single human who demonstrates the worst in all of this is Roger Goodell.

Roger Goodell runs the most powerful sports league in the world. This league also enjoys possibly the most diverse fan base in America, if not the world. The NFL is a marketing wonder. It also has a great game, and Mr. Goodell actually had a great opportunity. With the platform he had and a fan base of Americans across every economic and social strata, the NFL could have led the way to actually facilitating a real conversation on social change and racial issues. They could not do it. They caved and did the predictable—they pandered just like always. I have no idea why they pissed away an opportunity to make a huge difference and, while doing so, increase the value of their franchise globally. My guess is it could be fear, and because of the strength of their market position, they have little to no understanding of what integrity really is. There also is no greater demonstration of the absence of courage, stand, and masculine leadership than the collective ownership group of the NFL. They never miss an opportunity to choose greed and comfort over an opportunity to act boldly and make real change.

The definition I love of integrity (in our model, a positive phenomenon) is "being whole and complete—achieved by honoring one's word as we define honoring (creates workability, creates trust)." To operate with this level of integrity requires one to actually know who one is and then honor oneself while operating in alignment with that. It requires a level of awareness many don't yet possess, and it also requires, occasionally, passing on the short-term wins to create a long-term success. The perceived risk must have been too high. This time could have been one of the NFL really awakening and understanding the influence they have in the world. Instead, they elected to do what they always do: engage in the transaction and take the guaranteed money. They did not fail. They just missed. Like a long Tom Brady pass that missed Mike Evans—no real failure, just missed opportunity. That is also the nature of integrity.

As men we are never going to be perfect. It is not required. What is required now is that we become aware. We begin to understand our impact and influence. We notice our wake and become responsible for it. We begin to understand when we create messes. If we make a mess, we clean it up and move on. It's that simple. It's even stated in the Bible, Romans 8:1. Unfortunately in the gynocentric paradigm it has gotten quite fashionable to go around on the apology tours whining and expressing regret for all the actions we have taken in our attempt to build a better world. Have mistakes been made? Of course. But wallowing in pity and self-loathing is disgusting and completely unproductive. We have Barack Hussein Obama to thank for creating that as an acceptable tactic for feminized leaders throughout the world to follow. We also have him to thank for the shift to aiming low, accepting less, and creating a future vision of despair while being OK with it.

The second, equally ineffective, response is the double down. Donald Trump is the master of the double down: the best defense is a good offense and deny until you die. The unfortunate thing with this tactic, other than it is complete bullshit, is it can destroy trust. It can make you look like a complete asshole, especially when you did screw up. I think the most damaging thing about it is that to the untrained eye, it can outwardly be confused with standing for what is right.

Standing for what is right and what you are committed to is, in my opinion, one of the most effective ways to create change. Standing in the face of little to no agreement takes courage and self-belief at levels that are not common. Standing for what one believes is the bedrock to creating change and foundational to the movement we intend to create here. Great leaders like Dr. Martin Luther King, Mahatma Gandhi, Abraham Lincoln, and Aaron Burr (the master of the filibuster) have all been excellent at standing for what they believed in. Some think the filibuster is political grandstanding. Quite the contrary, it is a powerful delay tactic and a legitimate defense strategy as outlined in *The Art of War*. The filibuster is an action of standing one's ground. In the process of standing one's ground a funny thing happens. The people opposed to the filibuster get curious about how *you* can be so wrong *and* so passionate. The stronger you stand, the more curious they get. (I'm sure it has something to do with the law of attraction.) It causes them to begin the process of examining their own position. Just watch the 1957 movie, *Twelve Angry Men*.

The greatest statement of true masculine power, and the greatest expression of manhood, is to stand for what you believe regardless of popularity. To do that, one needs to understand what they believe and be fully aligned with that belief. When we get there, standing for our beliefs becomes natural. Standing for what we believe becomes honoring. It begins to build trust. In *Twelve Angry Men,* we can see it when Henry Fonda was first viewed as a crazy man. As he stood and expressed his beliefs, others began to look. This is not merely convincing; this is what enrollment looks like. This is how trust is constructed and coalitions are made. But before that can happen we must understand what our beliefs are and own them.

This is not bullshitting; this is *not* "fake it 'til you make it"; this is *not* performance. This *is* owning your word, your beliefs, and who you are—100 percent! In essence, it is willing to die for what you believe. That is some of the work for us to do. It is difficult work, but this work is required as we go on to fulfill on our promise to provide, protect, and leave a legacy. One of the hardest things we have to own as men is how unwilling we have been to operate at that level of commitment. We have to own our addiction to comfort and our fear of upsetting someone in service of doing what is right. We have to understand how soft we have gotten and how easily we will give up the ass. You don't have to go much further than look at our response to the Chinese virus lockdown orders.

Apologies, for the most part, are ineffective. We have worn them out. It is much more powerful to own the fuck-up and clean up the mess. No emotion, no judgment. Just being fully responsible and owning 100 percent of the outcome. No need for ego or concern, just ownership. I don't mean to be cold; however, the wimpy and lame "I'm sorry" just doesn't work anymore. That dog don't hunt. I am done with insincere, placating apologies.

I can accept a well-intended and authentic apology, but I have zero tolerance for the double down. Don't be *that* guy—we must stop this at once! It is obnoxious, and the impact on our credibility is too high. The impact on the practice of standing for what is right is devastating. I am a believer in never taking the first act of aggression, but if you see a guy do the double down, throat punch the douche. On second thought, no. Don't do that. Please confront the brother and educate him in the error of his actions. My guess? He is just scared.

After we create our purpose, we need to build the structure to deliver on that purpose. That structure begins with our relationship to ourselves. Foundational to that is our relationship to our word. We want to begin seeing how we relate to our word. The first place to look is how good you are at keeping your promises. Other simple places to look are things like showing up on time, paying your bills on time, and answering your emails and phone messages. There is an impact on not doing so and an impact on you. Begin to notice. You are going to want to throat punch me later on, and then you will love and thank me for it. The easiest way to build your relationship to your word and your relationship to integrity is to always do the simple stuff. A good place to start is to use your calendar as a structure. Do *what* you say *when* you say you will do it. If you can't, let those affected know and re-promise when you will. No apologies, no stories, no drama, no hiding, no double down (remember you are risking a throat punch on that). Just do what you say. When life gets boring, you are well on your way.

Another place to look is the relationship to yourself. How is your diet, how about your sleep, what about exercise? There are endless places to look. Your relationship with your friends, coworkers, how you perform your job. Are you aligned with the mission and vision of the organization? These are all places where we can grow, develop, and deepen our understanding of who we are and the opportunity to contribute to the lives of those around us. Thank you for being here, it is a blessing for me to do this.

You actually inspire me. Thank you so much.

CHAPTER 30

# Owning Our Voice

*"When the personality comes fully to serve the energy of its soul, that is authentic empowerment."*
—*Gary Zukav*

If there is one lesson I have learned from my years of leadership work and executive coaching, it is that owning one's own voice is one of the most emancipating experiences a human can have. It occurs when our expression is a direct reflection of our soul. There is little strategy and no performance, just pure expression in alignment with the fulfillment of our commitments. It is the source of building trust and partnerships. It is no longer about us, our identity. It becomes about us, our purpose. We have the ability to be bigger, more powerful, and more committed than ever before. It happens in service of that thing that matters most for you. It is sourced by love, and it is sourced by something way beyond us.

The process and achievement of owning our voice is at the core of stepping into manhood and masculine leadership. By owning our voice, we claim our individuality and install the structure to fulfill on the purpose we have created. When we are clear on our purpose and own our voice, we are now free to connect to the purpose of a group or community with which we can align. When our purpose is aligned with that of a group or community, we are positioned to make a contribution and impact the change on a whole new level. This is how a difference is made. This is how real success is gained. Through the joining of voices, ideas, and souls, there is no obstacle that cannot be overcome.

I have also never had anyone come to me directly and say, "Hey, Mike, what can we do to find my voice?" This issue of connecting to our voice and owning our authentic expression is an unknown problem—especially for men. So much of what we do and how we get rewarded is based on our relationship to the things around us. Our job, our friends, our community, and our family are all things around us. Seldom is it required for us to truly look in the mirror and ask, "Who am I?" Even less often do we ask, "Why am I here?" Occasionally we ask, "What is my purpose?" The more popular question is, "How do I...?" The best answer I have ever heard to these "how" questions is the book by Peter Block *The Answer to How Is Yes.*

Attending to the "how" is always an external process. It looks at strategy, tactics, resources, and skills. We have been trained that the answer is always in the "how." There are countless "how-to videos" on YouTube, and there are limitless how-to books and papers written. People love "how-tos" because it gives them the answer and stops the perceived uncertainty. People love to tell you "how to" because it makes them feel good and has them contribute and "made a difference." That is what "experts" do; they tell us "how to."

There is no "how-to" in discovering and owning your voice. It is highly personal and unique to you. *Your* way is *the* way. The path to discovering and owning your voice begins with discovering and owning who you are. The best way I have found to begin that journey is to discover your purpose. Access to your purpose is within. This journey within may be a difficult one. It requires courage and an ability to be with the uncomfortable. To own who we are, we must own it all. We must own our darkness, our weakness, our fear, our lust, our hate, our disgust, our anger, and all our flaws. Without owning those, we cannot own our strength, our light, our toughness, our love, our vision, our joy, our creativity, and all the power that is unique to all of us. It is through the complete understanding of all that we are and all that we are not that we can access our freedom to choose who we will be.

There will always be opposition, resistance, and obstacles on any journey. Sometimes those obstacle are unjust, unfair, and maybe even cruel. Sometimes those obstacles will occur as attacks. They are all gifts for us to learn and grow as humans. Yes, they are difficult. But the more difficult they are, the more valuable the lesson. I understand the call for justice and the demand to change. The calls of the current political left/gyno-centric paradigm are not unintelligent; they are just unworkable and coming from the mindset of a victim. If we come from a victimized mindset, we will always be reliant on the cavalry coming in to save the day. The current version of that is a reliance and dependence on the government to create new regulations and policies to solve the current woes of the day.

Unfortunately, when governments attempt to solve problems they only have two levers to use. Governments can supply resources or restrict freedoms. That is all they can do, because that is all they are set up to do. Therein lies the issue with social justice, which may be the loudest of all gynocentric agenda points. I get it, it makes sense. And from a victim's mentality there is no access to getting it done. To see a problem and have no access to solving it is a frustrating way to operate. It is completely congruent to then desire to put limits on the party that you view as the offender. It makes perfect sense to create prohibitions on the action that drives up fear. That is the reason for calls to end "hate speech" and "hate groups." It is also why those actions only create more division.

Currently we can see that the only solution provided by the gynocentric populations as it relates to "toxic masculinity" is the canceling of masculine expression. It makes perfect sense. They are victimized by it, so it must be wrong, and we need to eliminate it. From a place of paralyzing fear, those actions are cogent. Same goes with systemic racism. There are victims, and to support those victims and give them "the justice" they deserve, we must eliminate the villain. It sounds like vigilantism. I understand the thought process, but the only challenge is it cannot be done. Prohibition never works; it only drives the issue into the shadows. Driving issues into the shadows is not the solution.

The only way we can solve a problem is to own the problem. We need to be willing to "git some on us." We must engage. We must take on the issue of "toxic masculinity" and "systemic racism" the same way we address the issues with "the patriarchy." They are all the same thing. They are all complaints of the traditional way things have been done. That is why restoring manhood and masculine leadership is so important. I intentionally used the word *restore* versus *repair* or *replace*. Restore brings back the original greatness while addressing the issues of the contemporary world.

The best place to begin is the Four Noble Truths of Buddhism. The first noble truth is *dukkha*: "Life is painful and causes suffering." If we just get that life is painful and causes suffering, we can stop the never-ending process of trying to eliminate pain. If we own that pain and suffering are just part of life, there is no more resistance to it. As I mentioned earlier with owning our darkness to get to our greatness, if we own that pain and suffering are part of life, we can expand our capacity for joy and happiness. If we accept pain and suffering and stop the practice of avoiding it, we can then engage in life. Engaging in life is access to the discovery of "who we are" and "why we are here." It's through engagement that we get to test our purpose and practice fulfillment.

To begin, we must start with ourselves. Jay Niblick wrote a great book on success, and he has a simple formula for it: "Success equals our self-awareness plus our authentic expression." Simple, easy, awesome. The issue is, are we self-aware? We may or may not be. And what I will say is, there is no end to this road. This does not mean that the answer is endless navel-gazing and quiet contemplation on a mountain top. It just means we must be willing to own our blind spots. It simply means that we need to shift from cocksure ignorance to thoughtful uncertainty. This is the transition that can lead us from a dependency on "experts" and allow us to enter the realm of leadership. Leadership is going where we have never gone before, and I believe none of us have ever lived tomorrow. Leadership begins with thoughtful inquiry.

That existence in thoughtful uncertainty has us walk through the gate of courage and allows us to engage. It is through engagement that we build the muscles of understanding who we are and who we are not. Through the process of winning some and losing some, we discover what we are truly made of. We understand the characteristics and abilities we are blessed with. Through this process we can begin to learn. This process can be painful, and it can also be joyful. It is a far cry from the numbness that the narrative of safety and fairness provides. Through this process we begin to understand that the crashes and failures are gifts to be cherished, no matter how painful. Those crashes become milestones on the journey to discovering ourselves and our voice. This process is essential in the development of our authentic expression and understanding who we are as an individual.

Our forefathers who created this great country understood that our inalienable rights of life, liberty, and the pursuit of happiness were essential to our freedom, our personal sovereignty, and our liberty. They understood that to be a truly free nation, men had to be free to choose how they wanted to live. They understood that for freedom to exist, those expressions of freedom had to be responsible and aligned with a much larger purpose. It was inside that understanding that this grand experiment of freedom was constructed. It is through that experiment that we have discovered that with much freedom comes much responsibility.

We have been allowed to be free, but the level of responsibility we have demonstrated has not equaled the freedom we have been granted. We must take responsibility for that freedom now or risk losing what was granted to us. As men, we must up our game and restore our position of leadership, and do so in a way that is a contribution. Through that awareness and that process one's voice is revealed.

We must accept, without concern for the reason, that men and masculinity have been identified as the problem. Arguing about whether or not that is right and justifying our actions are a waste of time. To quote Mahatma Gandhi, "We must be the change we wish to see in the world." We must do that now. That change begins with owning our voice and providing responsible masculine leadership. That change begins with the authentic expression of manhood. The people we must begin to lead first are ourselves. Today is the day to begin that work.

What that work can look like is the practice of making "normal" normal again. Standing courageously for the unabashed and responsible expression of manhood. We must face the insanity and hold the crazies to account. We can no longer cower at the attacks of "hate speech," racism, and misogyny. Disagreement is not hate; it is disagreement. We must call out the double speak of "peaceful protest," the cries of systemic racism, and the calls for social justice. We must call out the aberration of gender fluidity and the absurdity of safe spaces. We must stand in the face of irrationality of ideas such as "flattening the curve" and the abuse of the application of unlawful lockdowns. We must stand in the face of the frenzied rage that makes baseless accusations of white supremacy. *"No"* is a complete sentence, and we must begin the practice of using that.

One of the characteristics of freedom is that we allow many things that are not in alignment with freedom. That is the nature of the freedom. It is completely consistent with freedom to let people share their thoughts and ideas no matter how differing they may be. The line is drawn when their expression interferes with the expression of others. I think that line has been crossed or at least straddled. Part of the expression of manhood is the development of healthy value-based boundaries. We are at that point where healthy boundaries can be a contribution to all.

I am clear that in our current politically correct/ gynocentric/ multicultural/extreme progressive/left wokeness existence, the call for diversity, inclusion, and equality does not include the voice of masculinity. That is the world of today. That is just more evidence of the cultural war waged against men—especially men who demonstrate any expression of traditional masculinity. So what? Permission and invitations are not required. We can actually be thankful for this because that narrative provides the perfect impediment to challenge our voice, sharpen our edge, and provide the grit to get very clear and responsible for who we need to be for ourselves, our families, our communities, and our country. This opposition is the perfect test to ensure that what we stand for is what we believe. This is a time of opportunity. This a time for clarity and it is clearly a time to share the *Manhood Manifesto: How Men Must Lead at Home, at Work, and in the Public Sphere*. Thank you, brothers.

## CHAPTER 31

# Doing Meaningful Work; Restoring Vitality

*"It doesn't matter how great your shoes are if you don't accomplish anything in them."*
—*Martina Boone*

The most distinguished means of expression for a man is in the work he does. I don't mean just in his career; I mean in the expression of his being. Men are often best expressed by their actions, oftentimes more than their words. Literature and folklore are filled with the "strong, silent types" or the famous expression "walk softly and carry a big stick," as said by Teddy Roosevelt. A great football coach summed it up, "You are what your record says you are." Jocko Willink said about leadership, "It's not what you preach, it is what you tolerate." In the world of masculinity, work, action, and doing are often the expression of being. The work, action, and doing are also a way to understand a man's commitment. Witnessing is access to believing. This is one area where masculinity differs significantly from the gynocentric paradigm. Working in the gynocentric paradigm may be a means to an end. Masculinity can be the end unto itself.

The state or condition of manhood is not an automatically achieved condition. It requires development. The most effective way I know of developing a boy into a man is through the process of doing work. Doing work is different from being a child. Work interrupts the comfort and safety of our domicile. Work pulls us away from our mommies and throws us out in the world, unsupported and emotionally naked. Work allows us to engage the world on its terms, not ours. It is a cause of struggle or resistance. It is often a source of failure and of disappointment. Work is also the opportunity to see ourselves as others see us and then check to see if our perception is a match. That is the beginning of self-awareness. If you are not sure the match is there, the real gift is noticing it and then doing something about it. Failure is seldom fatal, and this is a huge departure from the gynocentric paradigm of looking good.

The work we do is not as important as the drive and commitment we bring to our work. If we do this right, the work we do will source us throughout our life and be the platform for our continued growth, development, and lifelong learning. If you engage in that, you are a success. The work does not matter as much as who you get to be while doing that work. This is what W. Edwards Deming describes as *pride of workmanship*. One of the most successful and fulfilled guys I know works as a doorman at a hotel in downtown Chicago. He has done so for forty-one years. Some of the most unhappy and unfulfilled people I know hold positions of prestige with huge compensation packages. The work as we relate to it here is a vehicle for full self-expression. To do anything less than be fully engaged and expressed is a soul-crushing experience.

In my leadership work I am constantly fascinated and inspired by the skill, expertise, and commitment of many leaders.

Their level of passion and devotion is moving. One of the biggest challenges I have seen as the world gets increasingly more gynocentric, is that gynocentrism adds to the complexity and ambiguity in our culture. The primary value of gynocentrism is safety. Fairness is also a value that is very high on the list of what drives their actions and beliefs. An indication of people valuing "safety" and "fairness" is the way they communicate how they "feel" about it. Fairness and safety are feelings in and of themselves. Feelings are a huge driver in the gynocentric paradigm. You see it everywhere today in interviews and news analyses. One of the biggest questions used in political polls is, "Are you better off today than four years ago?" That is a feelings-based question.

I am not against feelings, nor am I anti-female, nor am I out to eliminate all things gynocentric. My intention is we need to understand these things and the impact they have so we can be responsible for them. Feelings are essential to the overall experience of life. Feelings are a gift from God that has us experience the journey of life. They are essential indicators to let us know if we are on track or not. They are the gauges and indicators of our existence. If you think of humans as machines, our feelings are the first indicator of how we are operating. All feelings are essential in the complete experience of life. The challenge? As our culture has become more gynocentric, we have made some feelings bad and wrong. In doing so, we have overemphasized others. Feelings have become an end to why we exist, not a means to live the most powerful and expressed way possible.

This focus on feelings can also interfere with the value and expression of work. When work is performed well, there is a return. We call that return profit. In the somewhat bizarre and twisted experience we see in the gynocentric paradigm, profit and capitalism have been villainized. Generating profit has been replaced with fundraising. The problem I see with fundraising is that people always want a return for their investment. That return now gets buried inside the process of raising funds and "doing good works." The mission and purpose can become a cover-up for the return on the investment. There becomes an absence of transparency that does little to build trust. There becomes a question of, "Who is behind the curtain?" The current gynocentric paradigm suggests it does not matter as long as good work is being done and people feel good about that work. I disagree. Good work is when our actions are aligned with our thoughts and words and they generate results that correspond to our commitments. How we feel about that has little to do with whether or not it is effective. This is just another example of the distortion created by the existing gynocentric paradigm that we must wrestle with every day.

By limiting our expression to what feels good, we have limited our ability to achieve our full potential as people and as a culture. This limitation on our ability to use our full potential has a detrimental impact on the pride of workmanship. When pride of workmanship is not valued, viewed as unimportant, or is not appreciated, the experience of work is negatively impacted. One of the things we must do as we begin to establish manhood and masculine leadership is to use feelings as indicators, not as an end product. Just because someone feels a certain way does not make it true, nor does it mean we all must follow that feeling. This is a formula for pure disaster! Establishing and reinstalling pride of workmanship is essential to our experience of manhood. When we understand that and are grounded in it, we then gain true access to our ability to self-assess. We must restore a healthy and normalized relationship to feelings. To do so we as men must lead by example because that is what we do.

*Longmire*, a series on Netflix, is a story of a contemporary Western sheriff. The background story is Walt is overcoming the loss of his wife. What makes this show great is it's really a classic Western—catching bad guys and righting wrongs—with a back story of traditional masculinity in the environment of modern culture. It shows the struggle of a really solid man grieving the loss of his partner, lover, and wife. It also shows all the judgments and assumptions people are making of him through the lens of the gynocentric paradigm. One of the most telling parts of the show is when Walt is in a field with his deputy and partner, Vic, who is a woman. He stops. She asks, "What's going on?" His response made me love the show. He said, "I'm thinking. I do that before I talk." That sums up traditional masculinity perfectly. Masculinity is rationally based. Gynocentrism is based in feelings and emotions. Neither is right or wrong. They are both required for the full experience of being human. These expressions speak to the differences of the genders. The work to do is to honor both and strive for balance.

The genesis of this book comes through my work with male leaders. They had the passion, skills, commitment, and desire to succeed, and many were struggling. They had a complete understanding of the job to do, the needs of their team, and how this all fit within the organization, and yet something was missing. Through my work I realized that men and women showed up differently. Most women had achieved a decent level of balance between the external world, the work they do, the organizations they were in, and their internal world. They understood who they were as people. I found this so funny because all we see in interviews is women talking about their struggles in balancing the external and internal world. That is what made *Becoming* by Michelle Obama an international bestseller. You don't hear men speak about this very often. When you do, at least for me, I usually reach for the gag bucket. Then it dawned on me.

Men are struggling now because our relationship to ourselves and the importance of some semblance of balance between the internal and external world has been missing. Men are expected to *"git shit done,"* to *"man the fuck up,"* to *"power through it."* That is how we have traditionally been judged. The world has changed, and if we did get the memo we did not understand it. So we have continued to do things we thought we knew worked, even when the feedback said we must change. The real confusion comes when results are delivered, yet the feedback says you are not delivering.

It happened to me. I was fired from a job where I was a top performer with breakthrough results. Yet I was not a fit to the new culture and the new leadership of the organization. I did not get the memo. When I asked about it, inquiring was more of an indicator of my inability to fit in. The tragedy of that is when I was hired I thought I would be there until the end of my career. I knew "I belonged." I loved working there and being part of the organization. It was a match to my expression. Then it changed: new ownership, new structure, and a new president came in. When that happened I was no longer a match, and I failed to adapt. The truth is I chose not to adapt, because I was not aligned with the new direction. The way I communicated my commitment was not seen as "positive." This is what happens when our identity and our expression into the external are not balanced with our internal awareness.

Working hard, generating results, achieving goals, and winning are what we as men have been trained to do. For a long time that is how we were rewarded. Western civilization developed through the Athenian mindset of rational and critical thinking and a Judeo-Christian ethic. Patriarchy is that structure of Athenian rationality and Judeo-Christian ethic. Our laws and Constitution are based on those two pillars. Feelings are OK, but they are not essential. They are primarily used as gauges. Victims are to be tended to, yet we must keep moving on. Progress, success, growth, development, and forward movement are what drives Western civilization. Individuality is honored and celebrated, and it is incumbent upon each individual to discover where they belong. That is what lies at the core of personal responsibility. Strong family structures and time-honored traditions are the pathways created to support people in that discovery. Bottom line, though, you had to be this tall to be on the ride, and one was required to *"man up"* to be successful. Victims were not celebrated. Nor was giving up. Your success was really up to you.

As previously stated, there have always been challenges to freedom, and freedom is not free. It requires work. The challenges to freedom are things like Marxism, socialism, and communism. All these belief systems value the state above the individual, and the payoff of these structures is you give up your individuality and responsibility so the state will take care of you. I think that is the same structure as prison. The ultimate punishment in our society is the removal of our freedom. Yet these political structures are basically offering the same thing. What has happened is the narrative of socialism, communism, and Marxism is one of safety, equality, and fairness. You don't have to go much further than your next BLM rally and listen to the rhetoric that is expressed there. The messaging of these ideologies is the same messaging you see on the late night "adopt a pet" or "contribute to these poor people" commercials. The messaging is simply that you should feel guilty for how good you had it. The messaging of socialism, communism, and Marxism is we are bad people for being successful, for achieving greatness, and for being able to live our lives as we see fit.

Messaging on feelings is highly effective in the gynocentric community. That is why, in the most recent election, a huge swing was seen in the voting practices of well-educated, white, suburban women. They looked around at their three thousand square foot houses and their brand-new fully loaded SUVs, and realized they could not go to Cabo this winter because of the global pandemic and so became aware that the world was not working. Of course, it was the fault of Western civilization and the patriarchy! In our desire as men to stem the upset, we agreed or at least attempted to appease them. The truth is, none of this makes sense. It certainly does not make sense through the lens of rationality and ethics. The way to deal with it is not to kill it or ignore it, because these responses are what has led to giving this stuff fertile ground in which to grow. The way we must address this begins with our own development and growth.

In becoming more self-aware we become more aware of our environment and have a greater understanding of what is working and not working. Our self-awareness supports us in being more confident. With confidence (not arrogance) we can inquire and do so with compassion. That honest inquiry has us look and question and get curious. The answers to those questions will tell us much. Our self-awareness actually allows for more access to critical thinking. It is through critical thinking we can share our vision in such a way that it can move those who do not see it yet. That is the distinction of enrollment, the most powerful leadership tool one can possess. For enrollment to be available, one must be willing to stand in the face of little to no agreement. It takes work to get here.

The work to do today is to just engage in whatever you are doing. What I mean by *engage* is really choose what you are doing. If you are a carpenter, celebrate being a carpenter and be present to the project you are doing. There is no nonessential work. All work can be an expression of who you are. Do that work well. One of my first jobs was as an apprentice in a tool and die shop. My job was drilling holes in steel blank rolls. Pick these blanks up, put them in the fixture, and have the drill press do the work. One after another, ten hours a night. To some that may sound boring. To me (I am not sure why) I found pride and satisfaction in it. I loved that job. I loved that job because I was learning, I had a great boss, and in my own small way at twenty years old, I felt like I was contributing, I was becoming a man.

Our work is an expression of who we are. It doesn't matter what the work is as long as that work is aligned with our purpose. If there is not a direct alignment, like the drill press job, have it be an access point to learning and discovering that purpose. Remember that everything can be a gift.

The biggest concern that I have with our contemporary culture is that the bias of gynocentrism and its feelings-based judgments are interfering with the learning, growth, and development of young men and boys today. My concern with that interference in the learning and development is it can impact their pride of workmanship. Pride in the work we do is essential in developing that self-confidence and self-assuredness that allow us to stretch beyond what is comfortable. Evidence of this is the elimination of shop classes and access to other ways young boys can develop. Add in the impact of absent fathers, the conditioning of the media, and the gynocentric indoctrination of the public school systems, and I have a huge concern about the development of our boys. Maybe this is where we should look at institutional sexism and misandry.

We have a bunch of work to do, and as men work is an expression of who we are. Our first task is to raise our own awareness of who *we* are. The good news is just *getting* that awareness is the win. From this place of self-awareness and connection to our purpose, we can now engage in the most empowered and empowering way. We live in a great time. Now is the time to restore masculine leadership in America. Now is a time to celebrate manhood and all it represents. Please join me.

## CHAPTER 32

# Leadership: Agreement Is Not Required; Inspiration Is

*"There are only two ways to influence human behavior: you can manipulate it or you can inspire it.*
                                    —Simon Sinek

Consider nobody really knows a damn thing about leadership. The reason is that leadership is not about knowing, it is not even about "doing." Leadership is about being. Being a leader. What does "being" even mean? There have been literally hundreds of thousands of books written on leadership. Hell, this is my second. Some of those books are great, others are epically stupid, and most miss the mark. The reason they miss the mark is the false belief that leadership and leadership development exist in some transfer of knowledge. That is a false claim. Leadership exists in engagement, in experience, and in our subjective reality. That makes it a real challenge. If leadership exists in each and every person's experience of their subjective reality, how in the hell can anyone lead a group of people in any endeavor and do so effectively? That is the universal question of leadership and why, so often, we have the experience of an absence of leadership.

That explains why we have so much disagreement on who and what makes a great leader. There is no greater example of this than our former president, Donald J. Trump. Some people viewed him as an evil despot. Other people viewed him as a savior of freedom and American greatness. Part of what caused this division is Mr. Trump rejected the traditional ways of communicating his ideas and vision. He rejected the standard practices of the presidency.

To some, that was to be celebrated. To others it was appalling and a threat. To everyone, we needed to look—not through the traditional lens of the media and standard practices—at him through our own lens and through our own perspective. Donald Trump shifted the game to a much more personal one. Our relationship to him, regardless of whether you loved him or hated him, was a personal one. Everything he did was personal. Everything he did was measured subjectively and was looked at through the lens of our own personal perspective. The result was he was viewed as a great hero or a crazy, racist xenophobe. Consider that neither view was true. Like most presidents, his actions were based on his commitment and what he thought was the right thing to do. I think history will show that, like most other presidents, he did some good stuff and he had some misses.

I bring this up to illustrate that leadership and leadership performance occur beyond us, the leader. Leadership, the act and practice, lives in the listening and the experiences of those we are leading. It has little to do with the leaders themselves. The mindset of the leader will inform their actions and practices, but the issue is the experience of the people being led.

As leaders we have no control over how people see us or hear us. We have no control over their bias or their opinions. We also have no control over their willingness to engage, participate, or be led. Leadership is not about control, yet so many leaders resort to manipulation, power, and control to lead. That is not leadership. That, at best, is management. At worst, it is dominating tyranny. Let's be honest: leadership is really hard. It is a tough thing to practice and a much more difficult thing to be successful at. To engage in leadership is to understand that you will fail. That failure will be met with harsh criticism and oftentimes fierce opposition. Because of this, a knowledge of oneself and an acceptance of oneself, flaws and all, are absolutely essential. In that process of self-discovery we must be crystal clear about our purpose and use that purpose as our North Star or lighthouse to maintain our pathway. If we lose sight of our purpose or succumb to the fear of self-doubt (we get really good at doubting ourselves), we will revert to the practices of control and management. Those practices can often occur as manipulation by those whom we will be leading. Leadership is the only mechanism we as humans have to create intentional change and achieve improvements.

That is what is occurring in America today. The pull toward socialism, communism, Marxism, or the progressive left is an indifference toward freedom and individualism. The people who align with this also align with the gynocentric values of safety and fairness. It does not matter what the objective reality is. The imperative here is that we live in the most fair and safe time in the history of man, but the constant messaging of doom and inequity leads to a desire of having someone else fix this problem.

One of the appeals of the gynocentric, progressive, socialist left is it requires little if any leadership. That mindset is run by policy and ideology. It is static, seldom-changing, predictable, and, therefore, safe. If it is safe, fair, and equitable, that should be enough to solidify the ideology. Subjective leadership, risk taking, and error making are replaced with "objective judgment" and "assessment." Perfection is their measure of success. Safe, fair, and equitable are impossible to guarantee all the time in a free society, so it becomes an easy target for that static ideology. Since the gynocentric, progressive, socialist left only trade in opinion and judgment and their strategy is to always apply pressure to their enemy, this is the perfect structure for them—at least short term. Since most everything is judged by emotions, there is no better short-term indicator than one's feelings.

As men, the message that the expression of masculinity is one of toxicity has also limited and repressed our expression. I don't care who you are. If you constantly hear that what you are doing is "toxic" you will put the brakes on. We just want the noise to stop. It does not. Appeasement never works. Appeasement, when discovered, is just more evidence that the original complaint is valid.

Let me tell you a story about appeasement in my hometown of Berwyn, Illinois. Berwyn is a blue-collar town west of Chicago. Like most towns in Chicagoland, Berwyn was highly segregated, and one could make the claim it was racist. Fast-forward forty years and Berwyn has intentionally evolved into one of the most diverse and inclusive towns in America. It is not perfect, and it has a community that celebrates all different expressions of the human experience. Berwyn has a large Hispanic, mostly Mexican, population. Berwyn is also a bastion of the LGBTQ community, all of whom live in harmony with a number of longtime residents. Berwyn also has a Black population whose numbers align with the Black population of the country. It is significant and recognized. The motto of Berwyn is a "City of Homes." It is where people live and raise families. The families today look much different than forty or fifty years ago, and yet they share many of the same values and desires as those who came before them.

During the summer of George Floyd, Berwyn also had BLM protests. Like many others, these "peaceful protests" erupted into rioting and violence. I am not sure why Berwyn was targeted. I think it was targeted because it was a symbol of how authentic diversity, inclusion, and equality could look and operate, which stands in the face of the narrative presented by BLM, Antifa, and other Marxist, hard-core political left ideologies.

Berwyn has a small but very left-leaning local radical population. The riots were not a problem for them, and they actually became a tool to mobilize this group. Part of the "plan" was to get a BLM mural placed in the city, much like was done in DC and NYC. They demanded a symbol of the collect "wokeness." (I think Berwyn was competing with Oak Park, a neighboring town to the north, to see which could be more "woke.") The Berwyn mayor and city council resisted and were quite adamant that this was never going to happen.

Like children who cannot get more cookies and candy at bedtime, the protestors threw tantrums and made more noise. The noise continued with constant protests and social media rants. In a desire to "end the noise" the mayor and city council succumbed to the acting out and installed a BLM mural in the east parking lot of city hall. The result did not end the noise. Now these radicals had a victory, and it gave them more fuel for the cause.

These radical woke folks had claimed that Berwyn was a racist and noninclusive city that was built on oppression and political corruption. Nothing was further from the truth. As we have shown time and again throughout the book, when one is operating from feelings, especially the feeling of safety and fairness, one never lets facts interfere with the narrative. Thus the phrase that drives so much today, "with an abundance of caution," is the phrase that allows the break from rational and critical thinking. I share this to show what happens when appeasement is a tool to end upset.

Appeasement no longer works. We must begin a new practice of leadership. Leadership is difficult and challenging. Leadership is always met with resistance. When we have a powerful sense of self, our relationship to resistance shifts. Resistance is now a tool to provide lift, much like the air pressure and the airplane's wings. Resistance also means to set one's course, much like the wind when we sail. Resistance is the mechanism to build strength and agility much like the kettle bells we toss around in the gym. When we get cool with ourselves (I don't mean arrogant), resistance becomes a gift and an indicator we are on the right track.

We can use that resistance to begin to authentically craft our message for those who have not or could not yet hear it. People's points of view occur through the lens of their beliefs, desires, and values. Not too many of us are able to see the world through the eyes of others. That is a big limit of humans. As a leaders, we need to be able to release our point of view, knowing we can always come back—it's not going anywhere. When we release that point of view, and we are cool with ourselves, and we are not operating from fear, we can really begin to inquire.

Through that inquiry, we will see and hear stuff we never have before. We begin to understand things differently. We begin to learn and discover. Again, we *must* release our own point of view to do this, or we will taint what we hear. The listening we are practicing here is not to understand or fit it into our structure. The listening we apply here is to learn with no judgment, assessment, or even shock. What we are striving for is to gain an insight into their perspective of the world, as unattached and unbiased as possible.

Once we arrive at the point where we are beginning to notice there are actually other people out there, and they see the world differently than us, and they are not all crazy, we can begin to ask how this aligns with our vision. How does this fit together? We can also see the ones who are in conflict with us. That discernment brings us to a point of choice. Viewpoints in conflict with our own have us look and inquire; can we work with them? Critical thinking is required here. Let's look at socialism. In urban areas, there are socialist activities that make perfect sense. Shared services like public transportation are a proven example. Other aspects, like public space, bikeways, and rest areas are all things required for a high quality of life in an urban environment. To accept them does not mean you are a communist; you may just be a pragmatist. This is why the process of leadership is so unique and dynamic. There is no one way.

This is also why an understanding of oneself and one's values is important. We all have biases, and we must own them. Bias is not wrong unless it is unknown. The unique thing I have found, as one understands and accepts their own unique qualities and characteristics and fully accepts them, we are more apt to accept the differences and unique qualities in others. What I have discovered is the more self-awareness we develop, the more empathy and compassion we gain for others.

The work there is to do, then, is to reach a consensus of how these different perspectives can be joined together into a workable solution. This solution will always exist in the future. We cannot fix the past, but we do not have to repeat the mistakes. Any plan that is based in the past is doomed to failure and argument. That is what the 1619 Project is, one that is fundamentally based in folly.

This is where the work begins. We must construct a message of leadership that is based in the future, a future desired condition, which is inclusive and meets the needs of those we are leading. Our job as leaders is to create a vision for the future. When we craft that message we must include those we are leading, consider their perspective and desires, and do so in a way that is authentic to our purpose and true to who we are. Others will be moved and inspired by that. When people are moved and inspired, they often want to join in and belong. We seek true belonging. That is the work of leadership, and that is what we as men must do to demonstrate the gift of manhood. The expression of manhood in our community is intended to be a gift. That gift is how we build a future for our children and our children's children. That is the expression of masculinity. This is the call of manhood.

CHAPTER 33

# The Only Way Out Is Through It

*"All right Mister, let me tell you what winning means...you're willing to go longer, work harder, give more than anyone else."*
— *Vince Lombardi*

*"The greatest accomplishment is not in never falling, but in rising again after you fall."*
— *Vince Lombardi*

*"It's easy to have faith in yourself and have discipline when you're a winner, when you're number one. What you got to have is faith and discipline when you're not a winner."*
— *Vince Lombardi*

When I was a kid growing up in Berwyn, Illinois, I fell in love with the game of football. Growing up, my team was the Chicago Bears. Gale Sayers, Dick Butkus, Mike Ditka, Mike Pyle, Doug Atkins, Doug Buffone, Rosey Taylor, and Dick Gordon were my guys. I loved the Bears. Their archrivals were the Packers. These Packers were led by the late, great Vince Lombardi. These Packers included Bart Starr, Paul Hornung,

Jim Taylor, Elijah Pitts, Marv Fleming, Jerry Kramer, Fuzzy Thurston, Forest Gregg, and Max McGee. The Bears-Packers rivalry was the foundation of my understanding of competition and rivalry. I hated the Packers and respected them. I loved those games.

The Bears won the NFL Championship in 1963. I was too young to remember it. The first football game I ever saw was at Soldier Field when the NFL Champion Bears played the College All-Stars to begin the 1964 season. This was how the NFL opened its season. I used the opening quotes from Vince Lombardi for two reasons. First, Vince Lombardi represented the biggest obstacle for success for the Bears. Being the biggest obstacle and the biggest source of resistance, I learned early that they were also the biggest opportunities and the biggest sources for growth, improvement, and progress. The games against the Packers became the measure to assess the level of performance the Bears had achieved.

Second, no one represented taking on issues, adversity, challenge, and competition in a more authentic, direct, empowered, and honoring way than Vince Lombardi. Coach Lombardi was a simple man; there were few surprises with him . The Packers were a simple team to figure out. Again, few surprises. Their strategy was excellence. Their tactic was flawless execution. They trusted themselves and respected and honored their competition. They showed up for every game prepared and ready to play. They were more concerned with their execution and focus than on the outcome. They fully understood that if they executed to the best of their ability and remained focused and present, the outcome would take care of itself.

Things were simpler then. They did not have analytics and computers, and iPads were decades away. Film study actually used film. Players had jobs in the off-season, so they were not football players all year long. It was a game, and it was great. I am sure I am bringing some romance to this, as we do whenever we reminisce. The players of today are far better conditioned, and far stronger, faster, and bigger. Yet, the game was just as great back then. I believe certain lessons from leaders of the past are as true today as they ever were. Vince Lombardi represents one of those leaders.

There is a need for leadership in the world. We are crying for it. It may be the one resource that we are in more need of than any other I can think of. People are also skeptical of leadership. They are tired of the abuses of leaders, the corruption of leadership, or the abandonment and betrayal of leadership. They are also weary of the lies and pandering of leadership, the empty promises, the failed initiatives, and the deflection of incompetence. Leadership is hard. Every day it gets harder because every day the puzzle seems to get more complex. Being a leader in the world today is tough. Being someone who is looking for leadership may be tougher.

Inside this world of confusion, people are angry—some could even say enraged. I believe people are really just heartbroken, disappointed, and too afraid to express how they really feel. We have lost our trust. We have lost our trust in our institutions. We have lost our trust in our democratic process. We have lost our trust in authority. In many ways we have lost our trust in God. Worst of all we have lost our trust in our fellow man. We are devolving into a culture of cynics that is fed by social media and cable news.

Now the new narrative is to trust the government. There is a popular definition that says insanity is doing the same thing over and over and expecting a different result. Any student of history understands that the great experiment of the United States began as an idea to become less dependent on big government. The idea of the United States is one based on individuals working in concert to build a more perfect union. That idea did not fail us; we failed that idea. The good news is as long as we have breath we can restore and reengage that idea. We are *not* hopeless. That is my request of you.

The idea I am offering is we men join together as brothers— as independent yet unified to restore manhood. We begin with restoring our masculinity in a responsible way. Not from anger and upset. We restore our masculinity through the practices described in this book. Restore by providing a space for all to grow and live lives of full self-expression that are unique and authentic to oneself. We restore the idea of protection, where safety is not a concern. We stand for what is right and we are a bulwark for those who desire to attack and destroy us. We do so in a way that lets others realize the absurdity of their abdication of responsibility. Finally we restore the practice of leaving a legacy, to leave a world worthy of our children and their children. To create a world that is inviting, healthy, sustainable, and self-sufficient. We begin with the practice of consensus and building a future in which we may not all agree 100 percent, but we can honor and respect. We build that in true partnership with the women in our lives, organizations, and communities. We build that partnership in balance and with equity.

This will require engagement and ownership of the intention. We must be "cause in the matter" of our life and leadership. That brings us to the fourth and final distinction of leadership: *"being cause in the matter."* Here is the definition:

*Being cause in the matter of everything in one's life as a stand one takes on self and life, and acting from that stand. It is not true that you are the cause of everything in your life, rather this is a place to stand—a place from which to deal with life that you have chosen for yourself. It simply says, "You can count on me (and I can count on me) to look at and deal with life from the perspective of my being cause in the matter." In taking this stand you give up the right to assign cause to the circumstances, or to others, or to the waxing and waning of your state of mind—all of which leave you helpless (at the effect of). When you see how this works it will be clear that taking this stand does not prevent you from holding others responsible. By contrast, when you have mastered this aspect of the foundation required for being a leader and exercising leadership effectively, you will experience a state change in effectiveness and power in dealing with the challenges of leadership (not to mention the challenges of life).*

Being cause in the matter of one's life, simply said, is just owning it all. No excuses. Being fully responsible for how things go. What does that mean? First, it means accepting things as they are. It means to understand what you have control of and what you don't have control of. Think about it, being 100 percent responsible yet realizing that you have no control. Notice that requires ownership and responsibility without control. Being at cause and being cause in the matter requires the release of control, and only through releasing control can we actually gain access to real leadership and gain access to our true power and authentic expression.

This is the money shot, my friends. This is the unreachable dream. It is not about attainment; it is about the journey, the idea, and who you get to be. That is the breakthrough. That is the opportunity. Things gets shifted by who we "be." That is why the "being" of *manhood* is so essential. To "be a man," to express the being of *manhood* requires presence and engagement. It is that easy. The only way out is through, and the only way through is to "git some on ya."

To do so will require engagement. We need to be willing to get dirty, to get some on us. It will be difficult, and it will be life-giving.

Nothing expresses this better than the poem by George Bernard Shaw, "The Splendid Torch."

We begin by getting clear on our purpose. If you have gone through this book and are still unclear on your purpose, reach out to me. I am committed that you get clear on your purpose. Once you are clear on that, then it is time for you to truly get in a relationship with yourself. The most important practice to take on is in maintaining a great relationship with yourself. Think about it, how in the hell can you be in relationship with anyone else if you don't have a decent relationship with yourself? It cracks me up when I hear people talk about the issue they had with this guy or that girl. If you listen to them, there are a whole series of villains in their stories: bad bosses, creepy exes, shitty landlords, and horrible teachers. Sometimes I like to ask them if they see the common thread of their stories. Of course, they want to know, and they always hate my answer. The common thread of all bad relationships any of us have is always us. Yep, whenever there is a recurring issue, the source of the issue is likely in the mirror.

We are getting near the end of my book. I said this was not a "how-to" book, and I am going to give you the way to get started. You ready? Let's go!

1) Distinguish your purpose. If you don't know, make something up that is bigger than you.
2) Look at what that purpose means to you. Why that? Then begin the process of getting to know you.
3) Go do something. "Git some on ya." What is something you care about that you always wanted to do but have not done? Do that.
4) Do that until you fail.
5) Repeat steps #2 through #4.

There is a chart in the appendix that shows the interrelationships of the four distinctions. I am not sure you will understand it, which is why there will be contact information and a "next steps" section.

Go live and be fully you, whatever that looks like. I don't care if you are a ballet dancer or a lumberjack. If that is what is in your heart and soul, go do it regardless of what anyone says. Do not hold back; if you need encouragement, reach out. Someone is there.

There are no shortcuts; there are no strategies. There is only engagement and slogging through the muck. Sometimes it may be easy; sometimes it will be a bitch. Never quit. Never quit on yourself or your commitments. Even if you want to, and you will want to. Never quit. God bless you, my brothers and sisters.

## CHAPTER 34

# Workability and the Truth

*"The truth at any cost lowers all other costs."*
*—Robert David Steele*

I have a commitment to limitless compassion for imperfection and zero tolerance for bullshit. I know it sounds cool. The truth is, as a practice it is a bitch. If you were to engage in this practice with me you would find the most difficult piece is the zero tolerance for bullshit. It is easy and joyful to have compassion for the human condition and celebrate the courage and vulnerability of imperfection. Bovine excrement abounds. Turn on the news, click on social media, listen to people in the stores. The volume of bullshit that is in our space is mind boggling. I challenge you to watch *Morning Joe* any morning on MSNBC and try to be with the bullshit that is spewed on that show. I try it often but cannot make it for more than ninety seconds. If Willie Geist is on, I have to leave in fifteen seconds or less.

First, let's define what *bullshit* is. It is the result of large animals mindlessly chewing their cud. The end product, which is excrement of the bovine, is warm and creates an environment perfect for the growth of fungus and mushrooms. Mushrooms, as a food source, are about 92 percent water, 4 percent carbohydrate, and 2 percent protein. A lot delivers a little, much like the product of the MSNBC show. The other thing mushrooms do is take on the flavors of the other foods in a dish, so they are absorbent and not really a source of their own, kind of like Willie Geist. Then there are "magic mushrooms." Those are the mushrooms that distort your reality. If you take them too much, you will begin to question what is real and what is the truth. That is what Joe and Mika deliver on their show, a distorted expression of the truth.

What is the truth? One definition of truth is "that which is true or in accordance with fact or reality." In the world today, what is fact? What is reality? There are so many reports and perspectives—what is true? Whom can we believe? Another definition is "a fact or belief that is accepted as true." Do masks work? Are lockdowns effective? How dangerous is COVID-19? Was the election stolen? Do any of us know?

Let's look at another truth that has been spoken about by our new president, Joe Biden—institutional or systemic racism. Systemic racism is now the cause of many of the social justice issues that exist in our world today. Or is it? The Southern Poverty Law Center (SPLC) has long been the source of identifying hate groups and racist organizations. The highest profile and most racist organization in America has long been believed to be the Ku Klux Klan. The "Klan" in its heyday was responsible for suppressing the efforts of Reconstruction after the Civil War. The KKK was driven into darkness, yet not out of business, by the federal government and President U. S. Grant.

The second wave of the Klan came around 1915, as it again was out to suppress the growth of an independent and growing Black community throughout the South. In 1916 there were an estimated four hundred thousand Klan members. They were partially successful through their tactics of terror, but the challenges of the economic depression suppressed their efforts again in the late 1920s.

The Klan reappeared in earnest in the 1950s as a result of the civil rights movement. By the mid 1960s, their ranks reached those of earlier in the century. This time, it was not government force but rather the voice of the people that provided the resistance necessary to stem the racist rhetoric and fear-based hate they were attempting to spread. It was through the leadership of Martin Luther King and other great leaders who stood in the face of this bullshit. Laws were changed, people were prosecuted, and change occurred. With that change came a shift of attitude and ways of living. Nashville, Tennessee, is one of the fastest-growing and most successful towns in our nation. Florida has become one of the most populous states in the nation, and Georgia has become a political swing state. The South is not a region of racism, segregation, and hatred. It is a region of growth, opportunity, and acceptance.

Do racism and hate still exist? Of course, they do—these are human characteristics. Unfortunately, in our current social and political environment, the gynocentric narrative of safety, equality, and fairness has seen fit to accuse the United States of America of being a place of intense systemic racism and a country defined by white supremacy. Their facts don't add up. If we use the SPLC as the source of the measure of hate, its 2017 estimate (the most recent estimate that I could find) of active Klan membership was between 3,000 and 6,000 members. I want to put that in perspective.

The gynocentric narrative of the far left progressives and BLM claims America is a country dominated by white supremacy and systemic racism. Yet the numbers provide by the SPLC says membership in the largest and most powerful of these groups is approximately 00.1 percent of the membership levels of sixty or so years ago. To put it in greater perspective, the WNBA, the bastion of gynocentric success, celebrated a breakthrough in attendance in 2018. The WNBA achieved an average attendance at their games of 7,500 people per game. The average attendance of any WNBA game is greater than the number of *total* active members of the Ku Klux Klan. The claims of systemic racism and the rise of white supremacy are blatantly false. Yet, if you look at the definition of the truth—"a fact or belief that is accepted as true"—then sure, there is such a thing as systemic racism. I also believed in Santa Claus until I saw all the toys in my parents' bedroom closet when I was ten.

As leaders we must not allow false narratives to gain momentum. We must stand for what is true and what is workable. We cannot succumb to the pressure, nor can we ignore the nonsense any longer. It is incumbent upon us to address these issues and do so in a way that provides an alternative and an opportunity. We must do so in a way that protects the truth, protects our freedom, and even protects those who are spreading the false narrative. We must interrupt the narrative and still love the people. It is also incumbent upon us to work together to create a future that does not require the fear and is not a fertile place for the mushrooms to grow. The best way is by operating with transparency and sharing all we are doing.

Here is the real problem with allowing a false narrative and signing off on bullshit: it uses resources that are intended to actually address the issue at hand. You want to know the source of the ever-increasing national debt? It is spending money where it does not produce an ROI. It is spending money to feel good or look good, but it does not get the result you desired. That is, by definition, wasteful. It is also incompetent. Nothing shows the unworkability of the gynocentric paradigm more than this: applying resources and making investments to "feel good" and "be inclusive" at the expense of solving the issue at hand.

The work that there is to do is not impossible. It will be challenging. Isn't challenging work what will call forth our masculine leadership? The work that there is for us to do is to "*be the change we wish to see in the world.*" As Simon Sinek said, "Let us all be the leaders we wish we had." That is it. It is time for us to be responsible American men and responsible American leaders regardless of our position. We won't be perfect. When we fail, we clean it up and get back to being the men we are committed to being.

It is our guilt, our triggers, our fear, and our need for agreement that feed this inaccurate narrative. I weep for the suburban men who now claim allied-ship. That act of appeasement is self-loathing and weak. I feel for the women and Black people who don't subscribe to the disempowering narrative. Who would want allied-ship with such weak-willed men, who are so frightened and emotionally frail, who are more willing to apologize than to actually do the work to create real shifts? I will fail on the side of compassion for them.

Our job is simple. Be the men we know ourselves to be. There are endless pulls for compromise. There is a powerful word in the English language: *NO.* No is a complete sentence. We can use it. Practice it, learn it, and be empowered by it. The more we connect to our purpose the more the use of the word *no* will become clear. The greater that we understand ourselves and accept all that we are and all that we are not, the clearer the path becomes.

It is our responsibility as men to bring healthy skepticism to the noise in our environment. Through our developed relationship with ourselves and our connection to a purpose sourced beyond us, we can begin to inquire in a new way. The purpose of this inquiry is to see what is really there, beyond the noise and the deception. This practice will also strengthen our muscle of being with what we discover. This will allow us to be able to engage with the newly discovered and the unknown. This practice is foundational to learning, developing, and growing. This will train us to not jump to the first conclusion and to practice acceptance. The purpose of this inquiry is to end the practice of accepting the expedient and safe over the right and powerful. Through the inquiry we can then begin the process of restoration.

Very few things worth doing are easy. We will not only restore masculine leadership at a time it is most needed, we will also restore access to our soul and spirit in a way we have not had for some time. This is the process of developing and restoring our responsible masculine leadership.

There is no top to this mountain; the journey ends when they put us in a box and throw dirt on our face. Just like a ride on my Harley, the true joy is the journey, and it is a journey worthy of us. The way to make this journey even more dynamic is to join me in creating a brotherhood of leaders. I look forward to that process.

The intention of this book is to create a movement. I have a request. Upon completion of this chapter, please reach out to me. My contact information can be found in the back of the book. Please join us.

Thank you.

## CHAPTER 35

# A Future Worth Living For

> *"Waste no more time arguing about what a good man should be. Be one."*
> —*Marcus Aurelius*

This nation of ours, the United States of America, is nothing but an idea, an experiment. It had never been done before. The idea of an independent, self-governing state flew in the face of convention. The idea of liberty as a right, bestowed upon us by our creator, was a breakthrough in the human experience. The idea of personal sovereignty and individual freedom has been under attack since the inception of man. The story of Adam and Eve is one of giving up one's freedom and personal sovereignty for the comfort and fun. Freedom has a price, and freedom requires choice and responsibility. It is not guaranteed. Freedom is fragile. Today more than ever, we are faced with the opportunity to choose how we want to live our lives. Today more than ever, we are faced with the responsibility of choosing our future. It is a big call, and it is ours to make.

Our forefathers declared independence from the king of England in July 1776. That was the birth of our nation. In their declaration the forefathers gave up the safety and protection of the king and his army for the freedom and sovereignty to live on their own terms. Free of the king's abuse and control, free of corruption, free of the limits to choose for themselves, without being under the thumb of his power. They understood the equality of men and that no man, no matter what his birthright said, was better than any other. They recognized that the rights granted by men can be removed by men, but our only true rights were bestowed upon us by our creator. In understanding that, the only way men can live in concert with the divine is for us to have the ability to choose freely and have the dominion to live as we see fit in alignment with our neighbors and environment. Our forefathers were beginning to see the delicate balance that it required and the never-ending growth that will always be essential. Since the inception of our county, we have both succeeded and failed in honoring that pact. We have a fairly good record of regaining our direction after failing and learning from the errors. That is the nature of freedom.

What makes the American version of self-governing so powerful and workable, though grounded in the idea of democracy, is that all men are created equal. What makes America work is a relentless stand for the freedom of individuals to live as they choose. That stand is demonstrated in the Bill of Rights and has been supported in countless decisions throughout time as we discovered the gaps in this great experiment. Most recently the Supreme Court upheld the freedom and the rights of the LGBTQ community in a 6–3 vote by a Court that is predominately "conservative." That speaks to the brilliance and workability of the system and the greatness of this experiment.

Today, as has happened throughout time, the idea of freedom and sovereignty is being challenged culturally, politically, spiritually, and economically. There is always some justification for the limitation of freedom. The current justification resides in cries of institutional racism and concern about climate change, along with the fear and the unknown of the Chinese flu. All are lofty concerns, and I have touched on them enough through this work that we do not need to dive any deeper. The real purpose of resistance and opposition is to provide the grit to sharpen our edge and develop us as beings. Remember, resistance and opposition are gifts from our creator that we should eagerly engage in and celebrate.

The resistance we are faced with today is the gynocentric narrative that values safety and fairness over freedom. Ben Franklin said, "Those who would give up essential Liberty, to purchase a little temporary Safety, deserve neither Liberty nor Safety." Dwight D. Eisenhower, former president and supreme allied commander, said, "If you want total security go to prison. There you are fed, clothed, given medical care and so on…The only thing lacking is your freedom." The final statement I will share regarding this is from C. S. Lewis. "Of all tyrannies, a tyranny sincerely exercised for the good of its victims may be the most oppressive." I believe this quote expresses the mindset of the gynocentric political left in America today. I do not doubt the sincerity of Barack Hussein Obama, Bernie Sanders, or AOC. OK, that's bullshit; I *do* doubt it. I see it as a well-constructed narrative to sell to the highly compassionate and empathetic. I see it as an emotional diversion to gain sympathy to gain power that will then provide access to more control and wealth.

Throughout history the only end game to the reduction of personal sovereignty and individual freedom is the gain of power and wealth for the select few who get to rule.

That is the game we are engaged in: the rule of a select few who will provide us with the basic needs and wants, safety, comfort and conveniences vs. our freedom. Freedom to live our lives as we desire with agency to choose. It is that simple. Thus, the title of the book, *Manhood Manifesto,* because it is time. This is a call for men to lead. To end the abdication of leadership and responsibility. It is time for men to own their voice, to share their vision, and to collaborate with other men and women to build that "shining city on a hill" that America is designed for. It is time to choose our freedom over free cell phones and free health care. It is time for us to own our lives. It is time for us to own our destiny. It is time to restore and own our manhood. It is time for us to lead and be leaders. This is not *cheer*leading; this will require work. There will be errors made and mistakes to overcome. Dealing with failure and breakdowns is one of the gifts of freedom. It is time to courageously begin that journey.

As we move into independence, we will move into a time of increased rationality and reduced levels of decisions made on emotions and fear. We will want to expand our critical thinking and our ability to see things differently than we have been trained. In the previous chapter we spoke of inquiry, discovery, challenge, and acceptance. One source that may be helpful on this journey is a selection of really good books written by friends of mine. Rollo Tomassi has written a book called *The Rational Male.* Rollo is one of the early contributors to the *manosphere.* The great gift of Rollo is to see him evolve and develop as a real agent and stand for responsible and effective masculinity. His book is a great resource for any man attempting to break the bonds of the gynocentric programming of the last twenty-five years. Another book that I believe should be required reading is by my friend Jason D. Hill, *We Have Overcome.* A book that speaks of personal sovereignty, freedom, and purpose, it inspires me every time I read it. I have read it three times. The final book

I would like to add to the required reading list is *Three Laws of Performance* by Steve Zaffron and Dave Logan. This book is so simple and elegant yet powerful and clear. It is filled with case studies that support their three laws. When you understand the laws you will have a moment of "duh," then laugh, then never forget them.

We are just about done here. Soon this is going to be on you. What you do will be a function of what future you want for yourself and your life. You have all you need to live the life of your dreams, the life that God intended you to have. All it takes is a little bit of courage, a sense of humor, and an unwillingness to stop. That practice will create the pathway to living your most authentic life. That, my friends, is the expression of freedom. If you do nothing else, understand your purpose and know your why. When you get that, the rest becomes blocking and tackling.

We have one more chapter. In some ways, the final chapter is an afterthought. In others it is a bit of a dessert and more of a celebration of manhood. I realize how I don't want to end this book, and I also realize I am close to being done. I don't have much else for you. It is time to hand the ball to you. Just like Ryan Tannehill handing the ball to Derrick Henry, I now will enjoy the best seat in the house to witness pure greatness and boundless expression. Go kick some ass, my brothers. Go Titans! #TitanUp.

CHAPTER 36

# The Final Word: Valor

*"Moral character is destiny."*

—*Jason D. Hill*

I have a friend who has been with me through most of the journey of this book. We have gotten to know each other pretty well. He is a man of incredible character and passion. It has been a joy to witness him move through his fears and concerns and begin engaging in life in a way that has him fully expressed. He is a lifelong learner and someone whose only desire is to contribute and be fully used up when this thing is over.

As we were discussing this project, he said there is only one word to describe it: *valor*. I was taken aback. *Valor* is not a word I use much, nor is it one I even consider. It's not in my word wheel. Knowing my friend as I do, an incredibly eloquent and quite verbose chap, I also realize he is not above a little "cock smooching." I bust him on that all the time and have requested he not do that with me. I have in the past been subject to that tactic. Every time I sensed it, things did not go so well. He assured me he was no longer practicing "smooching of the cock" as a way to achieve results and also let me know our friendship meant more to him than to resort to that. From that context I was moved.

Valor: "Strength of mind and spirit that enables a person to encounter danger with firmness; personal bravery."

When I take in that definition, authentic responsible manhood jumps out. That is also what responsible masculine leadership in America looks like. Men, leaders taking on issues and challenges with firmness and clarity. I see that, and I am so inspired by so many men in my life, so many men who take on the challenges of the world every day. They don't always get it right. Sometimes they fuck up or fail. So what? They clean up what needs to be cleaned up and get back at it tomorrow. Courage is the tool they use to get back in the game. In the gynocentric world, there is often talk of vulnerability. Courage is the masculine expression of vulnerability, and valor is the being of it. It is at the core of the three foundational roles of masculinity: *to provide, to protect,* and *to leave a legacy.*

Valor is sourced by the core leadership distinction of "*being given being and action by something greater than oneself.*" Only valor can express a person's willingness to sacrifice their own well-being for the good of a cause greater than themselves. Valor is essential to the structure of masculine integrity, and valor is at the core of legitimate masculine expression. Valor is the expression of authentic manhood.

Valor is also present in the practice of "*limitless compassion for imperfection and zero tolerance for bullshit.*" Valor is what provides the pathway for clarity to make that call. The leadership distinction of "*being cause in the matter*" is sourced by courage and valor. Valor is the "being" of genuine manhood and masculine leadership.

It's really simple, but it is not going to be easy. We need to choose courage over comfort and convenience. We need to choose valor over expedience. I think those choices become much easier with a growing relationship to our purpose. When we discover or create the reason we are here, things change. When we discover and connect to our purpose, we seldom hit the snooze. Hell, we won't even need an alarm. Each day becomes a gift to live our declaration of life. Shit gets way simpler and way clearer.

I think we are done. I once heard someone ask a painter how he knows he is done. That question so resonated with me because both my grandfather and my son are artists. The answer I heard made perfect sense. "When there is nothing else to paint." I have nothing else to share. I hope this book mattered to you, and I hope this book had value for you. Thank you for the gift of your purchase and more importantly thank you for the gift of your time and your mind. There is no more generous gift someone can give that that of themselves. It is honored and appreciated. I want to leave you with a final quote by a woman who represented the very best of feminism in the '70s. Thank you.

> *"I never understood the idea that you're supposed to mellow as you get older. Slowing down isn't something I relate to at all. The goal is to continue in good and bad, all of it."*
> —*Diane Keaton*

In honor of the great Warner Brothers cartoons: "*That's All Folks.*"

# EPILOGUE

# MY INVITATION TO YOU

Thanks for reading the book. Writing a book is a wild process, and this book was more wild and challenging than I could have ever imagined.

My vision is to build something here. I want to build a movement. What I really want to build is a brotherhood across the country. If this goes as planned, for some time after the book is released I will be appearing and "speaking" somewhere near you.

When that happens, please join. Join in the discussion. Join in the movement, and join in the brotherhood. I'm sure some of it will cost some money, and some of it will be free. Join in the community by sending me your email address. There will be a community newsletter that will be the backbone of this movement. The newsletter will be gratis.

I want to give you some ways of contacting me. Here is the website: www.MikeShereck.com (I know—it took tons of marketing research to come up with that website name). There will be a contact link you can use.

Here is my email, all I ask is you put something in the subject line that makes me know what it is about. I will respond: mikeshereck@gmail.com.

Finally, we will have a Facebook page. I am not a huge fan of Facebook groups, but until I get kicked off, the Facebook group is "Manhood Manifesto." Join in, I am sure it will be lively. Thanks again.

I look forward to connecting with you.

# BEER, BOURBON, CIGARS, AND MOTORCYCLES

*"Every action, thought, and feeling is motivated
by an intention, and that intention is a cause that
exists as one with an effect."*
                                    —*Gary Zukav*

Aside from these four things as being heavily associated with masculinity, these are also ways I love to recreate. As we move forward there will be gatherings with some or all of these items. I would love to have you join me and my buddies, both new and old, for men gathering in fellowship.

I especially want to invite you, if interested, to join me on one of the leadership rides. Each one is a unique experience that I promise will allow you to touch into a part of you that has yet to be discovered. I don't throw the "transformational" word around much. It has been abused and overused and nearly ruined by Barack Hussein Obama, but I do promise if you join us it will be transformational for you.

You can get a taste at www.rideoyl.com.

The website will also keep you informed as to the great beers, bourbons, and cigars we come across. As far as motorcycles, the conversation begins and ends with Harley-Davidson. (If you made less than an informed choice in rides, you are still welcome to join us.)

Join us and let's celebrate.

# AN IRISH TOAST

We are not here for a long time
We are here for a good time
And if we are blessed
We are here for a good long time
May God Bless you, my friends

# APPENDIX

# CHARTS, GRAPHS, AND
# VISUAL DISPLAYS

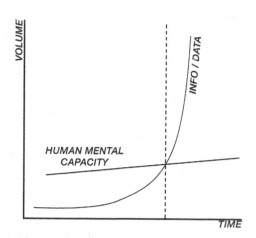

## MANHOOD MANIFESTO GRAPH:

I know you did not expect math in this book, but this graph is important. It outlines a shift in the condition of the human experience and why focus on leadership is so much more important today than on management or expertise.

There are really only two lines and the relationship says so much. The first line is the relatively horizontal line which represents man's intellectual capacity. You can see it does not change over time.

The other curved line represents the changes in information, data, and the shift in technology as represent by Moore's Law.

You can see that at the intersection of those two lines, the shit will literally hit the fan, and we'll enter into a new realm of human existence. (That is depicted by the horizontal dotted line.)

You can see if you attempt the apply the same thinking to the right side of the dotted line as you used on the left side, your ability to generate results will be impacted, which is a nice way of saying you will be fucked.

That is what this book is about—a call for leadership—not because it is cool, rather because it is required. We are in a new realm of human existence. I am not sure when that intersection occurred, but I will assert between 1999 and 2008. If someone forced me to pick a date, I would say 2004. Google started in 1998, Facebook in 2004, Twitter in 2006, and Amazon in 1994...2004 was a remarkable year of change. Ronald Reagan died, same-sex marriage was legalized, the tsunami hit in the Indian Ocean, the Red Sox won the World Series, and Janet Jackson's halftime performance at the Super Bowl, were all game-changing events.

When we can no longer control the flow of information. we must control ourselves and lead others. That is what we are calling for in this work.

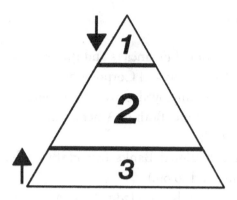

# TRIANGLE CHART:

What this chart shows is the pressure being established on the middle class, and small business by the current gynocentric globalist progressive agenda and the coalition that has been constructed.

In the top group, you have the elites, education, big tech, big pharma, big banks, political elites, and billionaires. They apply downward pressure. Lockdowns, tax policies, monetary policies, trade imbalance, etc.

The bottom group represents the "marginalized citizens" and "victims"—growing through recruitment efforts of government programs and grants. The top group needs this group as bodies to vote for their globalist programs.

The middle group is America. This group represents the people who desire and believe in liberty, life, and the pursuit of happiness. These are the people who work hard and pay the bills. These are the people who must stand up if America is to remain the bastion of freedom and liberty in the world.

## Group 1

- International Financiers and Billionaires
- Media Moguls and Corporations
- Lifetime Employed Government Bureaucrats
- Political Elite, Both in America and Internationally
- Big Tech
- Multi-National Banks (ex: HSBC; Chase; Deutsche Bank, and so on.)
- Hedge Funds and Hedge Fund Managers
- Big Pharma
- Big Insurance Firms and Health Care Organizations
- Multinational Global Corporations
- C-Level Executives of Large Corporations
- Board Members of Large Corporations
- State Funded Universities and Tenured Faculty
- High End Private Liberal Art Universities and Tenured Faculty
- Large Endowments and Not for Profits, (ex: Clinton Foundation, Gates Foundation, or Large Liberal Education foundations like the Harvard Foundation)
- Highly-Compensated and High-Level Corporate Executives
- Most Federal Employees
- Sucklers of the Corporate Teat: Well-compensated employees, subcontractors, vendors, and target acquisition companies.

## Group 2

- Small Business Owners
- Gig Workers (Not dependent on any of the people listed in Group 1)
- Privately Held Corporations
- Midsize Regional Companies, Management, Leadership, and Employees
- Employees of Large Companies
- State Workers
- Health Care Workers
- Most Working People, Regardless of Industry
- Police, Fire, and EMTs
- Construction Workers
- Union Workers
- Homeowners
- Retirees (Living on Pensions and 401k and Other Investments)
- Truck Drivers
- People in the Military Service
- Legal Immigrants and Naturalized Citizens
- Green Card Holders
- Farmers
- Ag Workers
- Independent Real Estate Investors
- Black Conservatives
- Gay and Lesbian Conservatives
- Most Able Bodied Adult Straight Men
- Conservative High School and College Age Students

## Group 3

- Underemployed and overeducated, Gender Studies Majors, Food Service Workers, Baristas, and so on.
- Multicultural People/Identity Politics Folks
- Teachers Unions
- Minimum Wage Workers
- Chronically Unemployed
- Forgotten People (the thirty-two year-old playing video games in his parents' basement)
- Welfare Recipients
- Students
- Undocumented/Illegal Immigrants
- Suburban Woke Housewives and Community Organizers
- Homeless
- BLMGN Members
- ANTIFA (I know it's just an idea)
- SSI Payment People
- LGBTQI2A+ (The Alphabet People)
- Professional Victims

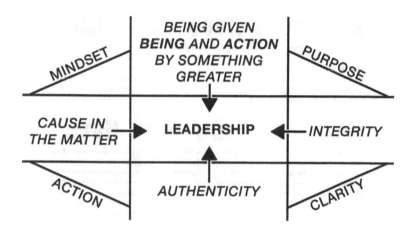

## Do

The action required
to achieve a goal or
respond to a stimulus.
Actions are informed
by what is needed to
"git er done."

## Have

The result derived from
that action.

## Be

The experience one
has from the result
generated (or not)
and the personal re-
ward achieved by the
result (or not).

## Be

The mindset and
commitment you have
to achieve a goal or
result. The approach
your bring to a project
or objective.

## Do

The actions used to
achieve the objective
or goal, and informed
by ones mindset.

## Have

The result generated
and the experience
one has generated by
the actions that were
were informed by the
mindset one brings to
the project.

# GLOSSARY

(Special words and phrases Mike uses that are common language for him, but that you may not have used much, at least not until now.)

***TRIGGER WARNING: THE FOLLOWING MATERIAL MAY CAUSE UPSET BY THE UNINITIATED.**

**1985 Chicago Bears:** Greatest football team ever assembled. Led by guys like Dan Hampton, Steve McMichael, Otis Wilson, Richard Dent, Walter Payton, Buddy Ryan, and, of course, Da Coach, Mike Ditka.

**Able-Bodied Men:** Healthy dudes born without any disabilities and who have not contracted any diseases that limit their physical abilities. Includes fat "fux" who don't exercise and who sit on their asses all day, and wimpy little pajama boys who sit and stare at screens nonstop.

**Action Bias:** A trait of many alpha males; a tendency toward action over planning; a ready-fire-aim approach to issue, a "git 'er done" mentality.

**Affordable Care Act (ACA):** The ill-conceived and more poorly executed health care bill that Barack Hussein Obama shoved down the throats of the American public. Its impact both made the government be the supplier of health care and lowered the standards of excellence; it also was the first attack on small and independent businesses by the Democrats.

**Alpha Male:** The authentic and natural leadership expression of a male leader. It must be an authentic expression of the individual.

**Authenticity:** One of the four core leadership distinctions in the book: "being and acting consistent with who you hold yourself to be for yourself, and who you hold yourself out to be for others" (which leaves you grounded and able to be straight with others without using force). This is the natural expression when you are connected to your purpose.

**Ally:** Feminized men and male feminists. They are the essence of male-dread and the lowest form of masculinity. This is the worst depiction of masculinity. These guys live in a constant state of fear and have succumbed to the radical feminist agenda. They serve no purpose but to live as subservient to women and are cuckolds. They have completely sold out on their masculinity in exchange for safety, protection, and acceptance by the women who use them. They have no backbone, stand, or real purpose (never mind no balls). Although we welcome them as the lost souls they are, they may be unredeemable. They have little respect for themselves, women have no respect for them, and men find them similarly useless. This is a pathetic way to live. These are also the readers of Michael Kimmel books.

**Ballers:** People who, by their very presence, get shit done. Not only do they drive results, but everyone within their sphere of influence grows, develops, and gets better. This is a result of dedication to their field of practice, along with the authenticity expressed while practicing in that field.

**"Being Cause in the Matter":** One of the four core distinctions of leadership in the book. "Being cause in the matter" of everything in one's life as a stand one takes on self and life, and acting from that stand. It is not true that you are the cause of everything in your life; rather this is a place to stand—a place from which to deal with life that you have chosen for yourself. It simply says, "You can count on me (and I can count on me) to look at and deal with life from the perspective of my being cause in the matter." In taking this stand you give up the right to assign cause to the circumstances, to others, and to the waxing and waning of your state of mind—all of which leave you helpless. When you see how this works, it will be clear that taking this stand does not prevent you from holding others responsible. By contrast, when you have mastered this aspect of building the foundation required for being a leader and exercising leadership effectively, you will experience a state change in effectiveness and power in dealing with the challenges of leadership (not to mention the challenges of life). What this looks like is you having complete ownership of your life and the results associated with it. No excuses, no bragging, no whining, no problem. It is just what's so: 100 percent ownership; 100 percent agency (past, present, and future of it all).

**"Being Given Being and Action by Something Greater Than Oneself":** One of the four core leadership distinctions in the book. Source of the serene passion (charisma) required to lead and to develop others as leaders and the source of persistence (joy in the labor of) when the going gets tough. Bottom line: one's own personal purpose.

**Beclowned:** The practice of making a complete ass of yourself, usually as a result of being consumed by fear yet pretending you got it handled. Another word for *asshat*.

**Beta Male:** Followers, good guys who will follow the lead. They can be susceptible to cock smooching and looking good, so they need to stay engaged or it can become problematic.

**Bitch:** Literally a female dog. It has many uses, second only to *fuck* in its versatility. It can be used to describe the process of communicating corrective action: "Please stop your bitching—I get it"; a complaint about a weak or wimpy man, "That dude is a bitch"; a task or a set of challenges one must meet, "Today was a bitch"; or a particularly direct and opinionated woman: "Yikes, she is a bitch."

**Bovine Excrement/Bullshit:** Currently one of the most abundant resources we have available to us. It is usually sourced by liberal media outlets, CNN, MSNBC, and in particular the *Morning Joe* show. Another great source of this comes in the form of the written word as published by Barack Hussein Obama, Robin DiAngelo, Ibram X. Kendi, Ta-Nehisi Coates, Michael Kimmel, and others; the works they author.

**Bluto Blutarsky:** A member of the Delta Tau Chi Fraternity, the "Deltas" at Faber College, the hero of one of the most iconic dude films ever, *Animal House*

**Cancelling/ Cancel Culture:** The act of diminishing and dehumanizing anyone or any idea that is not in alignment with the current and ever-changing woke/leftist/progressive/gynocentric narrative. This requires a constant state of anxiety to ensure you are never not aligned and a constant state of malleability to ensure perfect wokeness.

**Cock Smooching:** The act of appeasement to avoid conflict or curry favor. A survival tactic of beta males.

**Corporate Titty Sucker (CTS):** Can be anyone in an organization—it is particularly distressing when it is an adult male—and it is a survival tactic. It is an act of compliance. All it takes is complete abdication of anything that resembles leadership or masculinity. It is choosing to become a pawn and hoping that when they do come to eat you, you will be one of the last to be eaten. A despicable way to live. A life of complete and utter lack of fulfillment, chock-full of stress and depression. A gamma male.

**Cuck:** Becoming popular, it actually means a man whose wife is sleeping with other men. It is growing in use in the "manosphere" for a dude whose wife is the primary breadwinner and he needs her income to maintain his lifestyle. It can also be used as an expression for male feminist, especially if you suspect he is sucking up because he is on scholarship—someone who complies with less than authentic demands because someone else is footing the bill.

**Dean Wormer:** Dean at Faber College and the villain in one of the most iconic "dude films" ever, *Animal House.*

**Distinction:** We use the word *distinction* to bring clarity to something that can be seen as ubiquitous. Especially in the book, the word *leadership* can mean a bunch of things, in this book and our work there are four core distinctions that must be present for leadership to exist. Where these distinctions are absent, so is leadership.

**Fuck:** One of the most versatile words in the English language, of which millions of words are written, with millions more on the way. Fuck it.

**Feminism:** The movement that granted women equal treatment under the law: equal pay, voting rights, equality. These goals are close to being achieved, but as a result Cultural Marxism has emerged to take us to a new level of self-dread and ultimately destroy the more civilized societies. Since legal equality has been mostly achieved, it has taken on a more radical and now destructive movement momentum that is focused on some artificial side of social justice. (A *feminist* is a follower of feminism.)

**Giving Zero Fux:** Contrary to what many may think, this is not "not caring." It is the mindset that allows us to live passionately into our commitments with little to no regard for opinions, agreement, or popularity. It is standing in the wilderness, sourced by our internal knowledge connected to something far greater than us. Don Miguel Ruiz captures it fairly well in the book *Four Agreements.*

**Gynocentric:** Dominated by feminine interest or a feminine point of view. As used in this book, the gynocentric point of view is a fully approved modality of interpreting reality and views with any hint of masculinity as being "toxic." Being gynocentric is required to get any man access to news and television shows such as *The View,* MSNBC (especially *Morning Joe* and *Rachel Maddow Show*), CNN, and now ESPN.

**Gynonormative:** The taking of the gynocentric paradigm, and transferring it into doctrine, so there is no ability to question it or challenge it. Black Lives Matter is an example of an organization that lives by this paradigm, and you can see elements in the Green New Deal. Chicago Mayor Lori Lightfoot is a practitioner of a gynonormative agenda, one that requires 100 percent compliance with her vision or idea. Foundational to dictatorship.

**Hair Bun:** Long hair tied on the top of one's head. Often what women do before they perform fellatio, or oral sex, on a dude.

**IMX:** A profiling instrument created and delivered by Innermetrix. It uses the DISC profile, the Values Index, and the Dimensional Balance to provide three points of reference to a person's current state of performance.

**Integrity:** One of the four core distinctions of leadership in the book (in our model, a positive phenomenon). Being whole and complete—achieved by honoring one's word as we define honoring (creates workability, creates trust). Integrity creates the structure we live within. It begins with honoring our work as we would honor ourselves.

**International Harvester (IH):** The iconic manufacturer of farm equipment, founded by Cyrus McCormick. It was severely impacted by a strike with the United Auto Workers (UAW) in 1979–1980. It was the first attempt by corporate leaders, in this case Archie McCardell, to break unions. The strike nearly destroyed the company. IH sold its farm equipment unit to Tenneco and renamed the remainder of the business Navistar. Ultimately the result of the strike was the closing of many factories and the loss of tens of thousands of well-paying manufacturing jobs across America.

**Jag Bag:** A pejorative phrase used to identify someone of limited competence and awareness. Another word for jag off or ass hat.

**Libtard/Libtardian:** Someone who resides in the gynocentric paradigm and has no interest in inquiry of any perspective other than their own. This is evidenced by an amazing level of self-righteousness and a constant call for people to comply or a never-ending drive to convince people to "do the right thing." These people live in a state of always being right yet seem to always be unhappy, unfulfilled, and mostly miserable. Every day begins with a complaint.

**Man Bun:** See *Hair Bun*, but this is exclusive to men. Also a clear sign that a guy is a complete douchebag, especially if he wears it beyond 2017.

**Mangina:** The mythical body part of the highly feminized male.

**Manifesto:** A written statement declaring publicly the intentions, motives and views of the issuer. This book is a *manifesto*!

**Michael Kimmel:** Sociologist, ally, male feminist, the poster child for what a douchebag represents (without the hair bun).

**Mike Jensen:** Mike is one of the co-founders of the Being a Leader Program. He is also a professor emeritus from the Harvard Business School. Mike has done much work and is a foremost expert on the distinction of "integrity".

**Nissan Stadium:** Home of the beloved Tennessee Titans and the site of the 2015 Rolling Stones concert.

**Pajama Boy:** See *Soy Boy*.

**Professional Air Traffic Controllers Organization (PATCO):** This union was decertified by President Ronald Reagan when its members went on strike in 1981. The decertification opened the gates to antiunion sentiment throughout the United State.

**Pusillanimous:** A characteristic seen in men that is defined by a lack of courage and the presences of timidness.

**Pussy:** The most lovely of all the lovely lady parts. Should *never* be used as a disparaging comment toward men. Pussies, as Betty White referenced, are lovely things that can take a beating and keep on ticking. To call a dude a pussy would actually be a compliment.

**Political Correctness (PC):** The foundation of totalitarianism and the end of free speech. Foundational to libtardian politics, it is based in fear, word play, hypocrisy, shame, deception, control, and compliance. The most difficult thing about political correctness is that the rules are ever changing, and you never know you are in violation until just prior to being attacked. PC is an unwinnable battle, and the only way to deal with it is through authenticity, curiosity, and engagement. When that occurs PC usually disappears.

**Return on Investment (ROI):** A way to measure if the money you spent was worth it. Not all that effective, because you already spent the money. A way to keep score.

**Social Justice:** This is a radical new age form of social control that affirms the gynocentric beliefs of safety, fairness, and equality into our legal and social construct. Since justice was formed to protect individuals and their rights against a larger government entity, the idea of social justice is completely flawed and actually speaks to the foundation of Marxism and state control of behavior and choice. For the most part, social justice is antiliberty and anti-individual.

**Social Justice Warriors (SJWs):** Before BLM took hold, the SJWs were the *most annoying* of all creatures known to man. Armed with a limitless supply of self-righteousness, they know better than anyone else what the world needs at every moment. They are a true asset we have just not recognized as of yet. When we do, our appreciation will then come close to matching what they believe they contribute to the world through their omnipotence and inherent wisdom. (Sarcasm is free here.)

**Soy Boy:** A politically correct and socially acceptable way of identifying a cunt without creating the uproar of using that derogatory word.

**Slap Dick:** A fundamentally incompetent man, who is completely unaware of how terrible he is at what he might be doing at any given time, largely resulting from not even considering the possibility of his own gross underperformance. Your typical American large corporation is often a vast breeding ground for slap dicks. Greedy and back-stabbing, slap dicks also exhibit an absence of critical thinking and complete unawareness of how shitty they really are at doing what they do.

**Werner Erhard:** The founder and creator of *EST* and is often credited with being the leader and creator of the practice of *personal transformation.* Werner is also one of the co-creators of the *Being a Leader Program* which the four core distinction in this book are referred from.

**Wokeism/Being Woke:** the expression of the gynocentric and gynonormative experience all the time.

**Wrong-making:** This is the practice of making other people wrong and situation beyond oneself wrong. "Donald Trump was the worst president in American History." Wrong-making requires no personal responsibility or critical thinking. It is based in emotion and blame.

# ACKNOWLEDGMENTS

## Contributors (In no particular order) Knowingly or Unknowingly

Professor Jason D. Hill, PhD, author of *We Have Overcome*: This book and my relationship with Post Hill Press does not happen without Jay. I have had the pleasure of getting to know the amazing and complex man he is. I love this guy.

Rory Clark, founder of Focus Selling: I have known Rory way too long. I don't know how to describe him other than Rory. A man of God, funnier than hell, and a nearly scratch golfer, he is the power of one word. He is the most determined man on earth. He is my friend.

Peter Scott, coach, speaker, and author of *The Fearless Coach*: Peter has been my coach during a period of incredible growth and development for me. I met Peter at my most resigned. I had nearly given up on coaching and was actually in a fit of despair—I was about ready to quit. I love this guy and am so thankful for who he has been for me.

Christopher D McAuliffe, founder and CEO of Accomplishment Coaching: Without Christopher, none of this happens. I am not sure we can agree on what time it is, let alone on what is really important, yet he is a true leader who has created the space for creation to arise and blossom. Thank you, and I do appreciate you even when we don't agree.

Rocco Cozza JD, founder of the Cozza Law Group, author of *A.L.P.H.A.*: This man is a badass. He is powerful, committed, courageous, and the personification of strength. He is a brother and someone I respect and honor. It is a privilege to spend time and share space with him.

Robert Ponterelli, CEO, CBarts Building: Bob is my friend and inspiration. He is a symbol of courage and resilience. He is the most trustworthy man I know and I am blessed to know many. He too, is a brother and a man I love.

Derrick Green, President, Phi Kappa Sigma, Beta Lambda Chapter, NIU: Rick is a true leader. He is honorable, courageous, and undaunted. He is brilliant, clear, and the future of men. +LT

Tina Schulke, Change Management Communication Centre: Tina is a wonderful woman. She is graceful, committed, and a powerful leader.

David Bryant, DHB Change Advisors: David probably doesn't even know the impact he has had on me. David has challenged me in a ways that called me to refine, relook, and be responsible for my thoughts, words, and actions. There is no greater gift than that. Thank you.

Margaret "Magi" Graziano, founder, Keen Alignment, Inc., and speaker. This woman is a force of nature and seer of possibility. She saw something in me that I not only refused to see but resisted. She still hung in there. She is the greatest gift of my professional life. I am so thankful for the time we have had together and I look forward to what the future may bring.

Linal Harris, Inspirational Perspective, radio host, WVON 1690-AM, Chicago: This is the other guy who does not know the incredible contribution he is and has been to me. Linal is a brilliant leader, inspiration, and a constant stand for the greatness of people.

Kayla Acton, my daughter-in-law and the bride to my son Zack: She was a tremendous contribution to getting this thing started. Thank you so much. Zack is an amazing young man who has no idea the influence and impact he has had on my life. There are so many things I screwed up and yet he has become an amazing man.

For the multicultural and identity politics folks out there, there are thirteen acknowledgments, fourteen if you count Zack—seven white guys, four black guys, and three women. Clearly the numbers determine that I am a white supremacist, racist, and misogynist. Took care of that so you did not have to—one of the many services I provide.

I also want to really thank David Bernstein and all the people of Post Hill Press, who I have met and talked to, and who I will in the future. You guys are remarkable. And a special thanks to my editor who does the heavy lifting and who challenges my thoughts, my words, and my actions.

Finally there is another man I wish to acknowledge, Scott Kallick. Scott's strength, courage, and integrity are models of manhood. He is not perfect and that is part of what makes him a great man. He's a true "mensch."

I want to thank Stan and John for reading some of this and for the feedback

This does not happen without Jeannie. ILYOMT.

# Friends

Lauren Buckley, Gigas Collier, Amy VanderBerg, Michelle Jerbek, and Mike Strybel. Thanks to my friend Karen White for her warmth and friendship. Bob Trobetta, maybe you can get un-triggered long enough to get through this—one can only pray. All the bros: Mike and John, Ox, Gary, and Dennis (what a guy—the inventor of the fist bump, NO SHIT). There is Doc, Bob, Zel, Al, and Jim. I cannot forget Tommy, Ernie, and most of all, my idiot brother, who I love more than life itself, T.W. He may be the smartest and funniest guy I know.

I want to thank Fredo, Jason, Josh, and ShineBox, the Todd Father, and I cannot leave out the limey communist, Neil. I also want to thank Captain Nick Zuck of the US Army for his service.

I want to thank Marcus, Garrett, Joe, and Javy who work every day in law enforcement at a time where they are under-appreciated and at times targeted. I want to thank my guys in Berwyn, Richard, Scott, Mayor Bobby, and most of all, David and Troy (my roommates). I cannot have a shout out to Berwyn without thanking Lorene, and Berwyn is not Berwyn without a huge acknowledgment of Lucile Evans. You will never know the joy and passion you have evoked in me. Oh shit, I almost forgot! I want to thank my fellow writer and frat brother, Berwyn guy and longtime friend, TK.

There are so many who have touched me in my life, and I realize when you do acknowledgments, I will leave someone out—probably someone really important. If I did that, I am sorry, and know if you met me and know me, you played a role. Thank you.

# Shout Outs

I have been a Sox fan since I was eight years old. They are my guys and they are playoff bound as we are putting this thing together.

My adopted team, the Titans—my guys and the best running back since Jim Brown, Derrick Henry, #22. Titan UP.

Special thanks: If there is a soundtrack to this book, it's the music of Eric Church. Willie and Waylon have always been inspiration and I love this guy's music. Thanks Eric. I hope we get to meet soon.

They guys and gals at Little Italian Pizza on Route 59 in Naperville—that is the fuel that drove this machine.

To Accomplishment Coaching and the leaders there, especially Jodi Larson, Kerry Zurier, and yes, even Rodney. You guys make me nuts and aggravate the shit out of me, and you are the perfect force to keep my edge. Thank you for the work you do, and the gift you were to me. And a shout out to Kristine who is very cool.

The Bros—all of them—you guys are the environment of men that is my reality, each and every one of you is inspiring. Who'd a thunk that a fantasy football league could last this long.

This may be a bit of a fan boy shout out, but I want to acknowledge Mancow Mueller, Chris Platt, and the late and the great Rush Limbaugh. I listen to them on the radio during the plandemic and the Wuhan Flu/CCP biological attack on the world. This was during the time of the writing of this book.

Thank you for your stand for freedom and free speech.

# ABOUT THE AUTHOR

Author photo by Dan Lewis

Mike Shereck is a leader, father, partner, friend, brother, and coach. His work is dedicated to leaders understanding themselves and having them fully own their lives, career, journey, voice, and impact. Mike is a "dude"—a pick-up truck driving, Harley Davidson riding, blue jean wearing, cigar smoking, 100 percent alpha male. Mike is also someone who takes a stand for the greatness of all people, and someone whose heart and soul are open.

Mike sees the division in our culture to be one of the most destructive and disheartening events of his life. He also sees this as one of the greatest opportunities of our lifetime. Understanding that the only way out is through, Mike takes on this challenge every day in his work.

Mike works as a leadership coach and organizational consultant. He lives in Naperville, IL, and owns the credential of Professional Certified Coach through the ICF.